CAPTAIN COOK'S
MERCHANT SHIPS

CAPTAIN COOK'S MERCHANT SHIPS

Freelove, Three Brothers, Mary, Friendship,
Endeavour, Adventure, Resolution and *Discovery*

STEPHEN BAINES

You are a King by your own Fire-side, as much as any Monarch in his Throne:
You have Liberty and Property, which set you above Favour or Affection, and
may therefore freely like or dislike this History, according to your Humour.

(Cervantes, *Don Quixote*, from the Author's Preface, English Translation, 1725)

In memory of Peter Frank, author of *Yorkshire Fisherfolk*, academic, lover of Whitby, and
a man of great humanity, charm and wit.

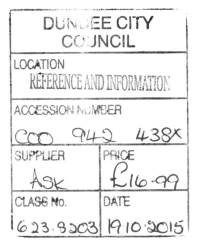
First published 2015

The History Press
The Mill, Brimscombe Port
Stroud, Gloucestershire, GL5 2QG
www.thehistorypress.co.uk

© Stephen Baines, 2015

The right of Stephen Baines to be identified as the Author
of this work has been asserted in accordance with the
Copyright, Designs and Patents Act 1988.

British Library Cataloguing in Publication Data.
A catalogue record for this book is available from the British Library.

ISBN 978 0 7509 6214 8

Typesetting and origination by The History Press
Printed and bound in Malta, by Melita Press.

Contents

Preface

There have been numerous books about James Cook, the first being the *Life of Captain James Cook* published in 1788 by the Presbyterian minister Andrew Kippis, which concentrated almost exclusively on the voyages, and was not the result of any great thoroughness of research, though it was much copied. The next biography of Cook worthy of note appeared in a fourteen-page entry in Volume II of *A History of Whitby* by George Young, in 1817. Although brief, it corrected some existing errors, and Young had done his research thoroughly even though he was not in Whitby at all in the eighteenth century. He contacted Henry and John, the sons of Cook's master and lifelong friend John Walker (1706–85), and persuaded them to lend him the letters Cook sent to their father, which he transcribed into the biography. Young was not only a historian but also the Scottish Presbyterian minister of Whitby, and he could not refrain from condemning Cook for 'the general neglect of divine service, too apparent from his journals' and for 'permitting the inhabitants of Owhyhee [Hawaii] to adore him as a god'; but his final opinion of Cook was favourable because he 'opened up' for the South Sea islanders 'the door of real bliss', asserting that 'The Society isles are now becoming happy isles indeed, rescued from absurd idolatries and abominable vices, and enriched with the blessings of Christianity and of civilization, through the arduous labours of faithful missionaries' – an evaluation of Cook's journeys which now finds few supporters.

Many books followed, some clarifying, some copying, some confusing; but it was not until the publication in 1974 of *The Life of Captain James Cook* by the New Zealander J.C. Beaglehole that a definitive, comprehensive and thoroughly researched account was available.

Much has been written since then about Cook on both the macro and micro scales; but the most popular format has been to tell the story of Cook's life, concentrating mainly on the three voyages. Although most of these included a brief account of Cook's childhood, this was a largely neglected area until Cliff Thornton's *Captain Cook in Cleveland*. Similarly, Cook's early years in the Royal Navy were overlooked until John Robson's *Captain Cook's War and Peace: The Royal Navy Years 1755–68*.

This book also seeks to fill a gap. Rather than tell the story of Captain Cook in which the ships have bit parts, I thought it would be interesting to tell the story of the ships in which Cook has a bit part. Cook sailed in or with eight ships which had begun as merchant ships: four in his earlier nautical career (*Freelove, Friendship, Three Brothers* and *Mary*), and four on the three voyages (*Endeavour, Resolution, Adventure* and *Discovery*). These ships have been written about before, but mainly sketchily and sometimes erroneously. Recently, some excellent work has been done on these ships, for example, John F. Allan's article 'Cook's Ships – A Summary Update' in *Cook's Log* (Vol 25, 2002), the magazine of The Captain Cook Society. But the real star in this sphere is Dr D.K. Abbass, director of the Rhode Island Marine Archaeological Project (RIMAP), who identified the transport *Lord Sandwich* as the terminally aged *Endeavour*, scuppered in Newport Harbour, where the ship probably lies still among the wrecks which RIMAP has discovered and which are currently undergoing thorough underwater archaeological excavation.

This book has a broader scope, covering the lives of Cook's eight merchant ships and those who owned them and who sailed in them. I have omitted retelling the story of Cook's three voyages for the same reason Young did not write a 'detailed account' of the voyage of the *Endeavour*: 'it is unnecessary … having been long known to the public'. However, what I think *is* necessary is placing these ships and people in the context of their times; so this book is also a story of trade, science, liberty and belief – vital themes in that exciting, violent, gossipy but largely untaught and unknown period through which these vessels and their people sailed literally and figuratively between the old world and the new. Kippis' biography of Cook was criticised because it omitted 'the appropriate philosophical perspective', and Young regretted he did not have space in his biography of Cook to discuss matters of 'commerce, science, civilization and religion'. I have attempted to remedy these omissions.

There are a lot of genealogies in this book – for which I make no excuses. In a society where business and family life were inseparable it was often the tangled webs of familial loyalty which made history. Historical genealogy is also interesting in itself, as Horace Walpole wrote: 'People don't know how entertaining a study of ancestors can be. Who begot who is a most amusing kind of hunting.'

Where contemporary sources have been quoted the spelling and punctuation are original, with occasional editing for clarification. Biblical quotations are from the 1611 Authorised Version (King James' Bible). The titles of the chapters use the names of contemporary Whitby ships, and the epigraphs are quotations from people who were alive in or before the eighteenth century. For information about money, weights, measures and the calendar, see the Appendix. Footnotes appear throughout; endnotes indicate sources, and are after the Appendix.

Stephen Baines

1

Present Succession

Trade, like Religion, is what every Body talks of, but few understand.
(Daniel Defoe, *A Plan of the English Commerce*)

When James Cook was born in 27 October 1728 Britain was a successful trading nation with a large number of Royal Navy ships and a larger number of merchant ships. Britons prided themselves on being a strong nation of free people, ruled by a Protestant monarch, governed by Parliament, with a state religion which was remarkably tolerant of other (Protestant) groups. It was noted for its free press, its freedom of speech and for its scientific achievements. How had all this come about?

In 1534, when the Catholic Henry VIII broke with the Pope in Rome and declared himself the Supreme Head of the Church of England, he was freed from the authority, expense and interference of the Vatican; but it was not clear what form the state religion would be. Henry persecuted both Catholics and Protestants. His son Edward VI was a Protestant, but he died young and was followed by his Catholic sister Mary. She sought to return England to the Roman Catholic fold, and her five-year reign was marred with hideous persecutions of Protestants. When Elizabeth I came to the throne she established a broad-based Church of England with the help of Thomas Cranmer; it was designed to be an inclusive religion to which a wide range of believers could assent: it was the nation's own brand of Christian belief tailored for England. There were many Catholics who simply wanted to practice their religion in peace and quiet; but the persecutions in Mary's reign and the attempts by Catholic terrorists to murder the queen put Catholicism beyond the religious pale. The defeat of the Spanish Armada by the English confirmed in the mind of many that God was on their side: if God was not actually an Anglican, he was certainly on the side of Protestants against the Catholics. The failed Gunpowder Plot reinforced this view; it was seen as a terrorist action fostered in Rome, and its prevention as an act of God. Catholicism became regarded by many as a serious enemy of the English monarchy, the Church of England, Parliament and the liberties of Britain.

Since the Middle Ages, it had been a principle of government in England that no new taxation could be imposed without the assent of Parliament. Elizabeth's Stuart successors James I and Charles I had not been brought up with this tradition and resented any limitations on their divinely appointed kingly powers. Between them they ruled without a parliament for twenty-one years, which meant that money was short, the navy was largely neglected, and neither could afford war. So when a Scottish army, incensed by Charles' high-handed attempt to force Anglicanism on largely Presbyterian Scotland, marched over the border, the king had to summon a parliament. The subsequent clash between King and Parliament resulted in some seven years of conflict fuelled by religious and political ideologies and entangled in traditional and familial loyalties, a war which was apocalyptically bloody and violent.

After the execution of Charles I, England and Scotland became republics with no established Church, and this fragile new commonwealth was protected by Oliver Cromwell in conjunction with Parliament. The favoured religious denomination was Presbyterianism, enshrined in *The Solemn League and Covenant* which asserted that the 'doctrine, worship, discipline, and government' of the English Church would be in accordance with 'the Word of GOD, and the example of the best reformed Churches'. Unfortunately there was, and would continue

The execution of Charles I.

to be, a wide range of opinion not only about which were the best reformed Churches but also about what the word of God had to say about Church doctrine, worship, discipline and government. The new regime replaced the majority of Anglican vicars with Presbyterians, and abolished bishops and other hierarchical Anglican positions. The *Instrument of Government*, adopted in 1653 as the British constitution, granted executive powers to Oliver Cromwell as Lord Protector, but also promised freedom of worship for all Protestants. However, the plethora of new and often radical dissenting groups was too much for the Commonwealth. In 1656, there were additions to The Lord's Day Act which made attendance at a (Presbyterian) church compulsory on pain of a fine of 2*s* 6*d*; but once the promise of freedom of worship had been made it was impossible to revert to 'one state, one church' politics. The Protestant Pandora's box had been opened; people felt free to think for themselves about what they believed, and how they interpreted the Bible. The result of this theological liberation was dramatic. It generated an ever-fragmenting sectarianism, with the growth of numerous religious groups: 'The Reformation continued to reform itself',[1] but with an unprecedented speed and fervour.

One of these 'seekers after truth' was George Fox, who came to believe that religion could not be imposed externally and had nothing to do with theological dogmatism or professional clergy. God was in all of us, and we must be guided by this 'inner light' to live a good and moral life in peaceable friendship with all others who must be treated as equals, as was believed to be the case among the early Christians. It was a simple and uncomplicated idea, and consequently a powerful message. Those who rallied to this new (or possibly old) belief called themselves 'Friends of the Truth' or simply 'Friends'; but soon were known as 'Quakers' or 'The Religious Society of Friends'.

George Fox found an eager response, especially in the northern counties. Quakerism soon established firm roots in Yorkshire, and firm they had to be. For a group whose way of life was predicated on peace, toleration and friendship, they did not find these virtues reciprocated by the authorities or by large sections of the population. Quakers refused to swears oaths (as it was forbidden in the Bible*), did not acknowledge hierarchies or titles (as all were considered equal in the in the sight of God), and saw churches (which they called 'steeple houses') and a paid priesthood ('hirelings') as unnecessary and decadent, corrupting the true spiritual life. So they did not swear oaths of allegiance, call judges 'Your Honour', doff their hats to officials, pay tithes or contribute financially to the upkeep of churches or clergy, nor fight or support warfare.

---

* 'I say unto you, Swear not at all … But let your communication be, Yea, yea; Nay, nay: for whatsoever is more than these cometh of evil.' (*Matthew*, 5.34–37).

Cromwell was interested in Quakerism, but there was no way that he would tolerate, let alone embrace, pacifism. He was a soldier, the victor in the Civil War and signatory to the king's execution; his crushing defeats of the Scots at Dunbar and the Irish at Drogheda were swift and violent, and the condemnatory biblical sobriquet 'man of blood' given to the former king could apply equally to Cromwell.

Cromwell understood that an island like Britain must be a maritime trading nation, and that to safeguard the wealth which commerce could bring, the merchant marine had to be supported and protected by the government. The common assumption was that there was only a finite quantity of commerce, so the more that was had by the Dutch (England's main trade rival) the less was available to Britain. Cromwell strengthened the navy, and Parliament passed the Navigation Act of 1651 which made it illegal for English overseas colonies to import or export goods except in English ships, and restricted the transport of imports from mainland Europe to ships owned in either England or the country of origin of the goods. This piece of legislation was aimed primarily and successfully at the merchant shipping interests of the United Provinces,* and was perhaps the main cause of the war (known as the First Anglo-Dutch War) in the following year. As befits a struggle between two maritime powers, this conflict was fought entirely at sea. It ended in 1654 with an English victory. Cromwell then turned his attention to the next two significant trading rivals: Spain and France. Cunningly he traded one off against the other, allying with France, on the condition she guaranteed not to support the Stuart claim to the throne. The English took Jamaica and Dunkirk (at that time part of the Spanish Netherlands). England, at the time of Cromwell's Commonwealth, could (albeit briefly) call herself the ruler of the waves without eliciting laughter. However, while the British, French and Spanish were destroying each other's merchant ships, the Dutch were able to recuperate all that they had lost in the First Anglo-Dutch War, and their trade flourished once more.

When the British seized land and established a colony, the main motive was trade and its consequent profit. Jamaica was to be particularly profitable in the eighteenth century, as new and valuable crops were imported and grown; these

---

* The Netherlands, or the Low Countries, were under Spanish rule until 1751 when seven provinces seceded and set up as a republic in the name of the United Provinces; Holland was one of the provinces and became, by a process of synecdoche, to mean all of them. The portion of the Netherlands which remained under Hapsburg control (roughly modern Belgium, Luxembourg, with a bit of France) was called the Spanish Netherlands. In this book, I shall refer to the Dutch Republic interchangeably as Holland, the Netherlands or the United Provinces.

included sugar, rice, bananas, mangoes, limes and breadfruit. Slaves to do the growing, tending and harvesting of these crops were also imported. Alongside the invading soldiers, governors, merchants and profiteers who founded British colonies were missionaries of the Established Church; but other religious groups were not far behind. Quakers arrived early in the Americas and were well received in Barbados and in Rhode Island which had 'no law … to punish any for only declaring by words, their mindes and understandings concerning the things and ways of God'.[2] However, the rigorous Erastian Puritan regime in Massachusetts, which had set up a religious domination every bit as repressive as the one they had escaped from in England, was obsessively antagonistic. In 1658 it passed a law outlawing immigrant Quakers, who were to be banished and not permitted to return under pain of death. Masters of ships that brought Quakers into the colony were to be punished.

Oliver Cromwell died in 1658 and rule passed to his son Richard; his succession was not a success, and he was forced to resign in 1659, leaving a power vacuum while Parliament and the army played a waiting game, both seeking their own advantage, but neither able to proceed without the other. The result was a state of nervousness and confusion which Pepys described in his diary: 'All the world is at a loss … the country … all discontented.'

The Restoration of the Monarchy on 29 May 1660 was greeted with general relief. It seemed to promise peace and tolerance in a united and strong

The Restoration. Charles II centre, with his brother James, Duke of York on his right.

maritime world power. As the diarist Evelyn retrospectively commented, 'never had King more glorious opportunities to have made himselfe, his people, and all Europe happy'.

Charles had promised that if he were to become king, he would:

> declare a liberty to tender consciences, and that no man shall be disquieted or called in question for differences of opinion in matter of religion, which do not disturb the peace of the kingdom.
>
> (The Declaration of Breda)

This may have reflected his real intentions, but was certainly not the mood of the largely Royalist Restoration Parliament filled with those who wished to restore the Anglican ideal of a country united within a single church, with Charles II at its head, sharing a single translation of the Bible and a single form of worship. Parliament erroneously believed this goal was obtainable and would 'not disturb the peace of the kingdom'. Parliament made the laws which the king had to sign. Far from being a time of 'liberty to tender consciences' there was an imposition of an exclusive, yet compulsory, Established Church of England.

Charles knew better than to challenge Parliament, but as king he had power and influence. However, he wanted an easy life and did not capitalise effectively on the mood of positive optimism in the country, letting many opportunities slip through his royal fingers. Evelyn wrote that Charles was of 'too easy nature' which allowed 'him to be manag'd by crafty men, and some abandon'd and profane wretches'.

The proclamation of April 1661 prohibited the unlawful assemblies of 'Papists, Presbyterians, Independents, Anabaptists, Quakers and other fanatical persons', and required anyone charged with attending such a meeting to be required to swear the Oath of Allegiance – which, of course, Quakers could not do. Several Acts (collectively known as the Clarendon Code, after Edward Hyde, Earl of Clarendon who was the king's chief minister) made it illegal for non-Anglicans to hold any government office, or attend any religious meeting of more than five people. The Quaker Act made it illegal to refuse to take lawful oaths, particularly the Oath of Allegiance. It became a catch-all piece of legislation for the authorities to discriminate against Quakers.

George Fox refused to 'take the oath' and was imprisoned from 1665 in Scarborough Castle. Leland, over a century before, had described it as 'an exceeding goodly large and strong castelle', but it had been dramatically battered when Sir Hugh Cholmley of Whitby had held it for the king during the Civil War for nearly two years before surrendering. It was dismantled to ensure it could never again be seriously defended and was in poor condition when Fox was imprisoned there, so it was hardly surprising that his health suffered.

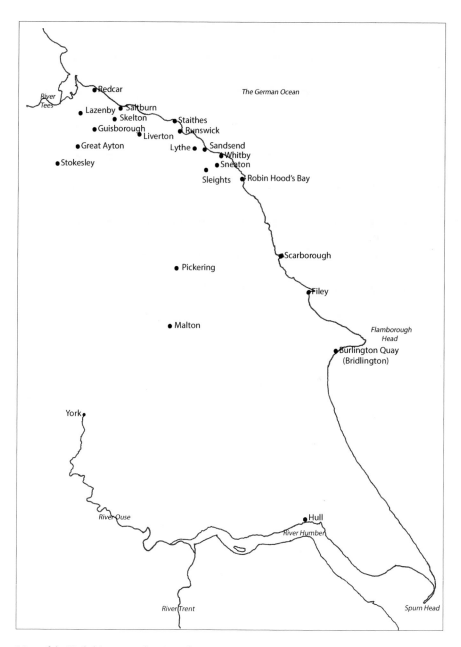

Map of the Yorkshire coast, showing places mentioned in this narrative.

Fox was released in 1666, after which he paid his third visit to the Friends at Whitby.

Three years later a plot of land on Church Street, Whitby, had been bought by Quakers as a site for a meeting house, which was finally completed in September 1676. The Conventicle Act was still in force at that time, so either it was felt that the mood of the country and/or county was more Quaker-friendly, or else that the risks of building illegal meeting houses were outweighed by the benefits.

Henry Compton, who had been appointed Bishop of London in 1675, was one of few leading members of the post-Restoration Anglican Church who had wished for greater inclusiveness and hoped that ultimately the Established Church could find a way of coming to a greater mutual understanding and union with other Protestant dissenters. However, his tolerant attitude did not include Catholics. His appointment may have been due in part to his impressive pedigree, being descended from Edward III through the Yorkist line, but he was certainly well trusted, as he was appointed to the Privy Council and chosen to supervise the education of Mary and Anne, the children of James, Duke of York.

Charles II had married Catherine of Braganza in 1662, a princess of Portugal, England's 'oldest ally'. Portugal had been an independent country since the twelfth century until she fell under Hapsburg rule in 1580 when Philip II of Spain also became Philip I of Portugal. Independence was declared in 1640 and the Duke of Braganza, father of Catherine, became King John (João) IV of Portugal. Catherine was a Catholic and therefore not a popular choice – even though she made the drinking of tea fashionable. Her dowry brought Bombay and Tangier into British possession. Although she had several pregnancies, they

The Quaker House at Whitby, which was rebuilt in 1813.

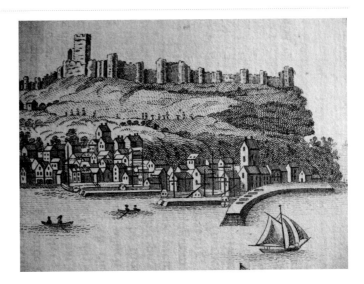

Scarborough castle.

had no live children, which must have been particularly galling to the queen as Charles had a series of acknowledged mistresses and a clutch of consequent acknowledged bastards.

By 1664, the commercial successes of the United Provinces once again stirred up feelings of envy and resentment among English merchants and Parliament. War fever gripped the country. The prevailing justification for the conflict was, as before, to extend English trade at the expense of the Dutch. Charles II also had personal and dynastic motivation: Cromwell's government had included a clause in the previous peace treaty insisting that the pro-Stuart House of Orange should be excluded from all public office in Holland, and this Charles wished to overthrow.

Quakers did not participate in this rage of militaristic aggression, but suffered as preparations were made by a nation which 'call'd aloud for war'.[3] Not only were they routinely accused of being traitors to their country but, as Besse records, their property was often seized 'for refusing to contribute toward the Charges of the County Militia'.

The Second Anglo-Dutch War officially began in March 1665, but before that there were government-supported piratical raids on territory of the United Provinces; for example, New Amsterdam, a Dutch city at the time, was captured by the British in 1664 and renamed New York after James, Duke of York. The English were arrogant and over-confident; they assumed that as they had beaten the Dutch very easily in the previous conflict victory in a second war would be a foregone conclusion. At first things went well for Britain; there was a resounding victory at the Battle of Lowestoft, in which William Penn fought with distinction. He later became an admiral and was knighted. He was Samuel Pepys' neighbour and former colleague at the Navy Board, and father to the William Penn who founded Pennsylvania.

Members of the Society of Friends naturally did not volunteer to serve in the navy, but the fighting ships of England were full of sailors who had not volunteered. Impressment was deemed necessary to keep the fleet manned, and many personal tragedies resulted, but a pacifist who fell into the hands of the press gang faced a serious test of his belief. It was not a good time for Quakers, especially those who lived in port towns.

In June 1666, the British navy emerged from the Four Days' Battle, one of the longest sea-battles in recorded history, in a position to claim victory, though it had, in fact, been a major triumph for the Dutch. A month after this, though, the Royal Navy had recovered sufficiently to defeat the Dutch and temporarily gain command of the sea off the coast of Holland, which enabled the British to capture a large number of Dutch merchant ships. These naval achievements were lauded by John Dryden, the first poet laureate, in his poem *Annus Mirabilis, or The Year of Wonders*. It is full of nationalist arrogance, and Dryden compares Holland's relationship with England to that of ancient Carthage with Rome:

> Thus mighty in her ships, stood Carthage long,
> And swept the riches of the world from far;
> Yet stoop'd to Rome, less wealthy, but more strong:
> And this may prove our second Punic war.[*]

Charles II was always short of money, and wars are expensive, so the king sold Dunkirk to the French for 2,500,000 livres (*c.* £350,000; in modern money £1.3 billion). Only a fraction of the agreed price was paid, and the money did not last long: the Great Fire of London had greatly reduced the Crown's revenue, and had brought additional government expenses. Add to this the ever-increasing extravagance of the court, and the result was that both king and country were seriously financially embarrassed.

Dryden was right about Britain being poorer than Holland, but wrong about the outcome of the war, and all his poetic pomp and spin came to look rather foolish. Pepys summed up the situation: 'the want of money puts all things, and above all the Navy, out of order'. Dryden had described the English navy which 'now at anchor rides' as 'vast'; in fact, England did not have sufficient wealth to continue the war, and several of the larger British warships were indeed riding at anchor in the Medway as they were too expensive to refit.

This allowed the Dutch, in June 1667, to sail to the mouth of the Thames with impunity, attack the fort at Sheerness, which was surrendered fairly speedily by the unpaid and ill-supplied garrison, and occupy the island of Sheppey. Then they

---

[*] The Second Punic War (218–201 BC) was fought between Carthage, led by Hannibal, and the Romans. Initially, Hannibal won some spectacular victories, but Rome fought back and the war ended with the complete defeat of Carthage.

Map of Kent and the Thames Estuary,
showing the Isle of Sheppey, the Medway
and Chatham.

sailed up the Medway and burnt many of the ships riding at anchor, towing away
the *Royal Charles*, which had been the ship in which Charles II had returned to
Britain in triumph in 1660. The diarist John Evelyn, who was a friend of Dryden,
wrote that this daring raid 'put both Country and Citty into a paniq feare and
consternation' with many 'fearing the enemie might venture up the Thames even
to London'. This was the most catastrophic destruction ever inflicted on the English
navy, and was also a successful (if brief) occupation of English territory. It was a
deep humiliation for the country, for the navy and particularly for the monarch.

   To add insult to injury the Dutch fleet blockaded the Thames for some days
afterwards. This caused a serious shortage of imports to London, particularly coal,
and led the king to consult John Evelyn, as an expert on trees and timber, about
his 'new fuell'.** The mood in the country turned against the government, and a

** A 'mixture of charcoal, dust and loam which burnt without smoke or ill smell' (Diary 2 &
8 July 1667).

peace treaty was signed in haste against a background of sullen discontent. Samuel Pepys wrote: 'In all things, in wisdom, courage, force and success, the Dutch have the best of us and end the war with victory on their side.' As Clerk of the Acts in the Navy Office, Pepys was responsible for the day-to-day logistics of the navy, something of a thankless task in a system that was riddled with incompetence, corruption and underfunding, though – as a result of his 'life-long labours' – Pepys eventually achieved his ambition of giving 'administrative discipline'[4] to the organisation of the navy.

The Dutch had won the war, and England was humiliated. Although England kept New York, the Dutch retained possession of the more profitable sugar-rich Suriname which they had captured a few months previously. The Indonesian island Pulau Run was officially confirmed as a Dutch possession, giving Holland a valuable monopoly on nutmeg for the next 150 years. Additionally, the English were forced to amend the Navigation Act to be more Dutch-friendly, and to sign an alliance with the United Provinces and Sweden in order to restrict France's territorial ambitions. The Dutch also abolished the position of stadtholder 'for ever'.

It was a disaster, and the public wanted scapegoats. One such was George Carteret of Jersey who had protected Prince Charles after the decisive Royalist defeat at Worcester. Later, after the execution of the king, Carteret had the prince publicly proclaimed as King Charles II at St Helier. At the Restoration, Charles rewarded him with a large grant of land in America (which Carteret named New Jersey) and the post of Treasurer of the Navy – and it was as such that Carteret was vilified as the man whose financial double-dealing and incompetence impoverished the navy into defeat.

The terms of the treaty had made another war inevitable. The Third Dutch War (1672–74) was meant to restore British prestige and to strike a serious blow at Dutch prosperity and trade, and at its current government. It was largely the brainchild of Charles II, who was also pursuing his dynastic interest in ousting the present Dutch regime and ensuring his nephew William of Orange, now come of age, should be appointed stadtholder. William had come to London in the autumn of 1670 in what was officially a visit to see his uncle, but which was no doubt something of a summit conference. Charles and William did not see eye to eye, but clearly had shared interests. Charles wanted William to run a puppet government subservient to the British in the United Provinces, which was not what William had in mind, and the visit, like many diplomatic missions, ended in mutual suspicion.

Charles persuaded William Temple, the British ambassador to the United Provinces (a man of probity who admired the Dutch), to pledge friendship with the government of Holland. The king then entered into a secret treaty with his first cousin and Britain's old enemy Louis XIV whereby the army of France and

Genealogy 1: Carteret Genealogy

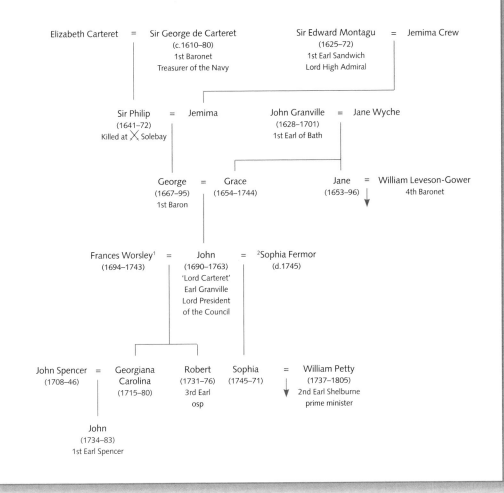

the navy of Britain would destroy the wealthy Dutch republican government. This was totally contrary to the alliance, made only three years before, between England, Sweden and the Dutch Republic to curb the territorial ambitions of France, especially in the Spanish Netherlands.

The idea of another war with Holland was not popular, and the country could not afford it. Evelyn captured the mood of much of the country when he wrote 'surely this was a quarrel slenderly grounded, and not becoming Christian [Protestant] neighbours'. Even before war was officially declared, the navy had been ordered to attack the Dutch merchant fleet sailing to the eastern Mediterranean while they were in the Channel. This was to be the

John Evelyn. Swaine after a portrait by Nanteuil.

pre-emptive strike which would seriously damage Dutch shipping and trade but was something of a fiasco due mainly to overconfidence on the British side.

The Dutch navy, however, was able to offer its own decisive strike, catching the British fleet unawares while the latter were still taking on supplies in Sole Bay off the Suffolk port of Southwold. The ensuing battle was fiercely fought. Edward Montagu, Earl of Sandwich commanded *Prince Royal*, which was set alight by fireships; he perished, along with his son-in-law Sir Philip Carteret, in the ensuing inferno. The Dutch had the advantage and might have inflicted massive destruction but the wind suddenly changed and ensured that the Dutch withdrew. This was neither the first nor the last time that England was saved by the weather; Sydney Smith was later to refer to 'those ancient and unsubsidised allies of England – the winds, upon which ministers depend for saving kingdoms as washerwomen do for drying clothes'.[5]

John Evelyn was one of the Commissioners for Taking Care of Sick and Wounded Seamen and for the Care and Treatment of Prisoners of War. It was his job to deal with the aftermath of the Battle of Sole Bay, having to look after 'many wounded, sick and prisoners newly put on shore'.[6] Naturally he was deeply affected by the tragic death of his 'particular friend' the Earl of Sandwich, whom he described as an 'incomparable person who was learned in sea affaires, in politics, in mathematics, and in musiq … [he] was of a sweete and obliging temper, sober, chast, very ingenious, a true Nobleman'.

Evelyn took his work very seriously, and he was concerned about 'the aboundance of miserably wounded' seamen irrespective of rank. He reported that:

I saw the chirurgeon [surgeon] cut off the leg of a wounded sailor, the stout and gallant man enduring it with incredible patience, without being bound to his chaire as usual on such painfull occasions. I had hardly courage enough to be present. Not being cut off high enough, the gangreen prevail'd, and the second operation cost the poore creature his life.

He added:

Lord! What miseries are mortal men subject to, and what confusion and mischeif do the avarice, anger and ambition of Princes cause in the world!

Later he commented on the war that it 'shew'd the folly of hazarding so brave a fleete, and loosing so many good men for no provocation but that the Hollanders exceeded us in commerce and industrie, and in all things but [except] envie'.

After Sole Bay, the British fleet was in effect useless. The French army had made incursions into the Netherlands, provoking a civil unrest in the country which toppled the existing government; William, Prince of Orange was invited to become stadtholder. By the end of 1672 the French and the British had come to distrust each other, and the war was doomed when Parliament refused to approve further funding. Taking advantage of the British weakness, New York was recaptured by the Dutch in 1673 and for a while was called New Orange after William, Prince of Orange. Britain made peace with the United Provinces in 1674 with the spin that their only war aim was the restoration of Prince William – which had already been achieved. The treaty was largely based on the pre-war status quo, so New York was handed back to Britain, which emerged surprisingly well from this total confusion of a conflict in which they had not won a single battle.

These wars disrupted trade; the Dutch blockading the Thames (1667) and the Battle of Sole Bay (1672) were serious problems for those ships engaged in the coastal coal trade between Newcastle and London, many of which were Whitby-owned and some owned by Quakers. During the wars, Dutch privateers had attacked and captured merchant vessels, deliberately targeting the East Coast coal fleet and ships trading with Norway and the Baltic. Peace brought an end to these depredations, and there followed some fifteen years in which Britain was free from war, much to the benefit of its trade. However, for those sailing in the Mediterranean, the Barbary pirates were a perennial danger, operating from various strongholds on the North Africa coast. They attacked merchant ships, plundering their cargo and taking the crew to be sold into slavery.

The walled and fortified city of Tangier, acquired as part of the dowry of Catherine of Braganza, was seen as having considerable strategic significance for the British trade in the Mediterranean and as a base from which the power of the Barbary pirates might be reduced. Samuel Pepys' administrative efficiency ensured that he was put 'into commission in the business of Tanger [sic]' by his patron and cousin Lord Sandwich. Other members of the Tangier Committee were Sir George Carteret and Admiral Sir William Penn.

A large force was sent out to garrison Tangier, but there was real antagonism with the local Portuguese inhabitants, who petitioned to be repatriated. This was granted, and Tangier ceased to be a city and became a barracks, surrounded by a rather unfriendly and uncooperative population. Sir Hugh Cholmley of Whitby had been appointed as the director of works at Tangier, with the responsibility of building accommodation for the men and improving the harbour by constructing a large mole. The impressive quadrangle of buildings was to be named 'Fort Middleton', but it was always known as colloquially as 'Whitby', as so many of the workers came from there.

Its isolation meant that Tangier had to be supplied with everything it needed by ship, which involved a lot of logistical work. Pepys, who had been appointed treasurer of the enterprise, receiving 'half the profit', became friends with Hugh Cholmley and it seems that the two of them had come to some mutually beneficial financial arrangement with regard to choice of suppliers. The mole was finished in 1676, and Sir Hugh Cholmley returned to England. Charles II, who was a keen supporter of the enterprise, granted him, as he was in possession of the old Abbey lands, all the rights and privileges 'in as full, free, and ample manner as any Abbot or Abbots of the said late Monastery of Whitby',[7] which included 'the sea-port and sea wreck through all his manor or Lordship of Whitby … with all the liberties, customs, and privileges pertaining to a sea-port', among which were taxes on boats and fish, and dues for the right of lying-up in winter.

However, despite Tangier's strategic usefulness, supporting the garrison there was expensive, and there were regular attacks from sea and land. Eventually, 'The English Parliament disgusted with the expense of maintaining Tangier, from which the nation had imagined it should gain great advantages, which, instead of being profitable, it was burdensome, resolved to abandon the place'.[8] In 1684, the English withdrew their garrison, stores and artillery, and blew up the mole and the fortifications.

During the Third Anglo-Dutch War, Pepys and Evelyn had both been employed by the Admiralty. They met on several occasions and discussed Evelyn's project to build an infirmary for sick and wounded sailors,* which Pepys 'mightily' approved of because it would be 'of use and will save money'. Evelyn lived in Sayes Court,

---

* The army had the Chelsea Hospital, but there was nothing equivalent for the navy. This was eventually rectified in 1694, by the initiative of Queen Mary II, in the founding of Greenwich Hospital. Evelyn was chosen as 'Treasurer to the Marine College erecting at Greenwich' with a salary of £220 (£26,000 / £565,000) pa. However, after two years he complained that he had not yet received a penny (Evelyn, Helen, p.76).

Genealogy 2: Montagu Genealogy

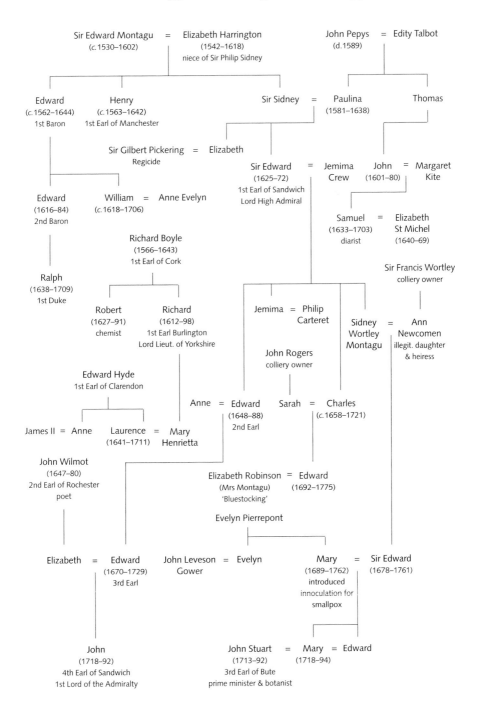

conveniently near the naval dockyard at Deptford, and was a Younger Brother of Trinity House:* Pepys at this time was an Elder Brother.

Like many intelligent men of the Age of Reason, Evelyn and Pepys were multitalented. Evelyn was a founder member of the Royal Society (of which Pepys was to be president in 1684), accumulated a large library (as did Pepys) and was a prolific author. They were passionate about science, trade and philanthropy – all of which were seen as closely related and intertwining: science was the means of promoting trade which in turn would bring wealth which would benefit the whole country.

After the Great Fire, Sir Christopher Wren's design for the new St Paul's Cathedral was (eventually) accepted, and numerous fine churches of his were built; however, his grand plan of totally restructuring the city with wide, straight streets, piazzas and public gardens to make a beautiful, practical, modern and efficient city was rejected.

Evelyn, who was a friend of Wren and a godfather to one of his sons, also wanted planning – in order to reduce the pollution in the city. In his work *Fumifugium*, he described the inhabitants of London as breathing 'nothing but an impure and thick Mist ... and filthy vapour ... corrupting the Lungs, and disordering the entire habit of their Bodies'. The cause was the burning of coal by the various heavy industries (e.g. 'Brewers, Diers, Limeburners, Salt, and Sope-Boylers') which were situated in the centre of the city, with the result that London resembled 'the Court of Vulcan ... or the Suburbs of Hell, than an Assembly of Rational Creatures'. Evelyn thought that the fire of London was an opportunity to do some real planning with all the main polluters resited in an industrial estate away from the residential and commercial parts of town, which would make living and working in the city more pleasant, and the relocated businesses would be able to operate more efficiently. Evelyn's utopian vision was also rejected, as there was neither the capital funding for anything so adventurous nor – more importantly – was there any precedent for King or Parliament to seize the necessary powers of compulsory purchase of private property, which would have been seen as a monstrous infringement of British liberty.

Rebuilding a city from an Enlightenment blueprint may be a fantasy, but making a garden could be a reality. And many strove to create gardens that

---

* Trinity House, which still flourishes, was founded according to its Elizabethan charter 'to erect and set up such and so many Beacons, Marks and Signs for the Sea, in such places of the Sea-shores and up-Lands near the Sea-Coasts, or Forelands of the Sea ... whereby the Dangers may be avoided and escaped, and Ships the better come unto their ports without peril' (Mead, p.20). They were later also involved in providing pensions for superannuated sailors and seamen's widows. The organisation was run by a Master (a post Pepys later held), four wardens and eighteen Elder Brothers. There were also Younger Brothers (usually between 250 and 400), who were assistants to the Elder Brothers but whose duties were largely honorary.

Cross section of
St Paul's.

were oases of delight and harmony, reaping the benefits of the twin sciences of horticulture and botany with plants often garnered from far-distant lands for their medicinal or culinary properties, their rarity or simply their pure beauty. The gardens were structured with avenues of trees, creating splendid vistas as well as having useful cash potential. A club of eager botanists, led by Hans Sloane, met at the Temple Coffee House near Fleet Street and acted as a hub for botanical information and exchange of plants. Members included Henry Compton, Bishop of London and his friend, fellow cleric and botanist John Ray.

Evelyn was one such enthusiastic gardener and he spent much time improving the garden at Sayes Court. His horticultural speciality was trees, and he wrote a book called *Sylva, or A Discourse of Forest Trees, and the Propagation of Timber in His Majesties Dominions*, which was both a comprehensive work on tree varieties and an appeal to landowners to plant trees to ensure that there would be sufficient timber in the future to replace the devastation (particularly of oaks) brought about largely by shipbuilding. He also favoured planting rows of fragrant trees beside roads in towns in order to improve the quality of the air. He had travelled in the United Provinces and visited the palace of Rijswijk, the home of the Princes of Orange, commenting that there was 'nothing more remarkable than the delicious walks planted with lime trees', which were both beautiful and a good investment. Sir William Temple, who had been the British ambassador to Holland, wrote his own contribution to the garden literature of the times with *Upon the Gardens of Epicurus*.

King Charles died in 1685, and was succeeded by his brother as James II. As Duke of York and Lord High Admiral, James had gained some popularity; and his first marriage was to Anne Hyde, daughter of Edward Hyde, Earl of Clarendon. James and Anne had two children who survived adulthood, Mary and Anne, who were brought up as members of the Church of England.

After his wife Anne died in 1671 James had 'come out' as a Catholic. Evelyn recorded the 'exceeding griefe and scandal to the whole Nation' when, on Easter Day, James did not receive 'communion with the King'. This clear and public statement of his Catholicism was shocking, particularly as Parliament had passed the Act for Preventing Dangers which May Happen from Popish Recusants, which required everyone holding any political or military office to take the oaths of supremacy and allegiance and make a declaration that it was their 'belief that there is not any transubstantiation in the sacrament of the Lord's Supper, or in the elements of bread and wine, at or after the consecration thereof'.

In the same year James had married the Italian Mary, the Catholic daughter of Alfonso IV d'Este, Duke of Modena. In 1685, the French king revoked the Edict of Nantes, thus making the practice of any Protestant denomination, in public or in private, illegal in France and its subject territories. In future, every French child born had to be baptised a Catholic. Protestant ministers had a fortnight to convert to Catholicism or leave the country; all other Protestants were forbidden to emigrate – though many did.

In England, Catholics flourished. Having a Catholic king who was *ex officio* head of the Church of England was a weird anomaly and one that generated a lot of bad feeling. However, as James wished to bring Roman Catholics back into acceptability in Britain, he was keen to reduce persecution for non-Anglicans. Consequently, religious persecution ceased with the Declaration of Indulgence. This was a welcome relief to dissenters, including the Quakers, though they were still liable to punishment for non-payment of tithes, which was a 'legitimate tax'.

The Declaration of Indulgence was not palatable to a sizeable proportion of the population, who feared it was a first step to reintroducing Catholicism as the national established religion, and consequently made an unpopular monarch even more unpopular. The Civil War had left still fresh and painful scars in the country's memory and consequently, while the ageing James II's sole heirs were

Genealogy 3: The House of Stuart

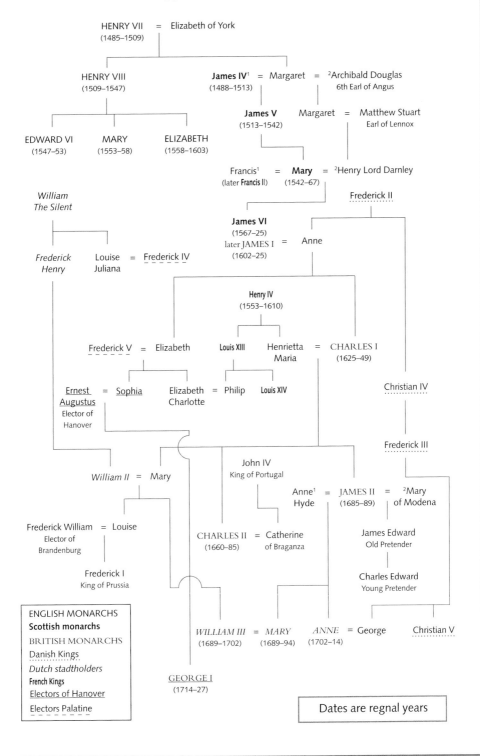

HENRY VII = Elizabeth of York
(1485–1509)

HENRY VIII
(1509–1547)

James IV¹ = Margaret = ²Archibald Douglas
(1488–1513)   6th Earl of Angus

James V   Margaret = Matthew Stuart
(1513–1542)   Earl of Lennox

EDWARD VI   MARY   ELIZABETH
(1547–53)   (1553–58) (1558–1603)

Francis¹ = Mary = ²Henry Lord Darnley
(later Francis II) (1542–67)

Frederick II

William
The Silent

James VI
(1567–25)
later JAMES I = Anne
(1602–25)

Frederick   Louise = Frederick IV
Henry   Juliana

Henry IV
(1553–1610)

Frederick V = Elizabeth   Louis XIII   Henrietta = CHARLES I
                                        Maria   (1625–49)

Ernest = Sophia   Elizabeth = Philip   Louis XIV
Augustus   Charlotte
Elector of
Hanover

Christian IV

John IV
King of Portugal

Frederick III

William II = Mary

Anne¹ = JAMES II = ²Mary
Hyde   (1685–89) of Modena

Frederick William = Louise   CHARLES II = Catherine   James Edward
Elector of   (1660–85)   of Braganza   Old Pretender
Brandenburg

Frederick I   Charles Edward
King of Prussia   Young Pretender

ENGLISH MONARCHS
Scottish monarchs
BRITISH MONARCHS   WILLIAM III = MARY   ANNE = George   Christian V
Danish Kings   (1689–1702) (1689–94) (1702–14)
Dutch stadtholders
French Kings
Electors of Hanover
Electors Palatine   GEORGE I
                        (1714–27)

Dates are regnal years

his two Anglican daughters, most people thought it better to weather out the storm until he died and was succeeded by Mary, the heir presumptive. In 1677, Mary had married William of Orange, stadtholder of the United Province. He had a good claim to the English throne in his own right, being the grandson of Charles I. This marriage had strengthened his claim, making it likely that he would sit on the English throne one day, provided James II had no male heir.

This situation changed in 1688 when it was announced that the Catholic James' Catholic wife had given birth to a son, James Edward, who would be the Prince of Wales and heir apparent to the throne. The prospect of England becoming a Catholic and, so it was feared, less free country under a repressive autocratic regime, like France, was more than most people could bear, believing it would undo the achievements of the Civil War and turn the clock back to the reign of Queen Mary.

Many read, or had read to them, the grisly stories of the Marian persecutions of the Protestants by the Catholics in John Foxe's book commonly known as *The Book of Martyrs*. It was regularly reprinted with appropriate illustrations and became, along with Bunyan's *Pilgrim's Progress*, one of the most influential books in British Protestantism after the Bible itself.*

Foxe fixed in the popular mind an image of what living under Catholic rule might be like, and immortalised such Protestant rallying calls as Bishop Latimer's last wordsto Bishop Ridley as they were both burnt to death at Oxford in 1555: 'Be of good comfort, for we shall this day light such a candle in England as, I trust, shall never be put out.'**

In 1688, many were looking to William of Orange to extricate the country from this gloomy possibility, and to ensure that the Protestant candle would continue to burn in England.

---

* John Walker had a copy of Foxe's *Book of Martyrs*; Gaskin records seeing it, 'with "John Walker" written on the title page' (Gaskin, p.386).

** These are the words attributed to Latimer by Foxe. Whether these were the bishop's words is debatable; but there is no denying their lasting efficacy as denominational propaganda.

2

Liberty and *Property*

How came we ashore?
By Providence divine.
(William Shakespeare, *The Tempest*)

On 1 November 1688, William of Orange set out from Holland to England. He had been invited: the *Invitation to William* was written by Henry Sidney, suggesting that if William came to Britain, 'the people are so generally dissatisfied with the present conduct of the government in relation to their religion, liberties and properties ... that your Highness may be assured there are nineteen parts of twenty of the people throughout the kingdom who are desirous of a change'. He added that many soldiers would desert, 'and amongst the seamen ... not one in ten' would stay loyal to King James.

The emphasis on liberties and properties reflects the claim of the philosopher John Locke that all people had the right to life, liberty and property. These ideas were enormously influential in political theory and practice in England and beyond for many decades. At the time of William's invasion, Locke was in Holland; he later sailed to Britain accompanying William's wife, the future Queen Mary II.

Henry Sidney, together with the six other signatories of the *Invitation* (who included William Cavendish, 4th Earl of Devonshire; Thomas Belasyse, Viscount Fauconberg; Richard, Viscount Lumley later 1st Earl of Scarborough; and Henry Compton Bishop of London), came to be known as the Immortal Seven. The *Invitation* was secretly smuggled out of the country to William by Vice Admiral Arthur Herbert, disguised as an ordinary seaman.

In spite of the promises of mass desertion from James' army and navy, William was taking no chances. He sailed with a massive armada of 500 ships (nearly four times the number in the Spanish Armada a century earlier) and a sizeable well-trained, well-equipped and well-supported army. Although this has become known as the Glorious (or Bloodless) Revolution, it was a real invasion force, indeed the last successful invasion of Britain. It had been assembled with speed

Genealogy 4: Belasyse (Fauconberg) Genealogy

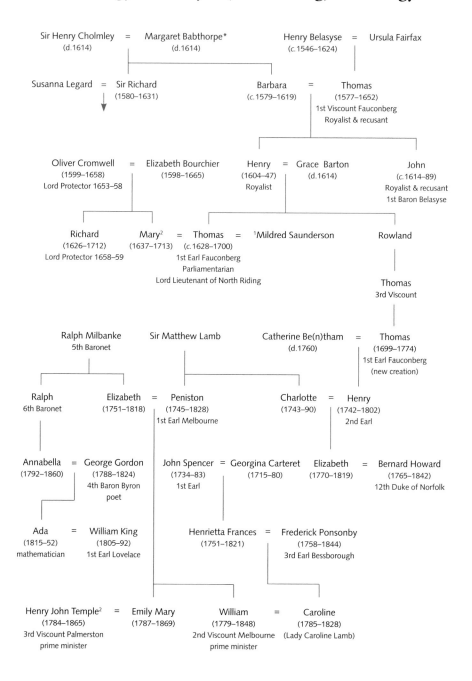

Sir Henry Cholmley (d.1614) = Margaret Babthorpe* (d.1614)

Henry Belasyse (c.1546–1624) = Ursula Fairfax

Susanna Legard = Sir Richard (1580–1631)

Barbara (c.1579–1619) = Thomas (1577–1652) 1st Viscount Fauconberg Royalist & recusant

Oliver Cromwell (1599–1658) Lord Protector 1653–58 = Elizabeth Bourchier (1598–1665)

Henry (1604–47) Royalist = Grace Barton (d.1614)

John (c.1614–89) Royalist & recusant 1st Baron Belasyse

Richard (1626–1712) Lord Protector 1658–59

Mary² (1637–1713) = Thomas (c.1628–1700) 1st Earl Fauconberg Parliamentarian Lord Lieutenant of North Riding = ¹Mildred Saunderson

Rowland

Thomas 3rd Viscount

Ralph Milbanke 5th Baronet

Sir Matthew Lamb

Catherine Be(n)tham (d.1760) = Thomas (1699–1774) 1st Earl Fauconberg (new creation)

Ralph 6th Baronet

Elizabeth (1751–1818) = Peniston (1745–1828) 1st Earl Melbourne

Charlotte (1743–90) = Henry (1742–1802) 2nd Earl

Annabella (1792–1860) = George Gordon (1788–1824) 4th Baron Byron poet

John Spencer (1734–83) 1st Earl = Georgina Carteret (1715–80)

Elizabeth (1770–1819) = Bernard Howard (1765–1842) 12th Duke of Norfolk

Ada (1815–52) mathematician = William King (1805–92) 1st Earl Lovelace

Henrietta Frances (1751–1821) = Frederick Ponsonby (1758–1844) 3rd Earl Bessborough

Henry John Temple² (1784–1865) 3rd Viscount Palmerston prime minister = Emily Mary (1787–1869)

William (1779–1848) 2nd Viscount Melbourne prime minister = Caroline (1785–1828) (Lady Caroline Lamb)

* Margaret was the gt-gt-granddaughter (in the female line) of Anne of York whose mother and father were both descended from Edward III, and who was sister of Kings Edward IV and Richard III. The skeleton of Richard III was identified conclusively by the mitochondrial DNA which had passed down from Anne of York's mother Cecily Neville through Margaret and her daughter Barbara in a descending female line to Michael Ibsen.

The eye of God sees and confounds Guy Fawkes' Plot.

and efficiency, and the rumours which circulated in England about it caused alarm and confusion at court.

When the fleet sailed, the plan was to avoid the south-east, where the British navy and most of its armed forces were assembled. If the wind was southerly, the Dutch would land in Yorkshire, where they believed there would be much support from Protestant dissenters; if the wind was easterly, which turned out to be the case, they would land on the West Country coast, where Monmouth's Rebellion had begun three years before.

William's armada sailed up the Channel in an ostentatiously magnificent display of power, and at some speed, driven by the same easterly wind which kept the English ships from leaving the Thames. Prince William's fleet moored at Torbay, but delayed disembarking until 5 November, a suitable propaganda gesture as this was the day when the British commemorated being saved from Catholic rule.*

William and his advisors were well aware of the power of propaganda (having brought a printing press with them), the most significant of which was the Prince of Orange's *Declaration of the Reasons inducing him to appear in Arms in the Kingdom of*

---

* The Observance of November 5th Act, which made 5 November a day of thanksgiving marked with ringing of church bells, a special service and an appropriate sermon, was passed in January 1606, sponsored by Edward, 1st Baron Montagu. His Royalist sympathies ensured his imprisonment by the Cromwell regime, and he died in prison in 1644. He was the uncle of Pepys' patron, the 1st Earl of Sandwich.

England, for preserving of the Protestant Religion, and for restoring the Laws and Liberties of England, Scotland, Ireland. This document had been months in the drafting and was the result of ideas and input from many sources, perhaps most importantly John Locke. This manifesto had been printed in vast numbers and had not only been brought over in the prince's ships, but also been previously and secretly sent to certain safe houses in Britain to be kept hidden until William landed. It began:

> It is both certain and evident to all Men, that the publick Peace and Happiness of any State or Kingdom cannot be preserved, where the Laws, Liberties and Customs, established by the lawful Authority in it, are openly transgressed and annulled; more especially where the Alteration of Religion is endeavoured ... those who are most immediately concerned in it are indispensably bound to endeavour to preserve and maintain the established Laws, Liberties and Customs, and, above all, the Religion and Worship of God, that is established among them.

William marched on London, taking time off to do a bit of sightseeing on the way, including a visit to admire the house and, more particularly, the gardens at Wilton, the family home of the Thomas Herbert, 8th Earl of Pembroke, to whom John Locke was to dedicate his *Essay Concerning Human Understanding*. This rather casual procession belied an efficient and well-executed takeover of the country; Dutch soldiers went on ahead, capturing Whitehall Palace and patrolling the streets of London, only twenty-one years since the Dutch fleet had sailed up the Medway and fourteen years since the end of the Third Dutch War.

On 13 February 1689, William and his wife were proclaimed as King William III and Queen Mary II, both to reign for life. The coronation, at which they vowed to uphold the Church of England, was held on 11 April with Henry Compton, Bishop of London, presiding: it must have been a special moment for the bishop when he put the crown on Mary's head, as he had nurtured her and her sister Anne in their youth, ensuring they grew up as true Anglicans.

Shortly afterwards, the Bill of Rights Act was passed, which established a constitutional Protestant monarchy, with a freely, fairly and regularly appointed parliament with fuller powers. In the same year, the Act of Uniformity and the Conventicle Act were repealed and the Toleration Act was passed, which allowed greater freedom of conscience and freedom of worship. The Bill of Rights also decreed 'that the subjects which are Protestants may have Armes for their defence suitable to their conditions and as allowed by Law'.* The threat of a Stuart

---

* This article was influential in the American states, granting similar powers to its (originally only white and male) citizens in the 2nd Amendment to the Constitution: 'the right of the people to keep and bear arms shall not be infringed.'

counter-invasion aided by the French was real; liberty must be protected, by force if necessary.

George Fox died in 1691, having lived to see an end to serious state persecution, but having the foresight to warn his followers that an easier life might lead them to backsliding, and prayed that they should not become one of those 'who embrace the present world and encumber themselves with their own business and neglect the Lord's and so are good for nothing'.[1]

James had escaped to France where Louis XIV supported his cause. The Stuart supporters did not give up easily, though the Battle of the Boyne was a decisive victory for William in Ireland – albeit a victory that bred long-term festering resentment. The Protestant song 'Lillibulero' was one of the early examples of effective propaganda. Sung to a tune attributed to Henry Purcell, it became the anthem of the Williamite Protestants, and it was said to have 'sung James II out of three kingdoms'. Certainly Uncle Toby in Sterne's *Tristram Shandy* seemed to think 'Lillibulero' had potent powers, as he would whistle the tune whenever he was in difficult or embarrassing situations.

Scottish Jacobites won the Battle of Killiecrankie but were unable to capitalise on it, so they agreed to peace provided that William ensured that the established church in Scotland should be in accordance with the Presbyterian order.

Shandy Hall, Laurence Sterne's house in Coxwold.

In England the country was more tranquil, the population eager for a less divided and more tolerant society in which people could get back to their business. Increasingly popular in the late seventeen and the eighteenth centuries, with the rise of the new science, was deism. The premise of deism is that God, all-powerful and rational, created the universe which runs regularly and effectively according to his rules, and consequently he would not and does not interfere with his own laws of nature. As Voltaire (who was influenced by Locke and Newton) was to put it: 'I believe in God, not the God of the mystics and theologians, but the God of Nature, the great geometrician, the architect of the universe, the prime mover, unalterable, transcendental, everlasting.'[2]

The abandoning of all miracles was never going to be acceptable to the Church authorities, especially as it would seem to deny the central Christian belief in the resurrection of Jesus. Mystics and theologians would continue to thrive, but aspects of deism's calm rationality, love of science and concern for morality rather than dogma certainly affected the beliefs of many Protestant Christians.

After the end of the Civil War, the Yorkshire-born rationalist and cleric John Tillotson had written: 'The manners of men have been almost universally corrupted by a Civil War. We should therefore all jointly endeavour to retrieve the ancient virtues of the Nation, that solid and substantial, plain and unaffected piety, free from extremes both of superstition and enthusiasm [i.e. fanaticism].' Some thirty years later he must have hoped that his much longed-for wish might at last come true. It was probably because of his toleration and compelling preaching that Tillotson was preferred over Henry Compton for the post of the Archbishop of Canterbury in 1691.

Joseph Addison, who in many ways set the pattern for the attitudes and beliefs for the reasonable person of 'the middling sort', wrote in the *Spectator*, that 'Faith and Devotion naturally grow in the Mind of every reasonable Man, who sees the Impressions of Divine Power and Wisdom in every Object on which he casts his Eye'.[3] In the same essay he included an ode (which became a hymn) based on the passage from Psalm 19 'The Heavens declare the Glory of God':

> The Spacious Firmament on high
> And all the blue Etherial Sky
> And spangled Heav'ns, a Shining Frame,
> Their great Original Proclaim ...
>
> In Reason's Ear they all rejoice
> And utter forth a glorious Voice,
> For ever singing, as they shine,
> 'The hand that made us is Divine'.

In 1695 Locke published (anonymously) his book *The Reasonableness of Christianity, as delivered in the Scriptures*, in which he sought to simplify Christianity which, he posited, the 'Writers and Wranglers in Religion' had made complicated, 'as if there were no way into the Church but through an Academy'. He pointed out that 'the bulk of mankind have not leisure for Learning and Logick'. Locke's dictum was 'Reason must be our last Judge and Guide in every Thing', and he aimed some of his argument directly at Quakers, explaining that they must bring their 'Guide of [the] 'Light within' to the Tryal [i.e. of Reason]' or they would be surrendering themselves 'to all the Extravagancies of Delusion and Error'.

Jonathan Swift launched a different attack on Quakers in his customarily vicious style in *Tale of a Tub*, written at Farnham when he was acting as secretary to Sir William Temple, who had retired from public life to write and 'cultivate his garden'. In Swift's book, Jack, in parody of the Quaker's central concept of the 'Inner Light', had a 'perpetual flame in his belly', generating a 'glowing steam' which he emitted as 'oracular belches to his panting disciples'.

How damaging this kind of attack was to the public perception of the Society of Friends is open to question; but Swift would not have spent the time and trouble over his hissing cauldron of satiric vitriol if the Society of Friends had not established itself as a sizeable and influential group in contemporary Britain. The Quakers were very much a minority group, but they understood publicity and the importance of keeping on the right side of the law. So far as influence went, they were punching well above their weight.

King William remained Prince Willem of Orange, stadtholder of the United Provinces, and, as such, was fighting a war with France in which England was necessarily involved. William would regularly travel to Holland each spring, and return each autumn. His wife Mary was joint sovereign but in practice William was the senior monarch, with his profile largely obscuring Mary's on the coinage.

Whenever William returned to Britain after his annual campaigning, Mary handed back the royal powers, acting more as a regent than a co-monarch. She died, childless, of smallpox in 1694. William's campaigning was not the only reason that he was an absentee monarch: he suffered from asthma and found the atmosphere in the city of London unbearable. When in London he stayed at Kensington, and whenever possible escaped to Hampton Court where he enjoyed the pleasant air and, of course, the wonderful gardens. William's absence from London ensured the growth in the prestige of Parliament, which in effect took over the daily business of running the country.

William, in armour with the victor's laurel wreath, almost totally obscures his co-monarch Mary.

Genealogy 5: Temple Genealogy

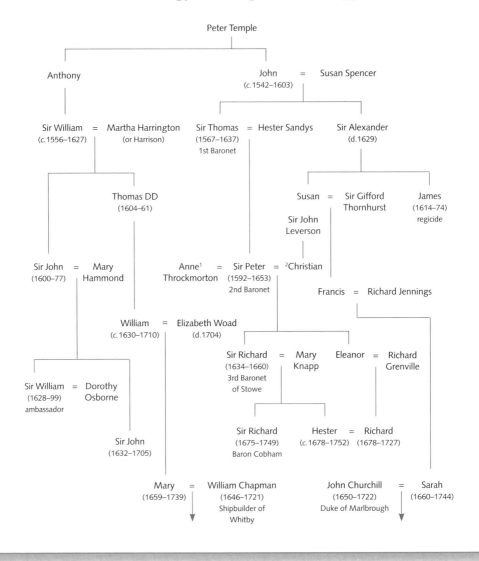

In 1694, Evelyn had let his house and garden at Sayes Court to Captain (later Admiral) Benbow and moved to the family house at Wotton in Surrey where he had been born, and where his childless elder brother George was living. It is probable that John contributed to the elaborate landscape gardening there, remnants of which still exist.

John Evelyn spent his retirement at Wotton researching and writing his book *A Discourse of Sallets*, a fascinating compendium of *Esculent* [edible] *Plants and Herbs, improved by culture, industry and art of the gardener.*

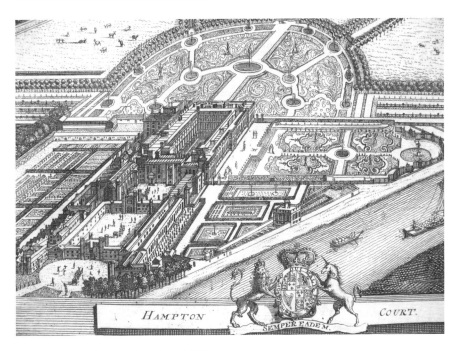

Hampton Court house and gardens, 1727.

Gardens at Wotton House.

3

Brotherly Love

Great kings are drawn to war
Like loaded needles to the North
(Matthew Prior, *Alma*)

Quakers regarded all people as equally valuable individuals. They
envisaged a society in which all should be bound together by brotherly
love and live in a peaceable kingdom. This ideal lay behind the
founding of William Penn's own personal colony of Pennsylvania, on
land donated to him by Charles II but bought from the local native inhabitants.
He established Philadelphia (which means 'city of brotherly love') on a rational
plan not unlike the ideas that Wren and Evelyn hoped to impose on post-fire
London with parks, gardens, straight avenues, and with the commercial areas
separated from the residential. Although Penn's enlightened toleration proved
good for business, the town plan of Philadelphia (without the restrictions of a
town planning department) succumbed to financial pressures. The Quaker
dream of governing an entire colony according to the principles of pacifism and
paternalistic benevolence dissolved in the face of *realpolitik*.

Quakers recruited mainly from the 'middling sort' of people: small farmers,
tradesmen, artisans and merchants. And, because – as Henry Taylor wrote – 'most
boys' who, like himself, were 'born in a sea-port town in the north of England
… incline towards a sea-faring life', the Quaker community in Whitby included
many mariners.

Quaker meetings had no formal prayers or form of service, allowing anyone
to speak as the spirit moved them. These meetings were open to all, and attracted
many curious outsiders; for example, Celia Fiennes attended one at Scarborough
in 1697 but was not impressed. She recorded that 'it seem'd such a confusion and
so incoherent that it very much moved my compassion and pitty to see their
delusion and ignorance'. [1]

The coal trade between Newcastle (and to a lesser extent Sunderland and
Cullercoates) and London thrived and more ships and bigger ships were busy in

this lucrative trade. Celia Fiennes, in her visit to Scarborough, saw '70 saile of Shipps pass the point and so come onward at some distance off from the Castle, supposed to be Colliers, and their Convoys'. The convoys were crucial in time of war as it would be impossible otherwise to get insurance for ship or cargo. A problem with convoys was that it meant the Port of London authorities would be inundated with colliers which would take two or three days to process, and then there would be a lull until the next convoy arrived; for example, the Port Book for London coastal imports[2] for 1697 records only fifteen vessels from Newcastle cleared between 13 and 15 April, but then a convoy arrived on 16 April and there were fifty-seven cleared that day and on the 17 April a further forty-six; then there was a lull until the next convoy arrived on the 19 April. The Port Book gives the names of the vessels, master and the cargo they carried: over the two busy days (16 and 17 April) the ships from Newcastle brought in 10,473 chaldrons of coal, with an additional 801 from Sunderland and 369 from Cullercoates: a total of 15,718 tons or 16,032 metric tonnes, 90 per cent of which was carried from Newcastle. The average load of those vessels carrying only coal was 100 chaldrons for Newcastle ships and 32.5 for those from Sunderland. Unfortunately, the Port Book does not give the port where these colliers were owned or built; however, for the three months April to June 1697, some twenty-two Whitby ship masters can be identified, of which five were Quakers. Although this is only a small sample, it is indicative of the importance of Quakers in the Whitby merchant fleet.

The war with France ended a few months later with the signing of the Treaty of Ryswick (Rijswijk), Matthew Prior being William III's secretary at the treaty negotiations. One of the terms of the treaty was that Louis recognised William as the rightful King of England, and undertook not to support the Stuart claim. Peace made the east coast much safer and colliers no longer needed to travel in convoy.

Most of the coal transported to London was for commercial use, though domestic consumption was not insignificant. It was not just London that was polluted by coal. Celia Fiennes described how, as she neared Newcastle: 'This country all about is full of this coale; the sulpher of it taints the aire and it smells strongly to strangers.'

Britain was growing rich on its trade, helped by the Navigation Acts and the establishment of the Bank of England in 1694. A small island with a large coastline needed a large and growing merchant navy for its trade to increase, and a large Royal Navy to protect the ships and to keep the seas safe. When funding became available, the Royal Navy shipyards improved and developed, becoming massive and complex organisations for the building and repair of ships.

The business of shipbuilding was becoming increasingly professional, more of an exact engineering project in material science. The new men were epitomised by Anthony Deane. Pepys had recognised his talents, and became his patron,

Portsmouth Royal Dockyard (the figurehead is of Admiral Benbow).

ensuring his appointment as Master Shipwright at the Royal Dock at Harwich. Deane became Mayor of Harwich and, with Pepys, was twice elected as MP for Harwich. In 1670, he published *Doctrine of Naval Architecture*, which Evelyn described as 'containing the whole mechanic part and art of building royal ships and men of warr … I do not think the world can shew the like'. With Deane, later Sir Anthony Deane, shipbuilding was transformed from a craft into a science.

Peter the Great, the modernising and civilising tsar of Russia, began his rule with only a single port, Archangel, which was frozen for some six months a year. He was determined to acquire ports on the Baltic and on the Black Sea, and to build a modern navy. To this end, he travelled to England in 1698, eager to learn how to build ships. This he did at Deptford under the guidance of Anthony Deane, residing the while at Sayes Court, Evelyn's house, which was conveniently close. The king had approved Peter's visit in the hope that it would bring greater friendship, and more trade, with Russia. In this, William was perspicacious, as in 1703 Peter gained access to the Baltic coast, previously under Swedish control, and started building St Petersburg, which became Russia's capital in 1721 and was to be a favoured Baltic port of trade with British merchants. Peter the Great was very busy while in London: he learnt how to repair watches, met William Penn, and visited the Royal Mint with Sir Isaac Newton. The tsar left England, rather reluctantly, in April 1698, taking a number of experts with him, including John Deane, Anthony's brother.

Evelyn thought Benbow was a poor tenant who did not take care of his property, but Peter the Great was even worse: the house and its contents were thoroughly trashed and the lovely and much cherished gardens were wantonly damaged. The tsar may have been great on modernising, but clearly still had much to do with regard to civilising.

Shipbuilding was a growing enterprise in the merchant navy as well. When comparatively small vessels were needed, it was possible to put together a seaworthy craft on any convenient piece of shore, and the shipbuilder could design and make it – to use an old Yorkshire phrase – 'by t' skeg o' t' ee' [by a glance of the eye],[3] that is, without working from a plan. However, the demand was for larger and more efficient merchant vessels. The Dutch had developed a type of merchant ship called a *fluit* (which the English called a 'flyboat') which was broader, longer and squarer than the British equivalent. Designed from the inside, cargo space took precedence over external beautiful lines; also it carried less sail and therefore needed fewer men, as 'sail area was the chief determinant of the size of the crew of any given ship',[4] which made them more economical.

The main British shipbuilding ports were in London and East Anglia, but the influx of captured Dutch *fluits* had caused something of a slump in these yards. As Defoe put it: 'Dutch flyboats taken in the war, thrust themselves into the coal trade … [they] were bought cheap, carried great burthens, and the Ipswich [ship] building fell off for want of price, and so the trade decayed.' 'However, some section of the English shipbuilding industry had begun to respond to the stimulus of new demands, and to produce ships which could compete with the Dutch.'[5] And those were the shipbuilding ports of the north-east: Newcastle, Scarborough and Whitby.

The French invasion of the Spanish Netherlands in 1701 meant the end of peace once more. To resist the French, the 'Grand Alliance' was formed which included England, Holland, Austria and Prussia. War was declared on France, and Louis XIV withdrew his acknowledgement of the Protestant Succession, recognising James Stuart as James III, rightful King of Britain. This war is known as the War of the Spanish Succession because Charles II, King of Spain, had died in 1700 with no direct heir to succeed him, and he had appointed the Bourbon Philip as his heir, who took the throne as Philip V. The Grand Alliance was formed of those countries which did not wish to see a King of Spain so closely related to a King of France, and therefore supported the rival Hapsburg claimant to the Spanish throne, the Archduke Charles of Austria.

Spain had a small army and a weak navy, and Philip V had to rely on the French forces, which were widely stretched. From the start, the Allies had the military advantage. On 29 December 1701, the occasion of his return from Holland after the season's campaigning, William III was inundated with loyal addresses, including 'An humble and loyal Address from the Inhabitants of the Town and

Genealogy 6: The Spanish Succession

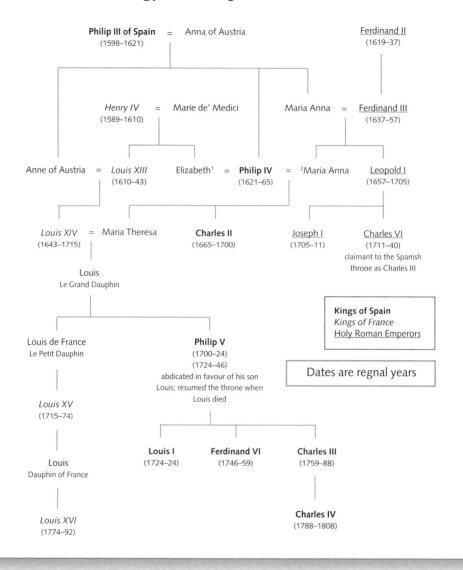

Philip III of Spain (1598–1621) = Anna of Austria

Ferdinand II (1619–37)

Henry IV (1589–1610) = Marie de' Medici

Maria Anna = Ferdinand III (1637–57)

Anne of Austria = Louis XIII (1610–43)

Elizabeth[1] = Philip IV (1621–65) = [2]Maria Anna

Leopold I (1657–1705)

Louis XIV (1643–1715) = Maria Theresa

Charles II (1665–1700)

Joseph I (1705–11)

Charles VI (1711–40) claimant to the Spanish throne as Charles III

Louis Le Grand Dauphin

Louis de France Le Petit Dauphin

Philip V (1700–24) (1724–46) abdicated in favour of his son Louis; resumed the throne when Louis died

Louis XV (1715–74)

Kings of Spain
Kings of France
Holy Roman Emperors

Dates are regnal years

Louis Dauphin of France

Louis I (1724–24)

Ferdinand VI (1746–59)

Charles III (1759–88)

Louis XVI (1774–92)

Charles IV (1788–1808)

Port of Whitby, which was presented to His Majesty by Hugh Cholmely Esq.', the Lord of the Manor. The Quakers also sent one which affirmed that under William's reign they enjoyed 'great Mercies and Favours; and particularly that of Liberty to Tender Consciences in Religious Worship as a proper Expedient to unite Thy Protestant Subjects in Interest and Affection'.

William III died the next year. The crown then passed to Mary's younger sister Anne. In 1702, an Anglo-Dutch naval force raided Cádiz and then sailed into

Castillo de Santa
Catalina, Cádiz.

Queen Anne's
coat of arms.
Quarterly: 1 & 4,
the English lions
quartered with
the French fleur
de lys; 2, the
Scottish lion
rampant; 3, the
harp of Ireland.

Vigo Bay capturing, plundering and destroying the Spanish treasure ships and the French warships that were protecting them.

On land, the Allied army, commanded by John Churchill, won some remarkable victories against the forces of Louis XIV. The first, in 1704, was the Battle of Blenheim. The Franco-Bavarian army, which was intending to capture Vienna and thus break up the Alliance, was massively defeated in a bloody battle, sustaining Somme-like casualties and with thousands taken prisoner. It was hailed as 'A Glorious Victory where with Almighty God had blessed Her Majesty's Arms over the French and Bavarians',[6] but it soon came to be seen purely as a battle between the English and the French, the most spectacular such land victory since Agincourt and a decisive blow for liberty and Protestantism against the superstitions and repressions of Catholicism.

Queen Anne bestowed on John Churchill the title Duke of Marlborough, and gifted him a mansion, to be named Blenheim Palace and built at Woodstock. The queen provided the land, and the house was to be paid for by the taxes of the grateful nation, the first instalment being £240,000 (c. £500 million) which the grateful nation could ill afford.

The queen had favourites. One was John Sheffield, 3rd Earl Mulgrave and Duke of Buckingham, patron of John Dryden and friend of Alexander Pope. He had been banned from court by Charles II for making advances towards Anne when she was a young princess; now that she was queen, she made him Lord Privy Seal.

The most influential of Anne's favourites was Sarah Jennings, of the Temple family. John Churchill married Sarah Jennings – a shrewd career move. Although Churchill was undoubtedly an excellent commander and strategist, it is equally undeniable that his rise to fame and power owed much to his wife's influence with the queen.

The queen also decreed a *General Thanksgiving to Almighty God* for the victory at Blenheim, but Robert Southey's poem 'After Blenheim', written at the end of the century, captures a more negative view of the battle:

> 'It was the English,' Kaspar cried,
> 'Who put the French to rout;
> But what they fought each other for
> I could not well make out.
> But everybody said,' quoth he,
> 'That 'twas a famous victory.'

The news of the famous victory of Blenheim arrived in Britain at the same time as that of the capture of Gibraltar by an amphibious attack of Dutch and British sailors. When the allied officers saw the extent of Gibraltar's fortified defences which had been taken they were amazed at their achievement, as '50 men might have defended these works against Thousands',[7] a comment that had an element of prediction.

There was much to be patriotic about. Marlborough led the allied army to victory after victory and in 1708 the British occupied Minorca, a valued prize because of its strategic value in the Mediterranean and its natural harbour – wide, deep and 3 miles long.

The Pope declared that the rightful King of Spain was Archduke Charles who, in 1710, triumphantly entered the recently captured Madrid. It looked as if the war would be over and the Archduke would be Charles III, King of Spain. It was not to be. Within months, Philip V had regained almost total command of Spain.

Genealogy 7: Sheffield/Mulgrave Genealogy

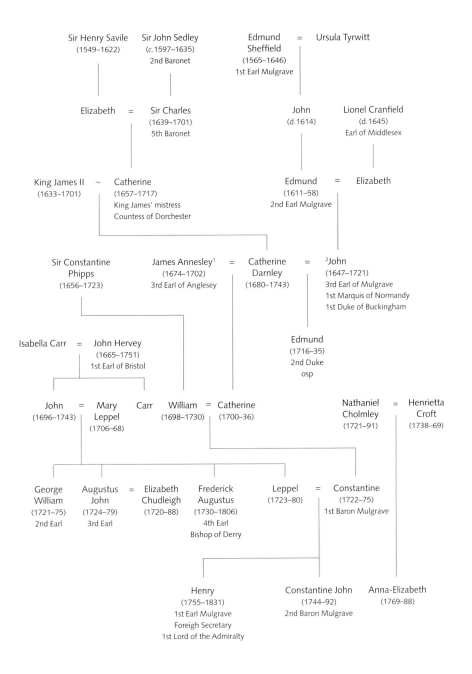

Sir Henry Savile (1549–1622)

Sir John Sedley (c.1597–1635) 2nd Baronet

Edmund Sheffield (1565–1646) 1st Earl Mulgrave = Ursula Tyrwitt

Elizabeth = Sir Charles (1639–1701) 5th Baronet

John (d.1614)

Lionel Cranfield (d.1645) Earl of Middlesex

King James II (1633–1701) ~ Catherine (1657–1717) King James' mistress Countess of Dorchester

Edmund (1611–58) 2nd Earl Mulgrave = Elizabeth

Sir Constantine Phipps (1656–1723)

James Annesley[1] (1674–1702) 3rd Earl of Anglesey = Catherine Darnley (1680–1743) = [2]John (1647–1721) 3rd Earl of Mulgrave 1st Marquis of Normandy 1st Duke of Buckingham

Isabella Carr = John Hervey (1665–1751) 1st Earl of Bristol

Edmund (1716–35) 2nd Duke osp

John (1696–1743) = Mary Leppel (1706–68)

Carr

William (1698–1730) = Catherine (1700–36)

Nathaniel Cholmley (1721–91) = Henrietta Croft (1738–69)

George William (1721–75) 2nd Earl

Augustus John (1724–79) 3rd Earl = Elizabeth Chudleigh (1720–88)

Frederick Augustus (1730–1806) 4th Earl Bishop of Derry

Leppel (1723–80) = Constantine (1722–75) 1st Baron Mulgrave

Henry (1755–1831) 1st Earl Mulgrave Foreigh Secretary 1st Lord of the Admiralty

Constantine John (1744–92) 2nd Baron Mulgrave

Anna-Elizabeth (1769–88)

Genealogy 8: Spencer, Temple & Churchill Genealogy

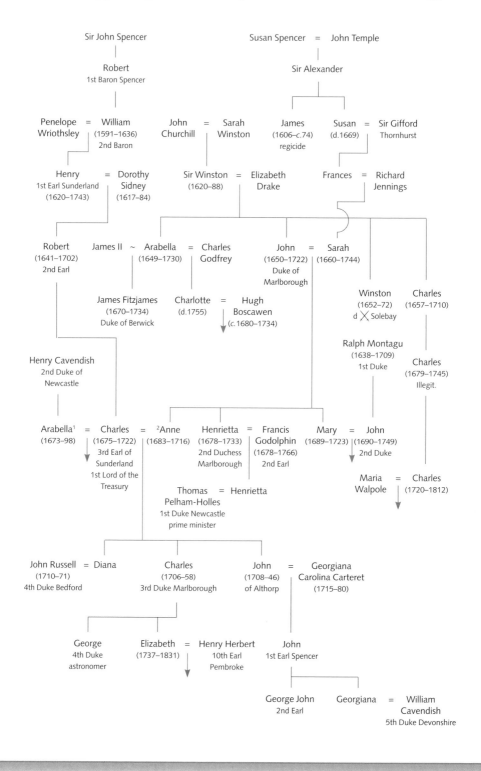

Cannon on the walls of Gibraltar.

Ruins of forts at the entrance to Mahón harbour.

The victories of the Allied army, under Marlborough, had at first stirred the nation to jingoistic enthusiasm. However, as the war dragged on it became increasingly unpopular: taxes became burdensome, and the Whig-dominated government was accused of incompetence and profiteering. The war had never been popular with the Tories, Jonathan Swift claiming that it was the war of Marlborough and of the Whig government and not of the queen or of the people.[8] Swift's description of warfare in *Gulliver's Travels* almost certainly reflected the horrors of this war: 'Sieges, Retreats, Attacks, Undermines, Countermines, Bombardments, Sea-fights; Ships sunk with a Thousand Men; twenty Thousand killed on each Side; dying Groans, Limbs flying in the Air: Smoak, Noise, Confusion, trampling to Death under Horses Feet … Fields strewed with Carcases left for Food to Dogs, Wolves and Birds of Prey'.

The trouble with favourites is that they can easily fall out of favour. The foundations of Blenheim Palace had scarcely been laid when Queen Anne tired of Sarah Churchill's constant interfering and strident anti-Tory nagging, and dismissed her from Court. The election of 1710 returned a Tory majority. Marlborough was accused of corruption and removed from his military post; with his wife he went into exile, not returning until after the Queen Anne was dead. The building of that impressively monstrous pile of baroque vulgarity that was to be Blenheim Palace had already consumed its £250,000 quota, and the government refused to grant any further funds. The new administration lost no time in setting up peace negotiations.

The war had meant more predations upon east coast shipping by French privateers. For example, in the spring of 1709 two vessels, one from Shields and one from Whitby, were captured and ransomed by one of several privateers based in Dunkirk. The former was ransomed for £240 (£600,000) and the latter £710 (£1,700,000); the shipowners must have regretted Charles II's sale of Dunkirk to the French.

Such attacks on merchant shipping presented an additional moral dilemma for Quaker owners and masters. As pacifists, they were not permitted to arm their vessels or defend their ships by force, but they had a moral (and financial) obligation to protect their sailors who would be unwilling to sail in a defenceless craft in privateer-infested waters. There was no absolute security, even in convoys, but because Quaker owners were always willing to surrender and pay ransom, some seamen considered this a good strategy as there was little danger of being wounded or killed in a sea fight. However, owners' pockets were not cash cornucopias, and paying licensed pirates to buy back their own ships and cargoes as well as the ongoing round of fines levied for not attending church or paying tithes was becoming too much to bear for some. Quaker Joseph Linskill was one of those who succumbed; when he bought a ship already fitted with cannon he 'did make use of them'.[9] He made a full confession and repentance which was recorded in the minutes of the Whitby monthly meeting. However, the repentance came only after the war had finally ended.

The War of the Spanish Succession was finally concluded in 1713 with the Peace of Utrecht. There were many issues of territorial gain, commerce and national pride to be considered. Matthew Prior – poet, politician, member of the

Board of Trade and arguably 'the best versed in matters of trade'[10] – was amongst those sent to Utrecht to negotiate terms which were mutually acceptable. The British acknowledged Philip V as the legitimate King of Spain, and in return France also accepted once more the legitimacy of the Protestant Succession, agreeing not to aid the Stuart claim to the British throne. Britain gained the most in terms of territory and trade, gaining Newfoundland, Nova Scotia, the Hudson Bay region and the island of St Christopher (St Kitts). Spain ceded Gibraltar and Minorca to the British, and granted her the *Asiento*, the right to participate in the profitable slave trade to the Spanish territories in the Americas. Spain lost all her European territories; those in Italy and the Netherlands became the property of Archduke Charles. The French agreed to dismantle the walls and forts of Dunkirk, which pleased the merchant traders of Britain and Holland. The Principality of Orange was ceded to the French and became part of France, though the Dutch Princes of Orange retained that title. The treaty was not popular with many in Britain, mainly because the French retained the valuable fishing rights off part of Newfoundland. It was particularly galling for the Dutch, who gained very little and felt betrayed.

Whigs were generally sympathetic to Nonconformists; but Tories, who had come to power, supported 'High' Anglican attitudes and introduced legislation to preserve and increase the authority and privileges of the Church of England. The Schism Act of 1714 deprived all but Anglicans of effective education by insisting that anyone who taught in or owned a school must obtain a licence – which was only granted to attested practising members of the Church of England. This did not please Scotland, united with England in 1707, who were mainly Presbyterians and Catholics.

Anne's reign was not all war and squabbling partisan politicians. London flourished and became one of the largest and richest cities in Europe. The fine new squares and town houses were elegant and stylish. But it has to be remembered that parts of the city were impoverished and unpoliced. Gin was cheap and devastating in its social and personal consequences. George Berkeley, the bishop and philosopher, wrote that gin was subverting the birthright of many citizens of free nations, making 'them, in spite of their liberty and property, more wretched slaves than even the subjects of absolute power'. His recommendation of 'tar-water, temperance and early hours'[11] was not a very attractive or popular alternative.

Queen Anne had married Prince Jørgen, brother of the King of Denmark, in 1683, when the chances of her becoming queen were considered negligible. The marriage was happy, and though he was no great character, he was an efficient and conscientious man. Anne endured seventeen pregnancies, but few of her children survived birth and just one, William, survived childhood – only to succumb to smallpox in 1700 before he even became a teenager. Anne died in August 1714.

In the absence of any direct heirs the crown went, as required by the Act of Settlement, to her second cousin Georg, Elector of Hanover, who became King George I. In her coronation speech Queen Anne had described herself as 'entirely English' (in contrast to the Dutch William III). George was entirely German.

Although he converted from being a Lutheran to an Anglican so he could fulfil his *ex officio* role as head of the Established Church of England, King George never made much effort to learn the English language, and communicated with his British subjects largely in French and Latin. His thoughts were with Hanover, and he spent much time there. In Hanover, he was absolute ruler; in Britain, he found Parliament restrictive, difficult and troublesome.

The election in early 1715 replaced the Tory ministry with Whigs. The new victors redistributed the spoils of power amid political infighting and retaliation, which included an (unsuccessful) attempt to convict Matthew Prior as an enemy of the state for his involvement in the Treaty of Utrecht – they failed, but Prior was not released until 1718.

Not everyone was pleased to have a German king, and in strictly biological terms his claim to the throne was weak – there being some fifty people, all Catholics, with a better claim; but none was prepared to change religion in order to become monarch of Great Britain. Top of the list was James Edward Stuart, the Old Pretender. Support for the Stuart claim to the throne had not died, particularly among the Highland Scots. In September 1715, the Earl of Mar raised an army, and at Braemar proclaimed James Edward Stuart as the rightful King of Britain. While Mar marched towards Stirling, another Jacobite army crossed over the border, meeting little resistance, or support, as it moved towards Preston. It was a dangerous time for the new king, and for those living in the north of England, who were probably grateful that the Bill of Rights had given Protestants the right to bear arms in anticipation of just such a Catholic rebellion.

But Britain was never going to become a Catholic country again. Christianity had originally developed and matured in a Europe which was feudal, aristocratic and autocratic, and had tended to cling to the structures and doctrines formed in that environment. But trade and business demanded a new set of values, not just the so-called Protestant work ethic, but – as Matt Ridley[12] has pointed out – new ethics: business probity, social mobility, and freedom of thought, speech and travel. It also required a greater understanding of the

George I.

Genealogy 9: The House of Hanover

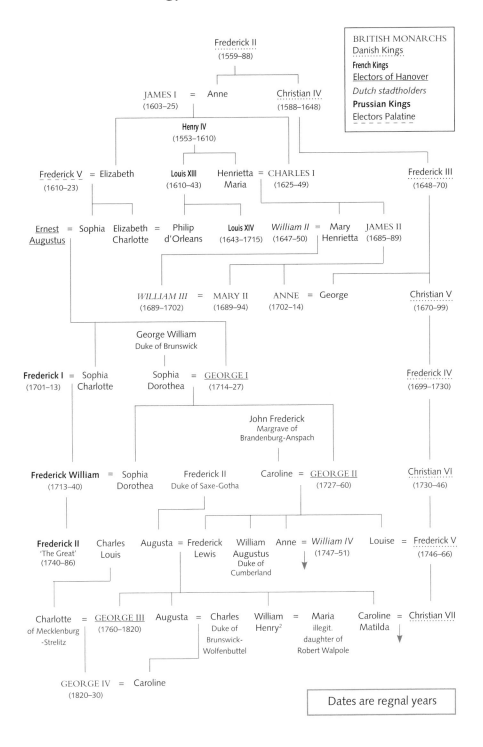

BRITISH MONARCHS
Danish Kings
French Kings
Electors of Hanover
Dutch stadtholders
Prussian Kings
Electors Palatine

Frederick II
(1559–88)

JAMES I = Anne
(1603–25)

Christian IV
(1588–1648)

Henry IV
(1553–1610)

Frederick V = Elizabeth
(1610–23)

Louis XIII
(1610–43)

Henrietta = CHARLES I
Maria   (1625–49)

Frederick III
(1648–70)

Ernest = Sophia
Augustus

Elizabeth = Philip
Charlotte   d'Orleans

Louis XIV
(1643–1715)

William II = Mary
(1647–50)   Henrietta

JAMES II
(1685–89)

WILLIAM III = MARY II
(1689–1702)   (1689–94)

ANNE = George
(1702–14)

Christian V
(1670–99)

George William
Duke of Brunswick

Frederick I = Sophia
(1701–13)   Charlotte

Sophia = GEORGE I
Dorothea   (1714–27)

Frederick IV
(1699–1730)

John Frederick
Margrave of
Brandenburg-Anspach

Frederick William = Sophia
(1713–40)   Dorothea

Frederick II
Duke of Saxe-Gotha

Caroline = GEORGE II
(1727–60)

Christian VI
(1730–46)

Frederick II
'The Great'
(1740–86)

Charles
Louis

Augusta = Frederick
          Lewis

William
Augustus
Duke of
Cumberland

Anne = William IV
(1747–51)

Louise = Frederick V
          (1746–66)

Charlotte = GEORGE III
of Mecklenburg (1760–1820)
-Strelitz

Augusta = Charles
          Duke of
          Brunswick-
          Wolfenbuttel

William
Henry[2]

Maria
illegit.
daughter of
Robert Walpole

Caroline = Christian VII
Matilda

GEORGE IV = Caroline
(1820–30)

Dates are regnal years

world, its peoples and resources. It would require flexibility in business practice and employment, increasing research into the development and manufacture of new products, better maps and charts, better transport and further developments into the science of navigation.

Whether Protestantism flourished in societies of this sort or created them is open to question, but they did tend to go together. Charles I's grandson, the Catholic James Edward Stuart, was not acceptable to most Britons as their king, even if the alternative was a foreigner who spoke no English. Indeed, when the pretender James landed at Peterhead in December of 1715, he learnt his army in England had surrendered outside Preston, and that the Earl of Mar's forces had been brought to battle at Sheriffmuir, near Dunblane, by an army led by the Duke of Argyll. The outcome was inconclusive but the Jacobites, hearing news of approaching reinforcements, melted away into the chilly uplands of North Britain. James returned to France, having been scarcely three months in the land he hoped would be his kingdom. For all his faults, George I was a Protestant and he supported freedom for Nonconformists. This was good news for Quakers, and all other dissenting groups. The government and the monarch realised that, then as now, attempting to create a unified country by forcing every citizen to adopt all the beliefs and to participate in all the rituals of one denominational religion was not going to encourage peace, harmony and unity. The Schism Act was duly repealed.

In later life, William Chapman, Whitby merchant and shipbuilder, looked back on the second decade of the new century as an ideal time for Whitby and the Quakers. He named exemplar Friends, particularly Gideon Meggison, Reuben and Thomas Linskill, John Walker, John Longstaffe and Henry Simpson, as men 'remarkable for their public spirit, hospitality and plainness and simplicity of manners', whose wives were 'neatly dressed, wearing black silk scarfs, which came over the shoulders and fitted close to the waist, and fastened before', which was a 'neat and becoming dress'. It was a time, he recollected, when 'tea was little used … the time of dining was ¼ past 12, and that of visiting at 2 in the afternoon, when the women always took their needlework with them'.[13]

4

The Prospect of Whitby

Industry, frugality, and a universal passion for what regards their marine, are said to be their [the inhabitants of Whitby's] distinguishing characteristics.

(*A Description of England and Wales*)[1]

Britain was always a land of traders; merchants and seamen have been the bedrock of its prosperity. It is interesting to note that the first map in the pocket book *Chorographia Britanniae* of 1742 is of the coast.

Whitby was one of many towns that lived off the sea, but real prosperity came with the discovery of alum shales nearby. Alum was mainly used in tanning and as a mordant for dyeing but was also an important ingredient in cosmetics, medicine and taxidermy. It was expensive to extract, but it was profitable. In the early seventeenth century, an alum works was set up at Sandsend, near Whitby, by Sir Edmund Sheffield, 1st Earl of Mulgrave. This, 'the first English chemical industry', created a demand for shipping to import the large amounts of coal, kelp and urine needed for the processing of the shales and to export the valuable end product.

One of the early Whitby master mariner shipowners who sought to benefit from this new trade was Luke Foxe in his ship *Allomes Amye* (Alum's Friend). He did not get rich from alum, so he sought to make a fortune by finding the elusive North-West Passage.* He received royal patronage and, with a letter from the king to the Emperor of Japan, set out from London in the 80-ton *Charles*. In this tiny vessel he circumnavigated Hudson Bay and reached further than any previous explorers. Much was achieved, and the crew arrived home safely; but he failed to find the North-West Passage and the Emperor of Japan never received his letter. Foxe died in 1635 and was buried at Whitby.

---

* A way in which ships could sail from the Atlantic to the Pacific via the north of Canada.

W.H. Toms' map of the English sea coast, from *Chorographia Britanniae*.

The town's fortunes received an added improvement with the work of Sir Hugh Cholmley (1600–57). He lived at Abbey House in Whitby, which he rebuilt in stone, the raw materials being plundered from the abbey ruins.

In 1632, he had a pier built on the east side of the river mouth, which prevented gravel and sand being swept round the cliffs by the tide and clogging the harbour entrance. Additionally, he embanked the eastern riverside making the land secure for housing and roads, and built a drawbridge over the river. All these actions increased the trade and affluence of the town, resulting in an influx of shipbuilders, master mariners, chandlers and other ship-related occupations.

During the Civil War, Hugh Cholmley, originally a Parliamentarian, changed sides. He defended Scarborough Castle and typically stripped the lead from the roof of Whitby Abbey to provide bullets for his soldiers. He was exiled, but when the war was over he was permitted to return to Abbey House. Sir Hugh founded an alum works at Saltwick Bay. In 1652, he laid out an orchard, known as the 'New Gardens', on the east bank at Whitby in order to provide the town with a healthy supply of fruit and vegetables. The following inscription was on the plaque that was placed on the wall:

> Our handy worke like to ye Frutefull tree
> Blesse thou O Lord let it not blasted bee.

Sir Hugh died in 1657 and his eldest son, William, succeeded him. William's second wife was Katherine Sedley; their only child was a son, Hugh, who died in 1665 aged 3, having been the 3rd Baronet Cholmley of Whitby for two years. The baronetcy then went to Sir William's younger brother, Sir Hugh Cholmley (1632–89), who 'became the first gentleman-usher to the Queen Catherine of Braganza and was a messenger from the King to her in Portugall'.[2] In 1666, Sir Hugh married Anne Compton, sister of Henry, the botanical Bishop of London. As a young man, Hugh no doubt helped his father's building works in Whitby harbour, gaining essential experience for his post as director of works at Tangier. Sir Hugh prospered, and so did Whitby. He died on 9 January 1689, leaving no son, so the title became defunct. However, his daughter Mary married

Whitby Abbey ruins.

Abbey House.

her father's cousin Nathaniel Cholmley, and the presence of the Cholmley family in Whitby continued. Their son Hugh improved Abbey House, the family home perched high on East Cliff with little shelter from the weather. He repaired existing damage, added a contemporary frontage and laid out formal gardens.

As Rosalin Barker has shown, the alum trade 'kick-started' Whitby's economy, which had fallen apart after the Reformation. What fuelled growth was her harbour. The River Esk, which divides the town in two, flows north into the North Sea (then called the German Ocean) in an estuary which provided a safe harbour for vessels seeking refuge from fierce storms. The bulk of the ships sailing past Whitby were carrying coal from Newcastle to London. As the metropolis expanded so did the demand for coal. The importance of Whitby as a harbour of easy access which could accommodate a sizeable number of ships escaped neither the government nor enterprising entrepreneurs. Consequently, in spite of objections by Newcastle and Scarborough, an Act was passed in 1702 for the repairing and rebuilding of the piers at Whitby.

This involved not only duties payable on a variety of goods shipped in and out of Whitby itself, but it imposed a duty on colliers sailing past Whitby of a farthing per chaldron on all coals shipped at Newcastle or its dependencies (e.g. Sunderland), except those shipped in Great Yarmouth★ vessels. The rationale for the government finding funding to enable Whitby's harbour was stated in the Act's preamble:

★ Great Yarmouth was paying for the upkeep and development of its own harbour, without any external contributions.

Whereas the Ancient Town of Whitby ... hath had Piers time out of mind, which are now very much Ruined and Decayed for want of an Income ... insomuch that though the said Harbour is capable of containing several Hundred Sail of good Ships, yet the Mouth thereof is so Choaked up, that none but small Ships can come in Loaded; and the want of the said Piers being kept in good and sufficient Repair, is not only very prejudicial to the said Town, and all the Neighbouring Country, but also to all the Northern Navigation, many Ships and Seamen having been lost near the said Port, not only by Storms and Stress of Weather but also Taken by Enemies within Sight of the said Port, which might have been saved had the said Piers been kept in good Repair.[3]

This Act was the saving of Whitby, and revealed that (in spite of having no particular representative in the House of Commons) the maritime interest in the town was able to provide sufficient evidence and pressure, possibly through the influence of William Cavendish, the new member for Yorkshire, to ensure the Act was passed. In December 1711, the newspapers recorded how a fleet of colliers was attacked by three French men-of-war and two privateers, and nearly all of them escaped by seeking refuge in Whitby harbour. The improved harbour proved its effectiveness, and the act was regularly renewed well into the nineteenth century.

Whitby had no real trade of its own, and was comparatively difficult to reach by road. The River Esk was only navigable inland for a mile or so. This would suggest that the town should be economically weak. But Whitby had a commodious and safe harbour. The port was well situated to trade with North Sea and Baltic ports, and was on the busy coal trade route. The town was on both sides of the Esk and the lack of through traffic on the river meant that Whitby had a disproportionate amount of river frontage, which was suitable for shipbuilding.

The shipbuilders of the north-east coast, especially Whitby, simply outbuilt their competitors, producing vessels that were perhaps not elegant, but whose available volume for cargo outstripped traditional ships of the same length. Many of the Whitby-built ships were Whitby-owned, but there was also a buoyant market for them elsewhere. So Whitby thrived.

The wealth thus generated ensured there was capital to buy even larger ships which were designed to be flexible in usage. Whitby ships were sturdy, could sail in deep water and could be safely beached on shore; they could be coal ships, timber ships, transport ships, whaling ships and, in later days, emigration and transportation ships.*

---

* The Whitby-built ships *Fishburn* and *Golden Grove* sailed with the 'First Fleet' to Australia in 1787.

Genealogy 10: Cholmley Genealogy

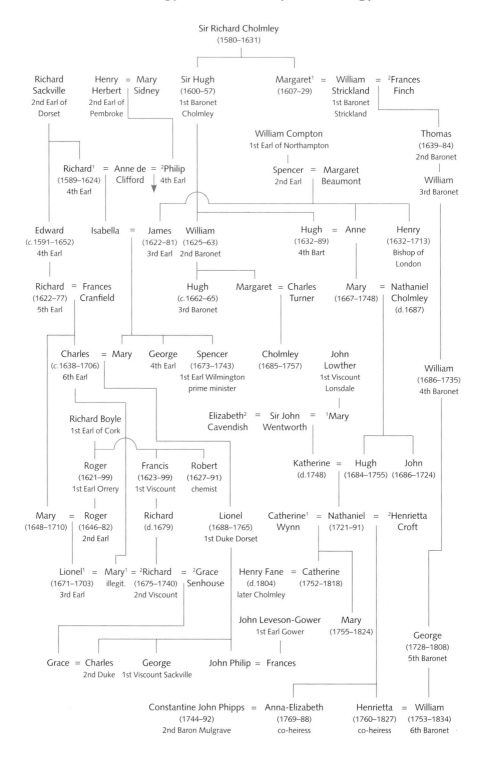

Whitby, like all ports, had always been something of a cosmopolitan town, but in the eighteenth century it was attracting more people and expertise from elsewhere: they came to Whitby looking to make money, and perhaps also for a better and freer life. With the new influx of talent and enthusiasm, the port expanded its trade and prospered.

While the north-east was flourishing, a few miles across the border in Scotland things were very different. After the union of Scotland and England in 1707 and the disruption caused by aftermath of the Jacobite Rebellion of 1715, the thought of moving over the border in search of work and better pay became an appealing prospect for many Scotsmen. One such was James Cook, born in Ednam,* near Kelso – just a short walk from England, and some 10 miles south of the latitude of the mouth of the Tweed, the coastal divide between Scotland and England. He settled in Cleveland and met Grace Pace; they took a liking to each other and married in Stainton church on 10 October 1725. They had a son, John. The Cook family then moved to Marton, roughly half way between Stockton and Guisborough. Their second son, James, was born in 1728 and baptised on 3 November at Marton parish church, the register recording that his father was a day labourer.[4] A day labourer was probably also what he had been in Scotland, but he had not travelled to England simply to spend the rest of his life moving from farm to farm being poorly paid in an insecure job and living in rundown cottages – especially as he was a family man. In 1736, he secured a job as a bailiff, a right-hand man to the tenant farmer at Aireyholme Farm in Great Ayton, owned by Thomas Scottowe, the lord of the manor.

Education was very important for the Society of Friends. Bible study was encouraged, so being able to read was seen as something of a necessity, particularly as the movement was involved in the printing and circulation of numerous books, tracts and 'Advices'. But to be a success in trade or business, a sound education was required. William Penn described, in a letter of 1682, what he wanted the education of his children to be: 'Let it be useful knowledge … I recommend the useful parts of mathematics, as building houses or ships, measuring, surveying … navigation; but agriculture is especially in my eye; let my children be husbandmen and housewives; it is industrious, healthy, honest and of good example.'[5] One way, irrespective of religious affiliations, to become educated in mathematics, measuring and navigation was to be apprenticed to a master mariner which, as it was not a school, had always been open to Quakers. In August 1703, Francis Salkeld, a Quaker from Kendal, came to Whitby to set up a co-educational school

---

* James Cook was baptised on 4 March 1694 by the Rev. Thomas Thomson, minister of Ednam, and father of the poet James Thomson, who was baptised there in 1700.

that taught 'useful knowledge' to Quaker children, years before there was any school like it for Anglicans in Whitby. Such education was high on the Quaker agenda – and, once the Schism Act was repealed, numerous Friends' Schools, often providing boarding accommodation, were opened.

Several Quakers made a success of their businesses. Being truthful was a central part of Quaker ethics. If they said they would do something, they would do it; they would give customers full measure and not seek to cheat or deceive them. Because they were committed to the truth they would price items at what they thought was fair, which customers would have to take or leave – on the basis that if they were prepared to accept a lower price they would have quoted that. In a world where haggling was normative, this was surprising, and refreshing.

By 1720, the prospect of Whitby was looking very good indeed.

5

Good Agreement and *Truelove*

Collateral love and dearest amity.

(John Milton, *Paradise Lost*)

Willaim Chapman (1646–1721), shipbuilder and Quaker, came from a long line of Whitby Chapmans. He married Elinor Smallwood, and they had two children, but she died in 1679. William wasted little time as a widower, and remarried in 1681. His second wife was Mary Temple, first cousin of Sir William Temple, ambassador and gardener.

Mary Temple seems to have become a Quaker, and this may be how she and William Chapman met. Mary's birth on 30 November is recorded in the Whitby Quaker birth register for 1659 but it is clear that this entry has been added later in a different hand. The birth of their eldest child Ingram on 8 April 1682 is entered in the Quaker register, so it is safe to assume that both parents were members of the Society of Friends before they married. It is interesting to note, therefore, that they were married in the Anglican Church at Egton on 21 July 1681.

The whole question of what actually constituted a valid marriage was far from clear at the time, and indeed is still debated today. In theory, a mutual contract between consenting adults (or if under age, also with parental consent) before witnesses would be sufficient, but over time there was an official and customary process which evolved into an accepted pattern for a legitimate marriage: first, that there were no legal barriers to the couple getting married; second, their intentions to get married (the banns) were read out in the parish churches of both the parties concerned for the three weeks prior to the wedding; third, that the wedding took place in one of these two parish churches (usually that of the bride); and lastly, the wedding service would be taken by a cleric of that parish, and the details would be recorded and witnessed in the parish register, which was available for public reference. However, if they wanted to be married out of the public glare and gossip, and if they could afford it, they could get an archbishop's licence. This involved a special legal document being issued to permit the marriage to go ahead at a particular time and church, and did not involve banns being read.

All this changed, albeit temporally, during the Commonwealth. The marriage act of 1653 effectively introduced secular marriage. Each parish would appoint a registrar who would ensure that couples wishing to get married had to submit the relevant details in writing at least three weeks in advance and their 'purposes' (i.e. banns) would be published in either the market place (on market day) or in the parish church (on a Sunday). The wedding ceremony itself was conducted by a Justice of the Peace before at least two witnesses. The details of the wedding would be recorded by the parish registrar. These secular weddings suited Quakers because it meant that a legal marriage did not involve clergymen or going into a church. Unfortunately for them, with the restoration of Charles II, the organisation of marriages reverted to the pre-Civil War situation. George Fox had encouraged his followers to keep sound records from the beginning, and had deliberately used the (once legal) Commonwealth pattern as a basis for the order of Quaker marriages, namely: a series of public meetings in which the intention to marry was published, a wedding which was open to all in which the bride and groom made reciprocal vows and signed the register, which was also signed by witnesses (of which there were several). The result was a system which was clear and which was generally accepted, but which was actually not legal.

This situation made the validity of Quaker marriages problematic. For example, in 1677, three Yorkshire Quakers were successfully prosecuted and imprisoned for cohabiting with their own wives because it was asserted that their Quaker marriage was not legal.[1] If a Quaker marriage was not accepted as valid, then the widow was legally a mistress and the children were illegitimate, which would mean they were not entitled to inherit. It was not unusual, therefore, for Quakers to marry in an Anglican church to ensure that they were truly married according to English law. Later, the Hardwicke Marriage Act of 1753 clarified what was necessary for a legal marriage. However, although Quakers were exempted from this Act, it did not actually state that Quaker marriages were legal, though it was generally seen as an unspoken acceptance of their legality.

Quakers were encouraged to marry Quakers, and as their numbers grew, this was enforced with greater enthusiasm. To 'marry out' resulted in being 'disowned' by the meeting, as it was seen as a threat to the purity and the continuing existence of the Society of Friends. Cousin marriages were common in the eighteenth century, and exceptionally so among Quakers. 'Quaker cousins' was a contemporary joke; however, it was clear that the Quakers themselves were aware of the inadvisability of such marriages – as early as 1675 their yearly meeting minutes show that they had decided against marriages between not only first cousins but also second cousins. This policy was reinforced at the yearly meeting of 1747 (which implies that the earlier injunction had not been widely obeyed) when Friends were told that 'whenever they know or hear of any 1st and 2nd cousins designing or intending to marry that they immediately advise them against it'.[2] The Whitby Quaker families intermarried, and most of the more prosperous ones eventually married into the Chapman family. As their family trees became progressively intertwined and tangled, they represented a solid and mutually supporting group; and as their business interests were mainly in shipping they were to form a powerful pressure group.

It has been said that all marriages are, to a lesser or greater extent, arranged marriages. This was certainly the case in the early eighteenth century. Many (the numbers increasing as the century wore on) dreamed of a love marriage but that was more hope than certainty, as pragmatic concerns were the major influence in deciding who was a suitable partner. In a society without pensions, a health service or unemployment benefit, the security which money could provide was always going to be an issue. In a society where wives were so dependent and reliant upon their husbands, it was crucial to marry a man who was dependable and reliable – and that meant a man who was able and willing to work hard, had saleable skills, and who was not prone to squander his earnings on drinking and gambling. In addition, he should be kind, faithful and considerate.

In this context it is worth noting that when a shipowner gave his craft a woman's name with a preceding adjective, the two descriptive words which were almost universally chosen were 'charming' and 'constant'; if they gave their ship their own first name the most popular adjective was 'constant'.

Parents – especially of the middling sort – were usually sensitive to their daughter's feelings about a prospective husband and were happy to agree to her choice – provided he was suitable. Many marriages became true love over time, fuelled not with romantic passion perhaps, but made strong with enduring amity, friendship, concord and good agreement – the latter perhaps including agreement that 'the woman is in the right, and the man in the wrong always'.[3]

In 1743, Thomas Herring was made Archbishop of York, in a splendid enthronement ceremony in the Minster at which the clergyman and novelist Laurence Sterne gave the sermon. Herring was a broad churchman with Whig sympathies. One of the first things he did in his new job was to find out detailed information about the religious situation in the archdiocese; he sent out a questionnaire to each of the parishes in his jurisdiction, the answers to which provide a unique picture of contemporary belief and practice. James Borwick, incumbent of Whitby parish church between 1736 and 1767, reported that in the town there were 1,325 Anglican families, 93 Quaker families, 39 Presbyterian families and 25 Catholic families.

Not only did Quakers have a sizeable community in Whitby itself but they were also great travellers; it was common for members of the Whitby Friends to attend meetings at Staintondale, Scarborough or Pickering where they could keep in touch with a wider circle of believers and to discuss religion, politics and business – and perhaps meet new prospective partners.

Although there could be antagonisms between the religious groups in Whitby, on a personal and business level there was much friendliness and cooperation. Families often had members of differing faiths, and religious loyalties often changed, which is hardly surprising when one thinks how much the official doctrines and practices of the Church of England had changed since the execution of King Charles I.

The eighteenth-century business world understood the importance of networking, and most areas of business and politics had their own networks. Whitby naturally had several interlocking interest groups covering the various aspects of the town's shipping industry. But religious affiliations were networks too, the Anglican being the largest, controlling all significant positions of power – both religious and secular – in the kingdom.

Being a member of the Society of Friends meant being a member of a different kind of network which spread beyond Britain to mainland Europe and the New World. Quakers were often to be found in occupations in the booming sectors of business, industry, shipping and finance. When Quakers travelled they would take a letter of introduction from their home meeting, so when they visited another town they had immediate help and acceptance from the local Quaker groups, which provided the opportunity to share good business practice and to make new financial and trading partnerships. If they were to be there regularly, or for any duration, the letter they carried might also contain information that the person concerned (be it a man or woman) was 'clear from all others' (i.e. unattached) in case they met a suitable Quaker marriage partner.

Whitby parish church.

Many colliers that were made and owned in Whitby did not enter Whitby harbour between the beginning of the sailing season and its end, and if the ships did not over-winter in Whitby it could be very much longer. As much of Whitby's coastal shipping trade was between the coal ports of the north-east and London, it is hardly surprising that Sunderland and Shields (the port for Newcastle) to the north, and Wapping and Shadwell (London suburbs) to the south were familiar to the nautical fraternity in Whitby.

In 1688, 'sundry of the masters and mariners of Whitby who were often by their employment obliged to be in Tynemouth Harbour' requested permission to build a gallery in the church at South Shields 'at their own proper cost' so they could worship on a Sunday without the embarrassment of taking someone else's seats. This was agreed and built, and proved so successful that a second gallery 'belonging to the masters of Whitby' was built in 1707 and a further one the following year. Building galleries and constructing pews did not come cheap. For the Whitby master mariners to go to this expense indicates the number of Whitby colliers arriving at Shields, the time it took negotiating with the factors in Newcastle regarding the type and price of coal being purchased, for the keels to ferry the cargo down the Tyne to Shields, and for loading the coal onto the ships. And it also indicates the great wealth which could be accrued in the trade, particularly by shipowning master mariners.

Not surprisingly, there was much intermarriage among maritime families of east coast ports. Quaker examples are: Richard Frost, mariner of South Shields, married Esther, daughter of Jacob Hudson, mariner of Whitby; Richard Vasey of Whitby, master of the *Owners Adventure*, married Margery Eden of Billingham, and Zachariah Cockfield of Whitby, master of the *Industry*, married Sarah, daughter of Joseph Sheppard, shipwright of Shadwell.

St Paul's Church, Shadwell, 1755.

It was also not unusual for people in London and the north-east ports to have a financial investment in Whitby shipping. By the 1740s, John Wilkinson was the ship's husband of the *Buck* of Whitby, owning some 60 per cent of the vessel, and the rest was divided among fifteen others including Robert Walker, butcher, of South Shields, Thomas Cockerill of Scarborough and three brewers from Wapping. Brewers and tavern keepers often controlled gangs of dockers and had agreements with particular shipowners and master mariners to use them exclusively. The stevedores were partly paid in tickets redeemed on the premises. The famous old Wapping pub the *Prospect of Whitby*, at that time known as the *Devil's Tavern*, probably had just such an arrangement.

The Chapman family were mainly master mariners and shipowners, and it was natural for them to marry not only fellow Quakers but also fellow Quakers in the same line of business.

On the tenth day of the eleventh month (January) in the year 1728* at the Whitby meeting house, the 33-year-old widower Abel Chapman, master mariner and shipowner, the son of William Chapman (by then deceased) and Mary née Temple, married Elizabeth Walker, the 26-year-old daughter of the master mariner and shipowner John Walker and his wife Esther née Stonehouse. The ceremony involved Abel taking Elizabeth by the hand, saying:

> Friends, in the Fear of the Lord and in your hearing whom I desire to be witnesses, I take this my friend Elizabeth Walker to be my wife, promising through God's assistance to be unto her a faithful and loving Husband till death separate us.

Elizabeth made a similar reciprocal commitment to be a 'loving and faithful wife'. And so they were married. There remained the signing of the register. It was signed by Abel and Elizabeth (who signed as Elizabeth Chapman), and countersigned by Abel's mother Mary, his older brothers Solomon and Ingram, and their wives Ann and Elizabeth, and his two younger brothers Aaron and Benjamin. Both of Elizabeth's parents signed, as did her brother Henry and his wife Anne. In addition, there were more than forty other signatures as witnesses; Quakers were keen to provide legal validation.

Noteworthy among the witnesses for both of Abel's marriages was Adam Boulby and his uncle Thomas Boulby. Adam's mother Esther Boulby (née Chapman) was a first cousin of Abel; however, Esther was part of the Anglican

---

* 1728, New Style. At the time, before the Gregorian calendar was adopted in England, it would have been 11 January 1727. See Appendix.

Genealogy 11: Walker Quaker Connections

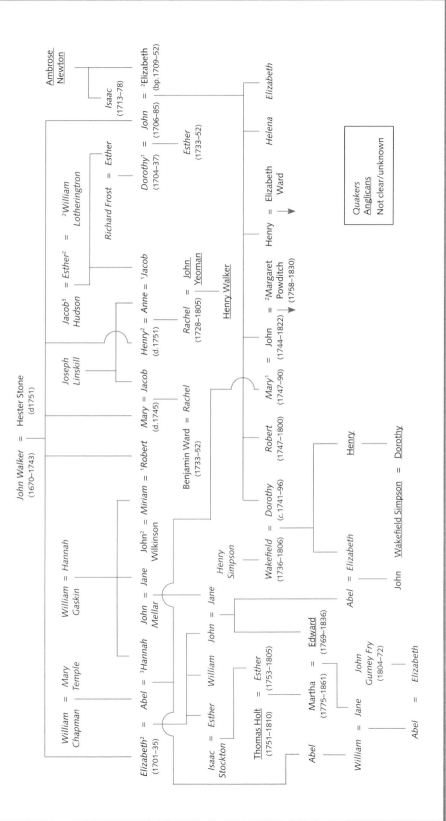

Chapmans. Also among the witnesses were Richard and Esther Frost, living in Haggersgate with their daughter Dorothy; she had been only 15 when she attended Abel Chapman's first wedding; at his second, she was 22, and she clearly caught the eye of the bride's brother John Walker. The Frost family came from North Shields, and probably knew the Walkers before coming to Whitby. John Walker and Dorothy Frost were married on 17 July 1730; not surrounded by their family and friends as his sister was, but quietly (and absolutely legally) at St Benet's, Paul's Wharf in London. By 1737, John Walker had moved into Haggersgate, living next door to his in-laws.

The family tree shows the Walker family marrying into other Whitby Quaker families. It is difficult to classify everyone's religious affiliations accurately; for example, Thomas Holt was baptised a Presbyterian, married a Quaker, and was involved in an unseemly squabble over the ownerships of a pew in the parish church. But it is clear that the two Walker weddings described above were part of a formidable series of intermarriages between some of the richest and most influential shipowning Quaker families in Whitby, frequently ignoring any injunctions not to marry cousins, and not to marry out.

6

Peace and Plenty

Generous commerce binds
The round of nations in a golden chain.
(James Thomson, *The Seasons*)

I n 1718, Charles Spencer, 3rd Earl of Sunderland, became the First Lord of the Treasury, the most important post in the government. He was neither particularly likeable nor particularly popular but held the position largely through the influence of his father-in-law John Churchill, Duke of Marlborough. The Whigs had gained power in 1714 and were to remain the party of government until John Stuart, Earl of Bute's appointment as prime minister in 1762. This did not mean that there was a constant amity and unity among the Whigs. On the contrary, there were myriad factions, changes of loyalties, bickering, squabbling and infighting – all the essentials of a parliamentary democracy.

Spencer was bitterly opposed by Robert Walpole, who had briefly held the post, but it looked as if Spencer was immovable. And then came the crash: the South Sea Bubble. In 1720, the value of the shares of the South Sea Company plummeted precipitately, causing a severe financial crisis with enormous personal and corporate losses, numerous bankruptcies and the failure of several banks. Among the victims of this financial scandal were Sir Isaac Newton and Jonathan Swift, both of whom lost sizeable amounts of money. Many politicians and 'moneyed men' were implicated in the fraud and corruption, including Charles Spencer.

Robert Walpole succeeded him as First Lord of the Treasury. Walpole was a moderate Whig, who had risen to power through eloquence in the House of Commons and royal patronage. He was a very able politician and he managed to save the situation from being a total financial and political disaster. He also contrived to shield several public figures, including the king, from official accusations of wrongdoing; this made him some very influential friends. By 1721, Walpole was also Chancellor of the Exchequer, and leader of the administration. He was de facto Britain's first prime minister (a title he hated and rejected). Walpole's supreme talent was his skill at playing politics: he knew how to treat people to ensure continuing loyalty and he knew how to neutralise opposition; he knew exactly when and how to use the carrot of promotion and the stick of sidelining.

Robert Walpole's ministry was at first popular; his policy of not getting involved in the numerous antagonisms of mainland Europe brought the country the longest period of peace in the century. Peace being much cheaper than war, he was able to stabilise the economy, lower the customs duties (especially on British exports) and foster trade. Peace ensured an increase in the trade between Britain and the Mediterranean, and the ships of Whitby took advantage of this: in 1727 *Friends Love*, John Medcalfe,* was trading with Bilbao, and ten years later *Buck*, Wilkinson, sailed to Alicante, Ivaca (Ibiza), Malaga and Fangerola (Fuengirola).

However, these were sporadic commercial ventures, convenient and profitable in the brief periods of peace. As the *Examiner* put it, 'our merchants were fix'd in the Business with other Countries';[1] trading with Portugal was more reliable. An agreement in 1654 had allowed British merchants access to Portuguese overseas markets in Asia, Africa and Brazil, and the Methuen Treaty of 1703 gave Portugal priority access to the English market for its wines, in return for abolishing their embargo on importing British woollen cloth. Whitby ships certainly traded with Portugal: in 1729, *Henry & Mary*, Robert Walker,** sailed from Shields to Lisbon, and two years later *Freelove*, John Walker, combined traditional trading partners with newly accessible Spanish ports, sailing between Majorca, Alicante, Cádiz, Lisbon and Amsterdam.

It does not seem that Whitby ships were to any significant extent involved in the lucrative export of English woollens (which were mainly produced in Yorkshire and East Anglia) or the direct import of Portuguese wines.

Drinking port wine became a patriotic activity. In 1704, it was noted that: 'French wine is laid by, and the gross [major] Draught of the whole Nation is upon Portugal Wines',[2] though this may also have something to do with the price, French wines being at least twice the price of the Portuguese ones.† Jonathan Swift encouraged the pro-port lobby in his poem 'On The Irish Club':

> Be sometimes to your country true,
> Have once the public good in view:
> Bravely despise Champagne at Court,
> And chuse to dine at home with Port.

---

* If a person's name follows a ship's name it indicates he is the master. This standard practice will be followed throughout.

** Brother of John (1706–85), Henry and Mary.

† In 1731, port wine cost 2*s* a quart in a tavern, equivalent to about £1.00 per 175ml glass today. Good strong beer would have cost the equivalent of about 35p per pint.

Genealogy 12: Prime Ministers

First Lord of the Treasury 1717–21
Prime Ministers from 1721
Leaders of Government
[Dates in office]

Robert Walpole

William Pierrepont

Sir John Leveson

Sir Edward Montagu
1st Earl Sandwich

William Cavendish
3rd Duke of Devonshire

William
4th Duke
[1756–57]

Robert
[1721–42]

Horatio = Rachel

Grace = Gilbert Holles

Thomas Pitt

Christian = Sir Peter Temple

Thomas = ¹Elizabeth Jones
Pelham

Grace² = Thomas = ²Dorothy
        Pelham

Elizabeth¹ = Charles = ²Dorothy Townsend
[1721–30]

Charles Spencer
3rd Earl of Sunderland
[1718–21]

John Churchill
Duke of Marlborough

Henrietta   Anne = Charles Spencer

Francis = Henrietta
Godolphin

Robert

Richard = Eleanor
Grenville

Hester = William
1st Earl of Chatham
[1766–68]

William
[1783–1801]

Thomas Pelham-Holles
1st Duke of Newcastle
[1754–56; 1757–62]

Catherine = Henry
[1743–54]

Henrietta

Sir Thomas = Frances
Gower

Jane = William John Manners
1st Duke of Rutland

Jemima = Sir Philip Carteret

John Granville

George = Grace

John = Catherine

Lucy = James Stanhope
1st Earl
[1717–18]

Philip
2nd Earl

George
[1763–65]

Charles = Hester
3rd Earl

Lady Hester

Evelyn

Sir Edward = Mary

Sidney   Evelyn

John
[1742–43]

John = Catherine

Evelyn = John Leveson-Gower

John
2nd Duke

John
3rd Duke

John
Marquis of Granby

Mary = John Stuart
3rd Earl Bute
[1762–63]

James Compton

Mary = Charles Sackville

Lionel

Spencer
[1742–43]

John Philip = Frances

Frances

Cádiz. John Walker in *Freelove* traded here in 1731.

Dr Johnson did his bit by adding that port was the liquor 'for men' and that claret was the drink for mere 'boys' as it was so weak that 'a man would be drowned by it before it made him drunk'. However, he did add, with a smile, that brandy was the drink for 'he who aspires to be a hero'.[3] There were enough boys and aspiring heroes in eighteenth-century Britain to ensure a steady market for French wines and brandy. As the duty on these items made them very expensive, there was a thriving trade in smuggling these, and other, items into the country.

The Collector of the Whitby Customs House reported in 1723 that 'there is constantly smuggling vessels on this Coast'.[4] Most of this smuggling was centred at Robin Hood's Bay, Sandsend and Runswick, which had many 'cobles', traditional Yorkshire fishing boats which could be manoeuvred close to the shore, were capable of sailing in rough weather and could easily be run ashore on a sandy beach. Such boats were comparatively cheap and could soon pay for themselves by smuggling: the customer could buy smuggled goods at least 20 per cent cheaper, but even that bargain price might be 500 per cent dearer than they could be bought abroad.

In November 1721, Richard Wilson, the Riding Officer of the Whitby Customs, found five half-ankers, containing about 20 gallons of brandy, on the shore at

Marske 'believed to have been run by one Thos Garbutt'. In August, 3½ gallons of *Genevas* (Dutch gin) and 36lb of prunes were seized from a fishing boat, William Moorsom of Robin Hood's Bay master, which was being landed from a Dutch smuggler. In the following March, the 100-ton Whitby vessel *Happy Return*, George Masterman, sailing from Dordrecht was caught with four half-ankers of contraband brandy. A fortnight later, twenty-two half-ankers of brandy from Holland were found concealed on the same ship with 'intention to be run'.

The custom records list illicit cargo found in the homes of various people. Some of the receivers were quite respectable: Miles Breckon of Newholm, master of *Elizabeth* (in 1731), was found to possess a half-anker of brandy and another of claret, as well as two canisters of Bohea (black tea) and a canister of 'Grene Tea'. Rather surprisingly, 23 gallons of brandy and 27 gallons of Geneva were found by the customs officer at the house of Catherine Lacy in 1729. The culprit was almost certainly Catherine, née Broadrigge (Brodrick), the widow of William Lacy, sailor, and they were both Quakers.

The Quaker quarterly meeting of 1723 sent questions to the monthly meetings, asking:

> Do your [members] take care to see none under our profession [Quakers] defraud the King of his Customs Duty or Excise or in any wise encourage the running of goods by buying or vending such goods? And do they generally reprehend and testify all such offenders and their unwarrantable, clandestine and unlawful actions?'[5]

Clearly, rumours had been circulating about Quaker collusion in smuggling, and equally clearly, these questions did not stop it. It has been claimed that about a quarter of all imported goods were smuggled – with tea, gin and brandy being among the most popular. With such a broad support for this illegal commerce, it is hardly surprising that the customs officers were rather unpopular. Perhaps it is not surprising that a payment is recorded 'for mending ye* Custom ho [house] Windows' at Whitby.

Breaking windows aside, Whitby was becoming more prosperous and more civilised: the roads and pavements were beginning to be improved, and the thatched cottages were gradually being replaced 'by neat and commodious dwellings, roofed with tiles'.[6] The first sash windows appeared in the 1720s, such an innovation that 'there were both town and country people gazing at them'.[7]

---

* An abbreviation for 'the', the 'y' acting as a stand-in for the Old English letter thorn (þ) which had fallen into disuse. The thorn was pronounced 'th' as in 'this', so, contrary to popular belief, 'ye' would have been pronounced 'the'.

The Old
Custom House,
Whitby.

Most of this increased wealth was due to the effectiveness of largely Whitby-based merchants, shipbuilders, shipowners, master mariners and sailors (and in many cases their wives) who made it all happen. The ordinary seamen and their families saw little of the prosperity and, in a society which had no welfare state,[*] accidents on board ship (and there were many), a propensity for drink, an addiction to gambling or a concatenation of incidents of sheer bad luck could precipitate a family into poverty, the workhouse and a pauper's grave; but for the able, ambitious, industrious and lucky the merchant navy could offer opportunities for promotion and a degree of affluence.

---

[*] Each parish was responsible for its paupers, supported by a parish tax. The Seamen's Hospital at Whitby provided lodgings and support for superannuated sailors and for the poor widows and orphans of seamen. Another possibility for them was to petition the Trinity House for a pension.

Many of those who did benefit from the increased wealth were often aware of their social responsibilities, undertaking local government duties (church warden, overseer of the poor, etc.) and making charitable bequests in life or (less painfully) in their will. But primarily they invested money to secure a comfortable future and spent – sometimes lavishly – on consumer items. Several of these newly rich Whitby families were members of the Society of Friends, a new generation who had no experiences of the savage persecutions endured by their ancestors, and who were at ease among other businessmen of different beliefs.★ Many of them were (comparatively) sophisticated, educated, urbane and godly 'men of the world', who no longer considered tea as the 'Broth of Abominable Things'.[8]

Due to the work of earlier Quakers there were meetings of the Society of Friends planted in many parts of the American colonies and in the West Indies. The Friends' Anglo-American contacts provided more than mutual spiritual support; from quite early times, many English Quaker merchants and shipowners traded with these areas where there was already a friendly network they could easily access. We learn from the Whitby meeting death and burial records that Richard and Joseph, sons of James and Hannah Marsingale, died within a week of each other in May 1703 'att nevis in amerrica & were Buryed there'. James Marsingale was probably the owner and master of the ship *Mary* which brought a cargo of 60 chaldrons of coal from Newcastle to London in 1697 (the year in which Celia Fiennes watched the colliers pass Scarborough). He married in 1698, so his two children who died must have been very young, which would imply that their mother was there as well.

In 1701, the Quaker Jonathan Radclife 'departed this Life … att Sea and was Buryed therein between Burbados & Maryland'. A more successful voyage was that of *Henry & Mary*, Walker, from Virginia in 1731, almost certainly carrying tobacco.

The Society of Friends were becoming increasingly anti-slavery in the early eighteenth century, and trading in goods that relied upon slave labour, such as tobacco and sugar, was developing into a tricky moral issue for them. George Fox himself had been somewhat ambivalent about slavery, merely encouraging masters to treat their slaves humanely. He seemed to envisage that after some years of education and religious development they would be freed – an idea he based upon the Old Testament concept of the Jubilee★★ year in which the Israelites were commanded by God to 'proclaim liberty throughout all the land unto all

---

★ This was made easier by the Affirmation Act of 1722, which removed many of the legal constraints against Quakers. They were allowed to affirm rather than take an oath, to institute legal proceedings and to exercise their right to vote unhindered.

★★ The jubilee year would take place after seven times seven years had been completed, i.e. every fifty years.

The Old Smuggler, Baxtergate, Whitby. Tiled and with sliding sash windows.

inhabitants thereof … and ye shall return every man unto his possession, and … every man unto his family'.[9]

Of course, the Quakers did not have a monopoly of the Whitby trade with the Americas at this time: for example, we learn of the round-sterned, 320-ton cat *Hudson*, William Livingstone, sailing to Jamaica in 1730. The master must have died on or shortly after this voyage, as the *Daily Journal* advertised the vessel to be sold 'by the Candle'* at Lloyd's Coffee House at noon on 10 February 1731. The vessel was 'well fitted' for her voyage, and was Whitby-built by Captain Thomas Grange 'deceas'd'.

Whitby was an important shipbuilding port, but we do not know much about the names of those who built the vessels until the late eighteenth century. Advertisements for the sale of ships routinely noted where a vessel was built, but hardly ever who built it, the mention of Thomas Grange being something

---

* Selling by the candle was the common way of auctioning ships. An inch of candle was lit, which would start the bidding, and the last bid before the flame went out was the winning one. Pepys witnessed such a sale of two vessels 'by an inch of candle' for the first time in November 1660, recording how the bidders 'do invite one another, and at last how they do all cry, and we have much to do to tell who did cry last'.

Shipbuilding.

of a rarity. Those who ran yards which built ships usually referred to themselves as a 'master builder' rather than as a 'shipbuilder'. The title 'shipwright' normally applied to the employees, such as Stephen Jowsey who is recorded as a shipwright in the Whitby parish register for 1738. His son William was born in 1701, and he is described as a 'carpenter' in 1738 and a 'master builder' in 1748.

The earliest mention in the Whitby parish registers of a 'master builder' is Matthew Shipton, who was buried in November 1723. He was married in 1678 and probably born in the 1650s, putting him of the same generation (and maybe a few years senior) to Gervase (or Jarvis) Coates, who is often considered to be the earliest of the named Whitby shipbuilders. Gervase appears in the Whitby parish records when he is buried in 1738; William Coulson, shipbuilder, appears in 1746 when his daughter Elizabeth was baptised; and Thomas Fishburn, 'm[aster] builder', when his son William was baptised 1750.

The 1730s brought about another improvement at Whitby when the Dock Company built three dry docks on the east bank of the Esk near Spital Bridge. The Company was founded by four entrepreneurial master mariners: William Barker, James Reynolds, Joseph Holt★ and John Watson. The latter's share soon passed to his

★ Young (p.551) lists the founder members as 'William Barker, John Holt, John Reynolds and John Watson'. John Holt was baptised in 1718, and John Reynolds in 1721. As the double dock – planned and financed by the Dock Company – was completed in 1734, it is unlikely that either of them would have been able to make much of a contribution to the proceedings.

Whitby. On the further bank far right is the site of the Whitehall shipyard occupied by Coulson after he had rented space in the dockyard complex. The Dock Company owned the riverside beyond the Whitehall Yard where the sailing boats are moored and beyond. Among those who built ships on the Dock Company's premises were Benjamin Coates and the Langbourns.

son-in-law John Kildill, possibly as a dowry for his daughter Isabel on her marriage in 1734. Many ships already over-wintered in Whitby and the new dry docks enabled them to be repaired more thoroughly, efficiently and 'at very reasonable Rates'.[10] They also provided winter work for ship's carpenters. In addition to the three dry docks, the Dock Company premises included two shipyards, a blacksmith's shop, various 'Messuages Houses or Tenements and the appurtenances thereunto respectively belonging'[11] – so it was quite an industrial complex.

From time to time members of the Dock Company also built ships, but mostly they rented out their shipyards, which enabled those who wished to set up as shipbuilders to develop a business without having to purchase a shipyard, examples being Benjamin Coates (the younger son of Gervase) and William Coulson, formerly of Scarborough. Shipbuilding and shipowning were flourishing in Whitby.

7

Fair Trader

To thee belongs the rural reign
Thy cities shall with commerce shine
All thine shall be the subject main
And every shore it circles thine.

(James Thomson, 'Rule, Britannia!')

In the eighteenth century, there were not many investment opportunities. Land was the most popular, as at that time 'ownership of landed property remained the greatest source of wealth, power and social honour',[1] partly because an owner of a freehold property was entitled to vote in the county constituency. Another form of investment was government bonds, which were introduced in 1751 and the following year were fixed at 3 per cent. These provided a steady guaranteed income.

Daniel Defoe wrote in 1728:[2] 'Trade is the Wealth of the World ... Trade dispenses the natural Wealth of the World, and Trade raises new Species of Wealth ... Trade has two Daughters ... namely Manufacture and Navigation.' When he wrote this he was not saying anything new; this was largely the accepted view, and the implications were clear: the country with the most trade would be the richest, and the most powerful. The logic was simple: the more territory Britain controlled which contained valuable raw materials, the bigger the trade and the wealthier the country would become, especially as the same controlled territory would be a secure market for English manufactured goods. In short: there was money in ships.

Investing in shipping was common. For example, George Fox had a $^1/_{32}$ part share of the ship *Pashant Triall* (Patient Trial) which was owned by John Cockerill of Scarborough. Such investment was high risk, but it has been estimated that the return on capital investment in east coast colliers was in the order of 6–12 per cent per annum.[3] A wise investor spread the financial risk by having shares in a number of vessels. A ship master would often invest any surplus income in a share of a ship which would increase his chance of being employed and maintained as its captain, and similarly sailmakers, rope makers, butchers, chandlers, farmers and anyone who was involved in supplying or servicing seagoing ships would purchase shares from a number of ships to ensure ongoing income and contracts. The partnership of Messrs John & Thomas Dawson, ropers, owned in 1737 (the year in which the latter died) shares in sixteen ships: ten owned at Whitby, two from their home town of Newcastle and one each from Shields, Sunderland, Scarborough and Hull. The Whitby-owned ships included *Gowin* (Gawain), Mark Noble; *Freelove*, John Walker; *Henry & Mary*, Henry Walker; *Constant John*, Robert Walker; and *Friendship*, Michael Boulby.

A common practice for a master mariner who owned his own ship was to enrol his sons, when each reached the age of about 11 or 12, on board as his 'servant' for a seven-year apprenticeship during which they should gain all the knowledge and skills needed to become a master mariner. A servant was not paid – indeed apprenticeships had to be bought and could be expensive.* The indentured servant would live at the expense of his master, who would supply food, clothing and other necessities, and in winter, when not at sea, would often live in his master's house. So being apprenticed to ones father or elder brother was clearly a cheap and convenient system for both parties. This would be followed by a year or two first as a sailor then as a mate to gain experience of responsibility and authority, after which he would become a master. Depending on parental wealth, it was a common practice for a father to give his master mariner son the main ownership of a ship as a coming-of-age present; this appears to be the case with Michael Boulby (*Content*), John Holt (*Olive Branch*), William Barker (*Mayflower*), John Wilkinson (*Buck*) and perhaps with Thomas Millner (*Mary Ann*). A master mariner who was the main owner of a ship was a very eligible bachelor, as can be illustrated by the sons of John Walker Senior: Henry, the eldest, was master of *Henry & Mary* by 1724, and was married by 1726; and John Junior was born in August 1706, was master of *Freelove* by August 1729 and married Dorothy Frost in July 1730.

Sailors who did not have wealthy, or well-connected, parents were often unlikely to rise much above mate, which was an achievement that marked eligibility: John Cremer records his uncle as saying, 'Now you are a Mate of a ship, I Suppose You'll Soon think of Marrying'[4] – something he was not keen to enter into. However, he did become a master and eventually married – twice.

---

* There was a whole range of types – and consequently costs – of apprenticeship. The main aim of an apprenticeship was to be taught 'the art of sailing and navigation' but with the caveat was that this was done 'within … the boy's capability' and also that of the master. The circumstances of an apprenticeship were very different depending whether the aim was to train a potential master mariner or a ship's carpenter or if you were a 'parish boy' who needed only sufficient skill to become an able seaman and therefore hopefully not be a burden on the parish poor rates. See Barker (2011), p.136.

Usually, the decision to commission a new ship was initiated by a single person who would persuade colleagues (usually family members, business partners, or both) to take shares in the enterprise. As the official owner, he had the main financial responsibility, found a suitable builder and enjoyed the privilege of naming the vessel. He was called the ship's 'husband', as he did the husbandry – the management of organisation and finance.

We do not always know what was in the mind of the initiating owner when he thought up a name for his new vessel. However, it should be noted that the eighteenth century was a time when puns, ambiguities and playing with words were a large part of wit. In an age when Sterne's 'Tristram Shandy' was a bestseller, it would be foolish to accept too much at face value.* The ship called *Prospect* would have been referred to as 'The *Prospect* of Whitby' a phrase which is ambiguous, and deliberately so. Similarly ambiguous is 'The *Liberty* of Whitby'; and there are other names which might have been chosen for how they sounded when spoken in this format: for example, *Commerce*, *Fortune* and *Success*.** *Noble Hope*, owned by Matthew Noble, is an example of a deliberate play on words. *Harmony* clearly has many resonances.

Ships not only had names, but they also displayed them (together with the name of their home port) on the stern and/or on the bows in letters large enough to be seen from other vessels or from the shore, when sailing by. It did not take owners long to realise that this rendered their vessel into a large travelling display board and their names of ships could be used for advertising. Surnames were used for the same reasons as traders' names are now painted on the sides of their lorries and vans: promoting the firm's name, and looking for business. Whitby examples are: *Addison*, *Barrick*, *Campion*, *Chapman*, *Middleton* and *Ward*.

The main business that Whitby ships were involved in during the early part of the eighteenth century was coal, and some of the colliers were named after collieries: *Bucksnook*, *Tanfield Moor*, *Wylam* and *North Seaton*. It would be surprising if the owners of these mines, or at least their agents at Newcastle, were not significant investors in these ships. Bucksnook colliery opened and laid a rudimentary waggonway to transport its coal to the Tyne in 1712. Tanfield Moor (near Beamish) was opened by George Pitt 1714, and he also built a waggonway. Wylam Colliery was owned by the Blackett family.† North Seaton was near Newbiggin, a few miles up the coast from Tinmouth.

---

* On 6 September 1769 the *Tristram*, Shandy, is reported to have sailed from Deal for Rhode Island.

** In the Receivers of Sixpences accounts for 8 December 1744 there is mentioned the 80-ton vessel *Thane of Fife*.

† William Hedley, the engineer there, built *Puffing Billy* in 1813 and Robert Stephenson worked as fireman for the pumping engine there. Robert was the father of George who was born at Wylam in 1781.

Genealogy 13: Coal Barons: Bowes, Lyon Liddell

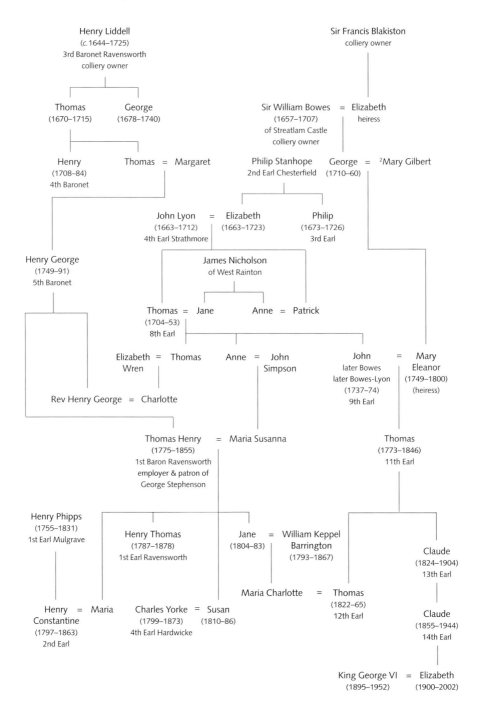

Three of the major colliery baron family names were Liddell, Bowes and Wortley-Montagu. These three families formed a cartel, the 'Grand Alliance', in the early eighteenth century, using their combined capital to buy up collieries and control waggonways. By 1750, they were effectively in charge of the majority of the collieries either side of the Tyne which used the river for export.[5]

Trade and profit were admired, and well-educated men engaged in business management could boast of their successes; Pope had made a clear distinction between those of noble and/or wealthy families who simply squandered their inheritance and those who invested in industry and agriculture:

> Why, of two brothers, rich and restless one
> Plows, burns, manures and toils from sun to sun;
> The other slights, for women, sports and wines,
> All Townshend's turnips, and all Grosvenor's mines.[6]

Unlike many other religious groups, the Quakers understood the importance of PR. Excluded from many careers apart from manufacturing and trading, they flourished in those. As the Religious Society of Friends, they often named their vessels using the word 'Friends'. *Friendship* was the favourite (on occasion the name appears on the muster rolls as *Friends Ship* in case the double meaning was missed). Thirteen Whitby ships had been named *Friendship* by 1789. Other Whitby Quaker-owned ship's names were *Friends, Friend's Desire, Friend's Love, Friend's Glory, Friend's Assistance, Friend's Adventure, Friend's Advice, Friend's Goodwill, Amity, Brotherhood, Brotherly Love* and *Brotherly Love's Increase*.

Freelove was another typically Quaker ship name, referring to the Christian belief that God's love is freely given to his people. However, the phrase 'Free Love' also had a secular meaning, implying that a lack of chastity before marriage and fidelity afterwards was not necessarily a bad thing. It seems likely that there was a certain amount of ribald jesting aimed at anyone associated with a ship called *Freelove*. How far anyone was upset by this is another question, but in some documents the ship *Freelove* is listed as *Truelove*.

8

Mars

When Trade is at stake, you must defend it or perish.

(William Pitt the Elder)

I t is often the case that peace treaties sow the seeds of future conflicts. The Treaty of Utrecht was not popular with any of the participants; the British had hoped – after so many victories – for more concessions, especially from the Spanish. Several British merchants acted as if such concessions had actually been granted, trading illegally with the Spanish colonies. At first this was overlooked by Spain, which was recovering from the war, but as she grew stronger and it looked as if Walpole's administration was committed to maintaining the peace at any price, she became bolder. In 1727, a Spanish attempt to retake Gibraltar was unsuccessful. Aggrieved, the Spanish government clamped down on illicit trading, using a stop-and-search policy towards British merchant ships, which was oppressive and at times violent. In such a fracas, a Captain Jenkins (allegedly) had his ear cut off by Spanish coastguards, the severed ear being kept pickled in a jar by the captain.

Walpole desperately wished to maintain the peace, but increasingly his administration came under attack for being too feeble and pusillanimous to protect British subjects and British trade. This mood was encouraged by the Stowe House Group, or 'Cobham's cubs', a group of opposition Whigs whom Walpole had excluded from government, and which met at the home of Richard Temple, 1st Viscount Cobham. In 1738, the House of Commons was shown Jenkins' ear, sparking the eponymous and inevitable war. Walpole sought the first opportunity to negotiate with the Spanish and, in return for niggardly concessions from Spain, peace was made. This produced outrage from the country's merchants and an impressive opposition speech from William Pitt, MP for the 'rotten borough' of Old Sarum and one of 'Cobham's cubs', in which he described the treaty as 'a surrender of the rights and trade of England' adding that 'the voice of England has condemned it'.[1]

War was renewed, but Walpole's administration, although it had maintained the Royal Navy ships-of-the-line in a state of some readiness during the years of intermittent peace, had made cuts in military funding for a peace dividend. Initial success by the British, the capture of Porto Bello (in modern Panama), was followed by some costly failures, notably the siege of Cartagena (in modern Columbia) which was recorded by Tobias Smollett in his novel *Roderick Random*. Smollett, one of the many talented Scotsmen coming south of the border to find his fortune, had enlisted as a surgeon's second mate in His Majesty's Ship *Chichester*, and was present at this catastrophe.

As the War of Jenkins' Ear morphed into the War of the Austrian Succession, Walpole stood down. His position as First Lord of the Treasury was taken by Spencer Compton in an administration led by John Carteret, but still very much influenced by Walpole.

The spark for the War of Austrian Succession was the death of the Hapsburg Charles VI, Archduke of Austria and Holy Roman Emperor, the same man who had claimed the throne of Spain and who had been the cause of the War of the Spanish Succession. His daughter Maria Theresa was his heir, but as by law and custom there had never been a Holy Roman Empress, there was the danger of dissention after his death. Consequently, he promulgated the 'Pragmatic Sanction' of 1713, which legalised a female heir to rule Hapsburg territories, and he ensured that it received the assent of all interested parties.

However, after his death, although Britain stood by its commitment, Frederick II 'the Great', King of Prussia, (George II's nephew) took advantage of the situation and supported the rival candidate Charles Albert, Elector of Bavaria. Frederick wished to consolidate scattered Prussian territories into a conjoined whole, to attain which he marched into the Austrian province of Silesia – thus beginning the war. France and Spain joined Prussia, so England supported Austria and the Netherlands. George II had tried to keep Hanover neutral, but Carteret persuaded him to change his mind and to set up the so-called 'Pragmatic Army' of Hanoverians, Hessians and British.

Mobilisation of the British army to fight on mainland Europe was no easy matter, requiring a fleet of transport ships. These had to be hired from the merchant marine by the Navy Board, who made a provisional selection of suitable ships which were later surveyed at a Royal Dockyard. The ships then had to be customised, with cabins for the men and stalls for the horses. All this had to be done as speedily as possible, ensuring the transports were ready when the troops were to be embarked.

Between July 1741 and December 1742[2] inclusive, 103 transport ships – mainly for ferrying troops to Flanders and Holland – were hired by the Navy Board and processed at Deptford. Their combined capacity was over 30,000 tons. More than 30 per cent of these transports can be identified as Whitby-owned ships – further evidence of the importance of Whitby as a shipbuilding and maritime trading port. Wars always raised ethical issues for pacifist Quaker owners and master

Genealogy 14: The Austrian Succession

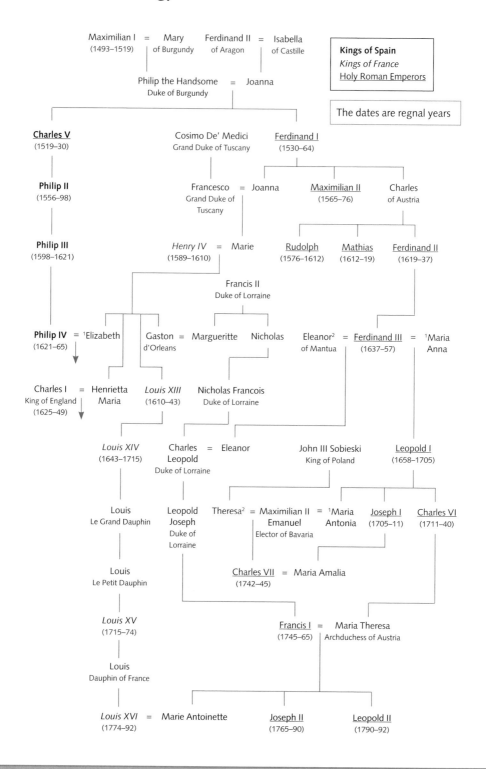

The Netherlands.

mariners. It is interesting, therefore, that five of the thirty-two Whitby ships in the above sample of transports were owned and captained by Quakers.

In 1742, 16,000 British troops were ferried to Ostend where they over-wintered as part of the Pragmatic Army. The following year they marched into Germany along the north bank of the River Main, making camp near Aschaffenburg, some miles east of Frankfurt, where they were joined by King George II with a welcome cavalry force and a cumbersome collection of waggons. The army's supply lines were extensive and consequently rather thin, and the French army cut them without much difficulty; the increasingly hungry Pragmatic Army had no option but to turn round and retrace their steps, marching into a larger French army waiting for them near Dettingen.

The ensuing battle could have ended badly for the Allies, especially if the king had been captured. In the event it was confused and clumsy. The French attacked first with some success, but a fierce though rather disorganised counterattack was decisive. The French suffered heavy casualties and the Pragmatic Army continued on its march back to Flanders. It was an important victory in that it averted disaster. Back in Britain, much was made of it with the dramatic and valiant image of George II brandishing his sword and leading his troops to victory. In reality, it was a somewhat dubious victory.

William Pitt denigrated the king's achievements at Dettingen. He was also appalled that George, as Elector of Hanover, was being paid large sums of money by Britain for the loan of Hanoverian troops in a war Britain was unlikely to win. He thought that Britain must be prepared, if necessary, to abandon Hanover, which could not be defended as it was entirely surrounded by other (often hostile) territories. Pitt's proclaimed policy was not to fight wars in mainland Europe but to ally with Prussia as the only country with a strong enough army to threaten the French and force them to keep substantial numbers of their soldiers in Europe. Britain would financially subsidise the Prussians, while using the Royal Navy to defeat the French and Spanish at sea, and the army to fight them on land in the West Indies, America and India thus creating the greatest empire since the Romans and 'control of the world's trade'. If Hanover was lost, he argued, it could be reclaimed in any further peace treaty.

This may well have been the wisest policy on offer at the time, but Pitt's attitude to Hanover made him a lasting enemy of the king who also did not relish the idea of an alliance with Frederick of Prussia, whom he referred to as 'a mischievous rascal and bad friend, a bad ally, a bad relation and a bad neighbour [to Hanover], in fact the most dangerous and evil-disposed prince in Europe'.[3] As the king had the final say on who was Prime Minister it looked as if William Pitt was doomed not to achieve any high office while George II was on the throne. Pitt had few influential supporters but he did have a keen admirer in Sarah Churchill, widow of John Churchill, Duke of Marlborough. She hated Walpole's policies, which she believed had unravelled the benefits accrued by her husband's victories, and consequently favoured William Pitt's vision. When Sarah died in 1744 she left Pitt a substantial legacy.

Carteret's administration only lasted a year, and was replaced by a coalition government (known, whimsically, as 'the broad-bottomed administration') led by Henry Pelham, and including all the significant members of the Stowe House group with the glaring omission of Pitt. George II had only agreed to the new administration on the condition that it was Pitt-free.

The war dragged on; the victory of Dettingen had merely allowed the Pragmatic Army to fall back to Flanders in good order. Some troops were transported back to Britain, as there were rumours of a French invasion on the south-east coast and of a landing in Scotland by Prince Charles Edward, the young Pretender, to claim the throne for his father James. In Flanders, the French army pursued their

Genealogy 15: Walpole Genealogy

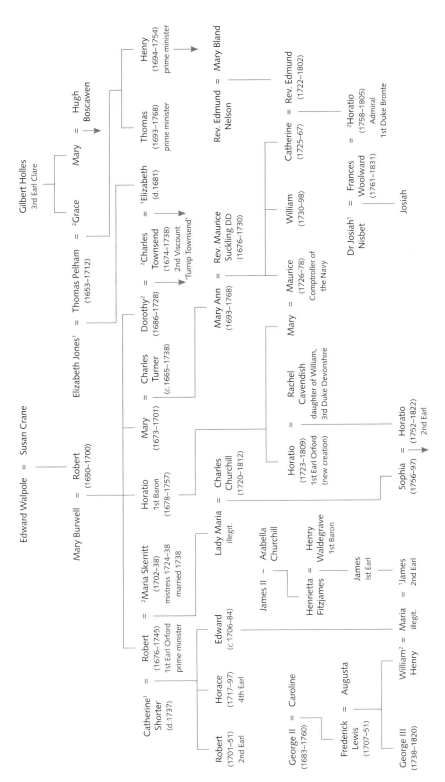

retreating enemy and in 1744, after a bitter siege, captured the underdefended town of Ostend. The Battle of Fontenoy the following year was a decisive victory for the French. Britain was very much on the defensive.

The mood of the country had changed since Thomson had written the words for 'Rule, Britannia!', but there may have been a comforting hope in his third verse:

> Still more majestic shalt thou rise,
> More dreadful from each foreign stroke;
> As the loud blast that tears the skies,
> Serves but to root thy native oak.

9

Enterprise

Frequently having a view of Ships sailing by … I thought sailors must be happy men to have such opportunities of visiting foreign countries, and beholding the wonderful works of the Creator in the remote regions of the earth … and indulging a curiosity which seemed implanted in my nature.

(William Spavens)

'At a little distance from this town [Guisborough],' wrote the almost certainly English author of *Letters from a Moor at London to his Friends at Tunis*, 'is Ounsbery or Roseberry-Topping, an high pyramid, which serves as a land mark for sailors.'

It seems to have had a variety of names: a roadmap of 1764 (overleaf) names it Rosemary Topping, and it was referred to as 'Osbury Toppin' by the diarist Ralph Jackson who climbed to the summit in July 1757 from which he 'view'd an open Vista to the West & North & N.E'. Its shape, with a gentle incline up one side and a steep precipitous slope on the other, was a feature which the Whitby master mariner, poet and customs officer Francis Gibson (1752–1805) made into the central simile of his verse 'On Passing Roseberry Topping':

> Supreme amongst the towering hills that shade
> Sweet Cleveland's fertile vale, see Roseberry
> Rearing its rocky front against the north;
> Gently inclining to the peaceful south.
> So stands the man with generous spirits fraught
> Superior to adversity's keen blast;
> Viewing with pity the disdainful eye
> Of opulence unmerited, the curling lip
> Of titled insignificance, the scorn
> Of little knaves in office; while the sun
> Of true religion on his features plays,
> And all th' expanded soul lies open to its rays.

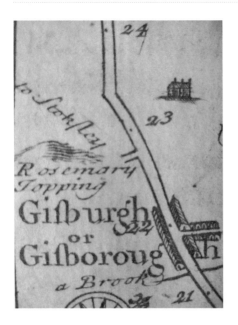

Road map showing
Guisborough.

While not great literature, this poem, with its passing homage to Shakespeare, far exceeds in aesthetic merit that of Thomas Pierson, schoolmaster of Stokesley, on the same subject, written in 1783:

> Of Atlas Mount let poets antique sing,
> Whose summit bare supports the bending sky;
> Of Roseberry's rude rock I deign to write
> The height of Topping, and its oozing rill.

There are times when one entirely concurs with King George III's exasperated outburst: 'Why will not my subjects write in prose?'[1]

Roseberry Topping towers over Great Ayton, and for the Cook family who lived in its shadow it would have been an ever present part of their life.

Being a lively and enterprising boy who enjoyed going his own way, James Cook would have, sooner or later, scrambled his way to the summit. From there he had a panoramic view of the coast, the port of Stockton and the ships on the crowded seaway. It seems certain that this was the first time that James Cook saw the sea,* but what he felt as he saw so much land and sea and what musings

---

* Contrary to Beaglehole's assertion that: 'Nothing can be more reasonably certain than that Cook had his first taste, as well as sight, of the sea at Staithes, and that the experience was convincing.'

Roseberry Topping and Aireyholm Farm by Barrie Wright.

developed in his mind over the ensuing years can only be conjectured. He would have returned to that summit when he was free to do so; clearly the horizons of this young farm boy were broadening.

Although James' father was employed as a bailiff to the tenant farmer, they were still fairly poor. Education was a problem; it cost money to go to school and when a boy was at school he was not contributing to the family budget. However, Thomas Scottowe paid the penny a week for young James to go to Great Ayton school. Scottowe would have been kept informed of the Cook family's arrival in the small town, but he may not have met the children. Whether Scottowe had already discerned particular talent in young James Cook is debatable; it is quite possible that he paid for all the poor boys of the parish to go to school, provided they were not idle, badly behaved or didn't regularly attend church. Such a situation might account for the comment that Great Ayton school took great care to instruct the children 'in the principles of the Christian Religion, according to the Doctrine of the Church of England'.[2]

Young James would have left school at about twelve, which enabled him to spend more time working on the farm helping his father and gaining useful experience. It is possible that his parents expected him to follow in his father's footsteps and become a bailiff, or even aspire to be a tenant farmer; but his son was perhaps already having feelings of 'being confined' and that the limits of Great Ayton were 'far too small for [his] active mind'.[3]

Networking and patronage were key elements in British society at the time covered by this book. Networking is still with us, but patronage (except by institutions) is often regarded as condescending and patriarchal. However, in the eighteenth century – although social mobility was becoming much easier than before – society was still clearly divided by class, education and affluence. It was almost impossible for the intelligent and gifted but ill-educated poor to reach their potential without patronage from those who had wealth, influence and connections. Patronage took many forms, from an introduction or recommendation, to personal funding or an appointment to a well-paid post. Indeed, it is often difficult to separate patronage from what we would call sponsorship, employment or just writing a positive reference.

Dr Johnson described a 'patron' in his dictionary as 'One who countenances, supports or protects', and there are many successful patron–client relationships which would be included in this definition: for example, Samuel Pepys and Edward Montagu, Jonathan Swift and William Temple, Joseph Addison and Charles Montagu, Robert Hooke and Robert Boyle, and Matthew Prior and Lord Dorset.

Although patronage is perhaps mainly considered from the position of the client, the patron was not usually acting solely from disinterested reasons or from the desire to be flattered. While busy networking, many businessmen in the eighteenth century were also searching out useful skill and potential. Even in a society which calls itself a meritocracy it is doubtful if talent will out, and eighteenth-century Britain was no meritocracy: talent had to be hunted and then nurtured, like a new plant from a far-off land. Arguably, the democratic practice of talent-spotting at many levels of society was crucial in the development of trade, culture and liberty in Britain.

The Walker family was a successful shipowning business. When John Walker Senior died in April 1743 he left two sons, Henry and John, neither of whom at that time had any male heirs and who between them had ownership of at least three ships. Ships were expensive; a newly built 300-ton ship ready to sail would cost approximately £2,000 (c. £4.6 million), and additionally there would be the cost of cargo, insurance and the food and wages for the crew.

The owners of a ship had to trust the master not only with the lives of all aboard but also with this massively expensive capital asset without any means of making contact and little chance of receiving any information until a brief line appeared in the newspapers or *Lloyd's List*, and sometimes not until the vessel reached its home port. And not all masters were worthy of this trust. The owners of *Buck* of Whitby clearly did not trust John Wilkinson, the master and part owner of the ship, whom they claimed had been secretly trading in contraband for his own profit and had consequently put the ship into jeopardy. This led to a Chancery case.[4] Shipowners needed to employ master mariners whom they could trust, and who had both navigational and people skills, and additionally who had experience, honesty, adaptability, enterprise and some knowledge of the language, customs and currency of those ports which are to be visited. A difficult task; but shipowners had to look ahead to the future of their business, and the best way to ensure that there would be a good supply of masters in the future was to find suitable children and take them on as servants, teaching them all the necessary skills and hoping that after their training they would be good captains for the owners' future ships.

The Walkers would have used their family connections to track down likely apprentices. For the Walkers, marrying into the Chapman family was pivotal in that it linked them not only to their influential Quaker family (replete with master mariners and shipowners) descended from William Chapman and his wife Mary née Temple, but also to the Anglican branch of the clan descended from Williams' older brother Ingram.

Ingram's grandson Adam Boulby's marriage to Margaret Spencer connected him with the Wards, Jacksons and Jeffersons. Ralph Jackson (the diarist) had in his youth been apprenticed to his relative William Jefferson, hostman of Newcastle. William Jefferson had two brothers: John, a master mariner of Staithes who married Margaret Spencer's sister Ellinor, and Anthony who married Sarah, daughter of Samuel Gill, the customs officer there. Samuel's daughter Ann married Augustine, son of Thomas Scottowe, and his daughter Elizabeth married William Sanderson.

Ralph Jackson's sister Rachel married William Wilson, and Ralph used to visit them at Great Ayton; in his diary he mentions that on 20 December 1768 he 'Drank tea with my Sister & the Children at Mr Scottow's' and a week later that 'Revd Mr Haswell, Captn Scottowe & his Bro Augustine (all of Ayton), dined with me [at Guisborough], and I went to Ayton with them in the evening, where I laid at my Bro Wilson's.'[5]

John and Dorothy Walker had two daughters: Esther (in 1733), and Mary (1736) who died in infancy. Dorothy died a few months later. John then married Elizabeth, daughter of Ambrose Newton of Bagdale Hall, who was related to the Chaloners and the Cholmleys. After the death of her brother Isaac (a Quaker), she and her sister Helena were his co-heiresses.

It is generally accepted that the young James Cook worked in William Sanderson's shop in Staithes, and then served three years' apprenticeship to John Walker of Whitby, ending on 20 April 1749.

Quite what led up to these events is not clear; the shop and the ships have usually been treated as two separate episodes, with James feeling dissatisfied with the former and then moving on to his true calling, in both stages being helped by Thomas Scottowe. But it has been cogently argued that they are two parts of a single plan,[6] which, perhaps, makes better sense.

Genealogy 16: Walker Anglican Connections

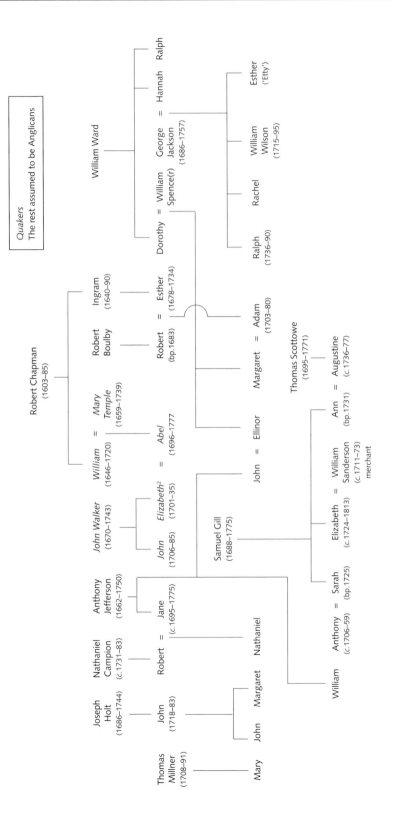

Quakers
The rest assumed to be Anglicans

Bagdale Hall, Whitby.

If a Lord of the Manor was approached by the bailiff of his tenant farmer to ask for help finding employment for his son, it is certainly plausible that help would be given. If after a matter of months the bailiff again petitions him for help because his son didn't like that job and wanted another, then the patron would be reluctant to help again unless either he was very good-hearted or the boy was exceptional. The evidence suggests that James Cook at this time was not academically outstanding, though he did have individuality, enterprise, ambition and stubbornness. Working on the land was tedious and not well paid, and many young men in that position, like John Nicol, 'longed to be at sea'. In his autobiography, Nicol added, 'My youthful mind could not separate the life of a sailor from dangers and storms, and I looked upon them as an interesting part of the adventures I panted after.'

If the young James Cook shared similar aspirations he would have told his parents. They may not have been very enthusiastic; after all, there were other children to support and the family relied on James and his elder brother John to contribute to the family budget. There was no money to spare for buying an apprenticeship. Once he had set his heart on being a sailor, James Cook stuck to his ambition with formidable resolution, whatever his parents might have said. Clearly, to have a career at sea he needed an apprenticeship, which would have to be paid for, so he had to take a full-time job to transfigure his hope into actuality. And ideally his new workplace would be near the sea so he could gain useful knowledge and experience of a sailor's life – or, as perhaps his parents hoped, be put off the idea of ever going to sea.

Either way, whoever thought that William Sanderson's emporium in the bustling fishing village of Staithes would be suitable was inspired. The shop was about as near the sea as possible – indeed it is now under the sea. Not only would almost everyone in the village (most of whom had maritime connections) come into the shop at one time or another; but also it was not uncommon for ships trading along the North Sea coast to provision at Staithes. Smaller vessels could moor on the quay; larger ships anchored offshore and sent a boat into port – several of both purchasing their supplies from Sanderson's. Working at the shop was the nearest James Cook could get to being a seaman without actually being one.

When Cook began working for William Sanderson, the latter had comparatively recently married Elizabeth Gill. Sanderson was a prosperous businessman and

Staithes.

almost certainly an owner or part owner of local vessels,★ which would not only be an investment in itself but would also guarantee that those particular ships bought their provisions from him.★★ James Cook learned about ships as well as provisioning them at Staithes. Young James was employed 'on the footing of a verbal agreement, without any indentures',[7] which might imply that he was not working as an apprentice but as a live-in employee. This would ensure a flexible outcome. If his new familiarity with the maritime life bred utter contempt, he could return to Ayton and the agricultural life; if it bred a passion to be a sailor then he had developed and learned much as well as accruing some savings to put towards his apprenticeship,† and John Walker had acquired a servant who had the capability of becoming a mate within six years or so and after that, he hoped, being a master for the Walker fleet of ships.

When James left Great Ayton with his few belongings on the road to Staithes in late 1744 or early 1745,‡ Britain was enmeshed in a war and looked as if she was going to lose. The French and Spanish planned to invade Britain with a force landing in the south-east (possibly at Maldon in Essex) and another with Charles Edward Stuart landing in Scotland. Dunkirk was being fortified and a flotilla

---

★ William Sanderson died in 1773 and the business was taken over by his wife Elizabeth and her eldest son John as 'Shopkeepers, and Partners, carrying on Trade and Business in the Name of John Sanderson only' (*London Gazette* 27 June 1789). The Ship Registers show that John had a half share of the brigantines *Dove*, Daniel Cole (58 tons, built 1777) and *Lark*, George Jefferson (62 tons, built 1783), in each case sharing the ownership with their respective master. John Sanderson was also the sole owner of both the sloop *Sophia Ann* (56 tons) and the boat *Nancy* (43 tons). As both of these were built at Staithes in 1754 it is safe to assume these vessels had belonged to his father William. All these vessels were small with crews of three or four men, and were possibly in the alum trade.

★★Documents, now in the Captain Cook and Staithes Heritage Centre, show that John Sanderson did business with the 40-ton sloop *Lively*, Edward Hurst, built at Whitby in 1786 (Boreham, Ian, 'William Sanderson of Staithes' in *Cook's Log*. Vol. 18. No. 4 1995). The ship served the Boulby alum works carrying coal and kelp from Hartlepool and Sunderland and shipping the finished product to London and Holland. The owners of this ship were George Dodds the manager of the Boulby alum works (who later married into the Sanderson family) and Ralph Jackson, the diarist, who had a considerable share in the business. *Lively* was long-lived and survived to be photographed by Frank Sutcliffe; she was finally wrecked on Bacton Beach in 1888. John and Elizabeth Sanderson went bankrupt in 1789.

† It would perhaps be unlikely he would have saved enough to pay for the whole fee. Maybe the ever-charitable Adam Boulby made up the difference, or John Walker gave him a discount.

‡ It is generally accepted that Cook's apprenticeship was for three years. His apprenticeship ended on 20 April 1749, so it would have begun on the 19 or 20 April 1746. If it is correct that his employment with Sanderson lasted about eighteen months, he would have started within this window. Hough's suggestion that Cook began work at Staithes in summer 1745 would appear to be too late.

of ships and transports were assembled there. Much of the British army were still in Flanders and the navy was scattered, some at Canada and some in the Mediterranean, blockading French and Spanish ships at Toulon.

However, Charles Edward, the Young Pretender, was delayed in his journey from Rome to Paris, so the invasion was postponed. By the time it was launched, British ships had arrived in the Channel from the Mediterranean. The French fleet sailed in February 1744 and managed to evade the British ships, but their plans were thwarted by that old friend of embattled Britain: stormy weather. Many ships were wrecked, the rest returned to France, and the French abandoned any plans for invasion, though rumours that the French had landed on the south coast continued to spread in Britain. The view of some, however, was that any invasion attempt by France would be a minor matter which could be handled easily without compromising the campaign in Flanders. Pitt argued that Britain did not need a standing army as there were not enough Jacobites in Britain to constitute a real threat. Henry Pelham, who had become the Prime Minister in 1743, was worried that this attitude was dangerous, remarking that, 'I am not so much apprehensive of the strength or zeal of the enemy, as I am fearful of the inability or languidness of our friends.'

Charles Edward Stuart decided to go it alone, imagining – with some justification – that he might stand a better chance of winning the hearts and minds of the British if he didn't arrive with an army of Frenchmen, and he set about buying arms and ammunition. On 5 July 1745, he set sail in a hired transport and landed in the Hebrides on 23 July, which was a surprise not only to his enemies but also to his friends.

At first the Scots were reluctant to rally to the Stuart flag, but when two or three Highland chiefs and their feudal clansmen came out for Charles Edward several more followed their lead and soon there was an army. It was not a massive army, never more than 6,000 in total, and they were not regulars but feudal levies whose chiefs argued amongst themselves about strategy, pride and precedence. Charles had virtually no artillery.

The British General John Cope, who was also short of guns and even shorter of gunners, had been sent north with a rather mixed body of largely inexperienced and untrained soldiers to deal with the situation. Better than nothing, perhaps, but certainly too little too late. Cope had no idea of the size of the rebel army, nor where they were. The hope was that Scotsmen loyal to King George would join his forces; but this was not the case, so he marched his troops to Inverness as a safe base from which to attack the Pretender's Highland soldiers. Charles Edward's forces, however, had turned south and entered Perth, where he was greeted with great enthusiasm. After a few days rest and training, he moved to Edinburgh where his reception was much more reserved, but on 17 September he moved into the city which (apart from the castle and its garrison) was his.

Philip Yorke (1690–1764), Lord Harwicke and Lord Chancellor, was very worried. He wrote to Herring, the Archbishop of York, on 31 August that 'There seems to be a certain indifference and deadness among many, and the spirit of the nation wants [needs] to be roused', adding, 'Is it not time for the Pulpit to sound the Trumpet against Popery and the Pretender?'

Herring was of a like mind, and needed little prompting; his reply was to be the beginning of a fascinating correspondence. King George, never one to spurn physical danger, had returned to Britain, and the Archbishop in his letter commented that 'His Majesty has fulfilled the duty of a good King in quitting his insignificant Electorate'. He expressed some grounds for hope in that Britain's allies the Dutch were sending soldiers.

Sir John Cope moved his army, which had already marched many hundreds of miles, from Inverness to Dunbar using transports. Similarly, a regiment of Dutch soldiers were moved in transports from the Netherlands to Leith to support the British; but in spite of so many hopes being pinned upon them, the Dutch were to prove a disappointment. Cope's dragoons were in poor condition: many of the horses were useless, several of the men's legs were so swollen that they could not wear their boots, and all were dazed with lack of sleep. This is hardly surprising, as they had been marched many miles across Scotland, and had twice retreated in panic at the rumoured approach of the Pretender's Highland army, whose reputation for ruthless brutality was fixed in their imaginative minds.

Battle between Charles Edward's army and that of the British king took place at Prestonpans on 21 September. The Highlanders ran speedily into battle, roaring and brandishing their claymores. The British dragoons and the conscripted gunners were the first to flee, and the rest were to follow, their flight impeded by the high walls of the estate of Preston Park. Some 700 were cut down, killed or horrendously maimed, and twice that number were taken prisoner. It was all over in about fifteen minutes. Fewer than 200 of the infantrymen managed to escape the battlefield but several of the dragoons were able to do so, hurrying to Berwick with Cope to bring the news of their defeat.

Berwick is less than 50 miles from Prestonpans and a mere 65 miles from North Shields: there seemed to be nothing but the stragglers from a defeated army between the north-east ports and Charles Edward's forces. The French had not landed an invading army but there were rumours to the contrary, and privateers were a constant threat. The inhabitants of Whitby and Staithes must have been very worried. How James Cook felt while all this was going on as he worked in Sanderson's sea-view shop we shall never know, though it is possible that he realised very vividly the crucial importance of the Royal Navy in maintaining peace and protecting trade.

The government was taking action, raising three armies, mainly using troops which had been ferried to the Low Countries so recently and were now being ferried back as swiftly as possible; but they were a long way from Charles Stuart and his Highland soldiers in Edinburgh.

The country seemed paralysed by the Young Pretender's successes, which few had anticipated. It appeared that against all expectation he had taken control of the Scottish Highlands and Lowlands and was now poised to march into England with his victorious troops. It was as if some folk tale bugaboo had suddenly become a reality.

The Archbishop had not been taken by surprise; he preached a stirring and much distributed sermon in York Minster the day after the battle, even before the news of the defeat had broken. Rhetoric, the art of making speeches which, with cogent reasoning and emotive use of language, can move and convince an audience, was an essential part of the Classical curriculum for a well-educated man. The Houses of Parliament were replete with oratory, and those who went to church expected the preacher to deliver not only godliness, but also good learning. There was a market for printed sermons, and even the ill-educated appreciated a good turn of phrase. The great movers and shakers of the eighteenth century were those who could use language to hold and persuade. William Pitt and John Wesley had this talent, and so had Archbishop Herring.

He praised Britain as 'the happiest Country under Heaven' which was ruled by 'the best of Kings and the most just and equitable Government' which together laboured 'for the Peace and Prosperity of the Publick'. He then went on to state that the rebellion 'threatens the very Being of our Nation, and the Ruin of every Thing which is dear and valuable to us' particularly 'a religion founded in

York Minster.

Reason and the Pure Sentiments of the Gospel', and a political system founded 'in the tenderest Regard for the Good and Liberties of Human-Kind'. And if the rebellion was to succeed:

> [a] fruitful and happy Country [would be] made a Place of Desolation and a Field of Blood … all Property confounded and our Goods and Possessions made the Prey of the next Invader…Houses torn down and rifled …Villages burnt up, Cities laid in Ashes … our Country ruined; our Religion, Laws and Liberties torn from us.

With this Churchillian rhetoric he emphasised the importance for all 'Nobility … Clergy, Gentlemen, Freeholders, and others, of the County of York' to attend the assembly at York Castle on the 24th to sign an Association, which they did in large numbers. The Association involved signing an undertaking to resist the Jacobite army 'as well by Force of Arms, as by all other Means'. The 'other Means' included contributing money.

The massive list of (male) signatories was headed by Archbishop of York ('Thos Ebor') and included: Thomas Belasyse, 1st Earl Fauconberg; Thomas Lumley-Saunderson, 3rd Earl of Scarborough; and Thomas Watson-Wentworth, Lord Lieutenant of the West Riding, Earl of Malton and 1st Marquis of Rockingham. The clergy included Jaques Sterne, Archdeacon of Cleveland, and Lawrence Sterne his nephew; Philip Kitchon, vicar of Marton, and 'Ja Berwick' (possibly James Borwick, incumbent of Whitby). Other signatories included Hugh Cholmley and his son Nathaniel; Cholmley Turner; William Chaloner, Lord of the Manor of Guisborough; Thomas Scottowe; Edward Montagu, wealthy coal owner; and Edwin Lascelles, wealthy plantation owner and MP for Scarborough, later 1st Baron Harewood.

The newspapers in October 1745 recorded how the inhabitants of Whitby, 'which are chiefly Masters of Ships', subscribed £1,000 (c. £2.5 million) 'for the Support of his Majesty and the Present Establishment', and that they would shortly have 'Fifty Men complete, who are to be commanded by Captain Nathaniel Chumley, who was at the Battle of Dettingen'. York and Hull formed volunteer troops, and Cholmley Turner planned to raise a thousand men in Cleveland. Regiments were duly formed and clothed but, as the regular army had first priority in receiving a limited supply of weapons, the volunteers were 'forced to exercise with broom staffs'.

Broomsticks or no, this military activity may well have deterred the Pretender's army from advancing into England on the east. Instead it went west, defeating another British army at Falkirk and capturing the city of Carlisle. Battles, even for the victors, are expensive in men, food and equipment, and Charles realised he could not afford too many costly battles. His army entered Preston and then marched on to Manchester, receiving a sufficiently mixed reception to buoy up Jacobite optimism, but certainly nothing like the large numbers of volunteers which he had hoped would rally to the cause of his father. The only hope for the Pretender was to avoid the government armies which had been sent to stop his advance, and march with all speed to London, seizing the capital in a surprise attack. He succeeded in the first, but only reached Derby.

Charles had no real supply lines and had not consolidated his achievements because he could not spare the manpower to garrison the towns which had submitted. Outwitting the forces of Wade and Cumberland meant the Pretender had two armies in his rear. Taking control of London was a fantasy. Britain, or at least England, was securely Protestant and dependent on trade and sound finance – and Charles Edward Stuart was not a sound investment. The merchants of London had underwritten the Bank of England to ensure financial stability during this crisis.

The Pretender's army turned round and went back to Scotland. Everyone, except perhaps Charles Edward himself, knew this was the beginning of the end. The Battle of Culloden (16 April 1746) was a total defeat for the Stuart cause, and the remains of Charles' army drifted back to the Highlands. Scotland was subjected to military occupation under the rigorous command of the Duke of Cumberland, the 'victor of Culloden', which involved the destruction of the last outposts of feudalism in Britain.

Whatever terror and atrocities were visited on the Highlands, the majority of people in Britain welcomed the final outcome of the rebellion, as was evidenced by the large number of petitions presented to the king congratulating him on his victory. The Merchants and Traders of the City of London expressed their pleasure that 'trade and public credit' which had 'so long flourished' under His Majesty's 'auspicious' rule was once again 'restored' and 'secured'.[8] More surprisingly perhaps, the Quaker General Assembly presented a Humble Address expressing their relief that 'the tyranny, idolatry and superstition of the Church of Rome' had not triumphed in Britain, and giving some praise to the Duke of Cumberland, but mainly their thanks were directed to the providence of God.

The Dutch regiments which had been sent had been hailed at first as a blessing; but they soon proved to be a problem. Herring had written to Hardwicke of the 'bloody frays every day between the Dutch and English'. The English seem to have been the aggressors, taunting their allies from Holland with their alleged inadequacy at the Battle of Fontenoy. It was clear that the two forces were not going to be able to fight effectively side by side, and the Dutch had to be replaced as soon as possible. Early in 1746, a fleet of transports was arranged to bring Hessians troops to Scotland and take the Dutch back home. These included a number of Whitby ships, including: *Concord*, William Chapman; *Henry & Mary*, John Jeffles; *Mary*, Thomas Linskill; *Mary*, John Coverdale; *Mermaid*, John Yeoman; *Noble Hope*, Noble; and *Three Brothers*, William Hill.

10

Freelove

I applied myself closely to learn every part of a seaman's duty.

(Henry Taylor)

The earliest record of the Whitby ship *Freelove* is on 16 August 1729 in London. On the 23 September, she was back in London where John Walker, the master, paid 8*s* 6*d* to cover the dues of his thirteen-man crew to support the Greenwich Hospital.[1] Although John Walker was the ship's husband, there were other part owners, including his father who bequeathed his 'right Title interest property claim and Demand whatsoever of in and to the Ship *ffreelove* of Whitby' to his son John in his will. It would be unusual if other members of the family were not part owners. We know that Joseph Colpits owned a ¹⁄₁₆ part and Thomas Dawson a ¹⁄₃₂ part, as their shares were advertised for sale in the *Newcastle Courant* after their deaths in 1729 and 1737, respectively.

Freelove was built in or before 1728, as she is described as being 30 years old in July 1758.[2] She was probably built by James Coates; an article entitled 'Authentic memoirs of the late celebrated Captain Cook' printed in the *London Chronicle* of 11 May 1780 stated that '*Freelove*, the first ship he [James Cook] sailed in, was built at Whitby, by Mr James Coates'. James Coates received £769 (*c.* £1.7 million) for building 'the ship's hold [i.e. hull]' of *Buck*, which was completed in early 1728, and owned a ¹⁄₃₂ share of her. It would seem likely therefore that he invested in *Freelove* as well.

The assumption must be that James Coates was related to the family of the Whitby shipbuilder Jarvis Coates, but this connection has yet to be made. When *Buck* underwent what seems to be a major repair at Whitby in 1742 both James and Benjamin Coates were paid for 'Plank and Timber' which might suggest some kind of partnership.[3] James was paid six times as much as Benjamin, which could suggest that James was the older – maybe a brother of Jarvis. Ralph Jackson's diary entry for 7 December 1757 records that he had 'dined at Mr Jefferson's wth Nathl Campion and Jams Coats late a Ship builder of Whitby'. Unless he gave up shipbuilding due to an accident or illness, James had retired to live off his investments – which would indicate that he was an older man.

Freelove was the first ship that John Walker owned, and it was in all probability the first ship which James Cook sailed in. Cook would have started his three-year apprenticeship on or before 19 April 1746, but the first documentary evidence we have of him aboard ship is on the muster roll of *Freelove*, John Jefferson, which began on Michaelmas Day, 1747 (as the Act* required), listing him as a 19-year-old 'servant' who, along with the rest of the crew, were aboard on 29 September, and had been in the ship before that date.

Freelove was a 'roomly' ship of 318 tons, and (apart from the brief exploration of the Iberian ports in 1731) she was engaged mainly in the coal trade and the timber trade with Norway. *Freelove* carried from 169 to 187 Newcastle chaldrons of coal (*c.* 440–490 tons), but mainly averaged about 175.[4] How many voyages a collier could do in a year varied enormously, depending on a range of factors including the weather, how many other vessels were in the same ports at the same time, the size and condition of the ship, the skill of the master and whether Britain was at war. Additionally, colliers were not always simply sailing back and forth between Shields and London (except, perhaps, during wartime when travelling in convoys) but might take on other ventures on the way. Hausman lists the number of trips a year made by four Whitby colliers:[5]

Ship	Dates of sample	Average number of trips	Maximum trips per year
Diamond	1756–59	4.5	8
John & Sarah	1756–59	5.0	8
Sea Adventure	1756–60	6.8	8
William	1756–59	2.7	5

These are war years. *Freelove*, in peacetime, made seven voyages in 1753 and five in 1752.**

The Walker family, probably originally from Newcastle or its environs, had gradually moved their capital into Whitby and had settled down there. The Poor Law provided for those in the parish in need, funded by a tax on property. The Poor Rate Assessments therefore give a fair indication of wealth if not of income.

---

* The Act of Parliament for the Relief and Support of Maimed and Disabled Seamen and the Widows and Children of such as shall be killed slain or Drowned in the Merchants Service. The Act required a deduction of sixpence a month from all merchant seamen; the muster rolls were the associated paperwork.

** The year 1752 was short of 11 days. See Appendix.

The 1720, Whitby Assessment suggests that John Walker junior was living with his parents and brothers in Flowergate, and he did not have to pay anything. In 1728, he was still in Flowergate with his parents but paid 3*d* per week, presumably based on his share in *Freelove*. In 1733, he was living with his wife Dorothy in Haggersgate and paid 5*d*. In 1737, John Walker senior and his wife Esther were living in Church Street (assessed for 10*d*), with their soon-to-be-married son Robert (4*d*). Their son Henry (11*d*) and his wife Ann (née Linskill) were near neighbours also living in Church Street with their children Esther, Mary and Rachael. John junior was still in Haggersgate (6*d*).

John Walker junior's younger daughter Mary died before she was a year old and was buried on the 12 January 1737; his wife Dorothy died five months later. By the end of 1737, the Haggersgate house contained, apart from any live-in servants they had, only John and his 4-year-old daughter Esther – and John had been at sea for much of the year. At the end of 1737, John Walker, now 31, decided to retire from active captaincy. In 1738, *Freelove* set out again on voyages to Norway and Newcastle as before, but captained by Thomas Williamson. In 1743, she went on a voyage to Riga, returning to Gravesend, probably with materials for shipbuilding.

It was in 1746, at about the time that the Young Pretender's army was being crushed at Culloden, that the (probably) 17-year-old James Cook began his three-year apprenticeship with John Walker. Compared to the small village of Staithes, Whitby was a large town, a bustling and busy port with flourishing and noisy shipbuilders' yards.

James Cook's indenture would involve John Walker having to provide accommodation, food and clothing in addition to instruction. A master's provision for his apprentices' accommodation did not necessarily mean that he had to have them all living in his house, but it is fairly certain that James Cook took up his residence in the Walker home in Haggersgate,* which included John, his daughter Esther by his first wife, his new wife Elizabeth (née Newton) and their

---

* John Walker senior died in April 1743. It has been suggested that John Walker junior then left his house in Haggersgate and moved into his parents' house in Grape Lane, and therefore it was in this house that James Cook spent his apprenticeship. This has to be wrong on many counts. It was not the custom then, any more than it is now, for a husband to move his wife and family to live with his mother when his father dies. The Whitby Poor Rate Assessment for 1743 noted the death of John Walker senior and crossed out his name as payer for the Grape Lane house, inserting Esther's name instead; her son John was still at Haggersgate, where he ran his business. Widows were quite happy to live alone, in the house, and with the servants that they were familiar with. The same assessment listed forty-five women as 'widow' who paid poor rate, and there were several other women, like Mrs Esther Walker herself, who did not have the tag 'widow' and who may well have been so. It is true that John Walker in his will had not given the house to his wife but to his sons John and Henry as tenants in common, adding

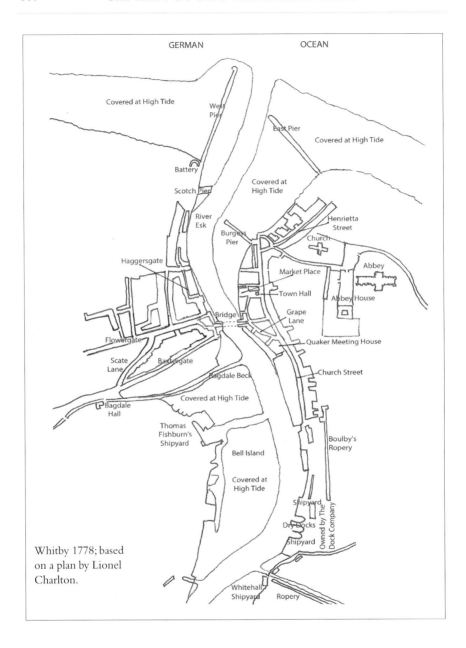

GERMAN   OCEAN

Covered at High Tide   West
                              Pier
                                        East Pier
                                                   Covered at High Tide

                              Battery

Scotch Pier   Covered at
                     High Tide

                River
                Esk   Henrietta
                     Burgess   Street
                     Pier   Church

Haggersgate   Abbey
                     Market Place
                              Town Hall   Abbey House
                              Grape
Flowergate   Bridge   Lane
                              Quaker Meeting House

Scate
Lane   Baxtergate
                Bagdale Beck   Church Street

                     Covered at High Tide
     Bagdale
     Hall
          Thomas
          Fishburn's
          Shipyard   Boulby's
                                Ropery
                     Bell Island
                     Covered at
                     High Tide
                              Shipyard
                              Dry Docks   Owned by The Dock Company
                              Shipyard

Whitby 1778; based
on a plan by Lionel
Charlton.
                     Whitehall
                     Shipyard   Ropery

that they would pay, after Esther's death, £5 a year each to Esther's brother Richard. This suggests that that John Senior expected his wife to remain in the Grape Lane house, after which it would be let and the profits to be divided equally between John and Henry; in other words, he was thinking of the house as an investment rather than as a home (John and Henry already had homes). If he intended either of his sons to live and work there he would have left it to one of them and compensated the other, or at least to have bequeathed it to them as joint tenants.

children Dorothy, John, Elizabeth and (probably) baby Henry. Hough claims that Cook had 'a room of his own', but more probably he shared a room with some of the other Walker apprentices.

There would also have been servants in the house, among whom was the 38-year-old widow Mary Prowd, whose prime duty was probably to look after the children but who also kept an eye on the apprentices. Mary was one of eight children of John Hardwick, a carpenter. In 1732, she married Mark Prowd, a sailor, and had two children: John and Mark. Unfortunately, her husband died in 1737, his pauper's burial being on the same day as the baptism of their son Mark – who died within the year. If Walker employed this single mother out of charity, he was well repaid; she seems to have been a cheerful woman who coped well with a house full of children, and James Cook became something of a favourite.

For a life at sea, Cook would need new clothes. At Sanderson's shop he would have worn the standard men's clothing of the time: knee breeches, waistcoat and a coat – either full down to the knees or cut away. Sailors had distinctive clothing: a short-cut jacket (with a slashed sleeve and buttons), waistcoat and trousers,[6] as is shown in contemporary prints and – more impressively – from the unique collection of eighteenth-century sailors' clothing excavated in the 1990s from the wreck of the Whitby ship *General Carleton* by a team of underwater archaeologists lead by Dr (now Professor) Waldemar Ossowski of the Polish Maritime Museum in Gdańsk.[7] Such clothes would have been purchased by Walker. Although ordinary sailors had no official uniform in the eighteenth century, once Cook

Whitby from the north; drawn by Westall, engraved by Findern.

Whitby looking across the Esk to the west side. The church, abbey and abbey house on the top of the hill. Below on the left are the backs of houses in Grape Lane, on the right Church Street.

was suitably kitted out, it would have been clear to all that he was a member of what William Cobbett called 'the tarred and trousered crew'.

Walker would also have provided Cook with a sea chest and bedding – these were manufactured locally in sufficient quantity to satisfy the local demand and to export to Hull, Newcastle and even London. Suitably equipped, James Cook was enrolled on the crew of *Freelove* as a 'servant'.

By 1746, the master of *Freelove* was John Jefferson of Sandsend, a man of much experience whom Walker knew and trusted. His first command had been *Constant John*, owned by John Walker's brother Robert. James Cook was apprenticed to John Walker, who was therefore responsible for his training; but once *Freelove* was at sea it became Jefferson's job to make a seaman of this young servant. Andrew Kippis, in his biography of Cook (1788), was right when he wrote that 'the greatest part of his [Cook's] apprenticeship was spent on board the Free-love': Cook sailed for an estimated nineteen months on board *Freelove* and only some four months (14 June to 14 October 1748) in *Three Brothers* during his apprenticeship. It seems that while Cook sailed in *Freelove* she was a full-time collier: protections from press (to exempt the crew from being impressed into the

A sailor's jacket, from *General Carleton*. The white parts are reconstructed; the darker parts are all original. James Cook would have worn a coat like this when at sea. (Photograph by E. Meksiak)

navy) were issued to *Freelove* on 2 July and 28 August in 1746 as she was in the 'coal and coasting trade', a reserved occupation in times of war. Apart from their start and finish locations, *Freelove*'s muster rolls for 1747 and 1748 mention only one other port: Shields.

The master was king of his ship and of those who sailed in her, and he made the decisions, but the mate made things happen, and often set the tone of the vessel. The mate should be able to do anything the master could, as he would take over command if anything serious happened to the master. The mate of *Freelove* was Robert Watson. James Cook had three excellent mentors: John Walker, John Jefferson and Robert Watson, and he was a quick learner. During his Whitby years he spent some thirty months at sea with Jefferson, and some twenty-three with Watson (if he was mate of *Freelove* from 1746).

Cook spent about thirteen months of his apprenticeship with John Walker in his house at Haggersgate.* It is possible that for some of that time he was tutored by one of the local teachers of maths and navigation; however, Walker became lifelong friends with his apprentice, so it is likely that he spent a considerable

---

* Not the 'nine years living in Walker's Grape Lane house' claimed by Richard Allen, p.25.

amount of time with him, teaching the skills necessary to become an effective shipmaster.

Freelove carried ten 'servants' in 1747, constituting more than half the crew. This would have been an unusually high proportion for peacetime; in wartime the percentage of apprentices tended to increase as servants could not be impressed into the navy provided they were under 18 or in the first three years of apprenticeship. They would have been a mixed bunch. Not all would have been apprenticed to John Walker, and not all his servants would have lived in his house.

From a fellow apprentice, Thomas Gibson, who was an exact contemporary, Cook would probably have learned much useful wisdom, like the chanted *aide memoir* of the order of places passed on the way up the Thames:

> Hole Haven, Shell Haven and Mucking Creek,
> Tilbury, Gravesend and Northfleet,
> Gray's, Greenhithe and Purfleet,
> Rainham and Bugsy Hole,
> Greenwich and Limehouse, and into the Pool.

or the rhyming quatrain of what to look out for in the last stretch before reaching Whitby:

> When Flamborough Head we pass by,
> Filey Brigg we mayn't come nigh,
> Scarborough Castle lies out to sea,
> Whitby three points northerly.[8]

The voyage between Shields and London was a difficult one, with shifting sandbanks and narrow passages. The sea coast of Yorkshire was deemed:

> one of the most dangerous parts of the kingdom to ships … The mouth of the Humber is very difficult for ships when the wind blows strong at East, unless the pilot be well acquainted with the shoals that be scattered about the mouth of that river. Ships … must be careful of a shoall called the Dreadful which lies about three miles and a half from the Spur-head, and on which there is no more than six feet.[9]

There were other dangerous sandbanks, particularly round East Anglia. Henry Taylor, some nine years younger than James Cook, describes how badly kept were the lighthouses on that coast, commenting of the Cromer light that 'there was not a worse light on all the coast and that owing to its badness many ships had been lost on Sheringham Shoal, and the north-end of Hasbro' Sand'. He added that 'Orfordness and the North-Foreland lights were also very bad ones,

The High and Low Lights at Spurn Head, 1829. The High Light is Smeaton's Lighthouse, built 1776. Smeaton's Low Light was destroyed *c.* 1778; the one shown here was built in 1816.

and Winterton was little better'. Because of the bad lights, timing was crucial; the master had to ensure that the dangerous sandbanks off the coast of Norfolk were traversed in daylight as it was almost impossible to travel at night unless there were clear skies and a full moon. If a ship arrived too late to navigate through before it got dark, it had to ride at single anchor overnight, Taylor adding that few knew how to manage ships at anchor, except those bred in the coal trade.★

Added to these difficulties was the suddenness and ferocity of North Sea storms. The Norfolk shore was notorious; Daniel Defoe travelled along the coast from Winterton to Cromer and remarked that:

> the farmers, and country people had scarce a barn, or a shed, or a stable; nay, not the pales of their yards, and gardens, not a hogsty, nor a necessary-house, but what was built of old planks, beams, wales and timbers, &c. the wrecks of ships, and ruins of mariners' and merchants' fortunes.

When James Cook arrived back in Whitby after his first few months on *Freelove* he had seen much, done much and learnt much. He was probably exhausted

★ Henry Taylor spent much of his later life campaigning for better navigation lights, with considerable success. He became known as 'the seamen's friend'.

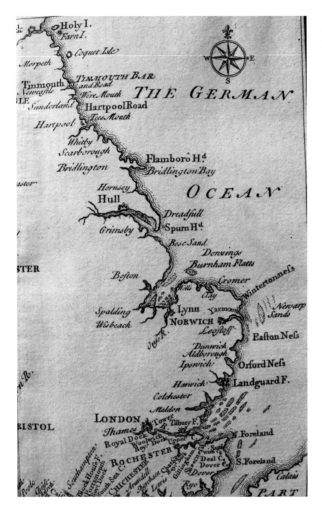

The dangerous east coast, including the 'shoall called the Dreadful'.

and with chafed hands, but pleased to have made the first step towards being a sailor. He would also have heard the news that Sir William Murray, cousin of Lord George Murray (the leading general in the Young Pretender's army), had been arrested at Whitby while trying to escape to Holland in disguise. Murray had aroused suspicion mainly by offering too much money for his passage. He was arrested by the local constables and delivered to the Castle of York where he awaited trial for treason.

The war in Europe staggered on, as all sides lumbered towards a treaty. Finally, in October 1748, peace was signed at Aix-la-Chapelle. The issue of the Austrian Succession had been sorted out with the death of the Charles VII. Prussia and Austria had already come to an agreement that Prussia would keep its conquests in Silesia and recognise Maria Theresa's husband Francis Stephen as Holy Roman

Emperor. Apart from this already done deal, the treaty required all concerned to return to the status quo before the war.

All those deaths and all that money wasted for nothing – no wonder that no one was happy with it. The British were especially angry with the surrender to France of Cape Breton Island and Louisbourg, both hard-fought victories. Louisbourg guarded the entrance to the St Lawrence and hence to the control of Canada. The much lauded naval victories off Cape Finisterre seemed to have been in vain. France was no more pleased than it had been in 1713; it had not beaten Britain. The French once more agreed to recognise the Hanoverian succession, which was an embarrassment as Charles Edward Stuart was in France still hoping that the French would help him restore the Stuart monarchy. When he was told by Louis XV to leave France he took no notice, and had to be arrested before he realised that the king was in earnest.

There was peace but it was evident it was no more than a break during which the major powers tried to reduce their massive national debt and prepare for the next war. Once again there was a flurry of contracts as transports were needed to bring troops home from the Flanders front. But there are no forces like the force of nature; as troops were being brought home, a storm of ferocious violence struck with little warning and disastrous consequences.

Ship in a storm, by Harvey Taylor.

A first-hand account of this terrible storm was written by Nathaniel Othen[10] of the Welch Fusiliers, some of whom embarked on *Sea-Flower* of Whitby at Williamstadt, with forty-one horses. They sailed on 18 December 1748 for Burntisland (Fife). A few hours later the hurricane struck and before the sailors could furl the sails 'the wind tore them all to pieces'. Othen went below and discovered 'that seven of the horses had broke loose, which made the rest so wild, that we were obliged to kill them all but one. But it was six days before we could get them overboard; during which the smell was so offensive, that it made the whole ship's crew sick.' The ship was blown they knew not whither, and the 'steward perished with cold, as did the carpenter soon after' and 'several of the boys had their limbs frozen, so they were unable to work'. After seemingly endless days without sighting land, they eventually reached north Norway where they were allowed to disembark, and a special hospital was erected for them; but many lost the use of their limbs, and several died in the hospital. After a month they set sail once again, with a repaired ship, finally reaching Leith on 9 April 1749.

Freelove was not a transport at this time, but continued as a collier ship. She started her season on 28 February 1748 with the crew much the same as before with John Jefferson, master; Robert Watson, mate; and Thomas Harwood, carpenter. Matthew Hill, the 56-year-old cook, had been replaced by the 41-year-old John Presise [Percise]; the servants were largely as before but Robert Chandler had left – presumably because his apprenticeship had ended. Seamen were discharged and signed on at the convenience of the ship in order to save money, so tended to lack continuity of employment. It is difficult to make sense of what happened on this voyage from the muster roll. As a suggestion, *Freelove* sailed to Shields to load with coal, then to London, and back in ballast to Shields for more coal. At Shields on 5 April, John Johnson, seaman, and Thomas Dodds, servant, were added to the crew. Five days later the ship was at Whitby where Robert Watson and five servants, Donald MacDonald, James Cook, Ralph Newby, Thomas Gibson and Edward Smith, were disembarked and John Percise the cook was discharged. With this now mateless crew, Jefferson sailed to London and returned to Shields, perhaps via Whitby where James Dunn, mate, and William Burkill, seaman, were added to the payroll on 15 May. Then to London and back to Shields where all the crew were discharged on 7 June. The reason for all these strange crew changes was that John Walker's latest acquisition, the new ship *Three Brothers*, had been launched and Robert Watson and the five experienced apprentices who disembarked were preparing her for work. Jefferson was to be master of *Three Brothers*, taking with him the aforementioned five servants.

Nearly everyone was where they should be, except that Robert Watson, who was to be master of *Freelove*, was in Whitby with the *Three Brothers*, and John Jefferson, master of *Three Brothers*, was at Shields with *Freelove*. *Freelove* set sail on

Genealogy 17: Gaskin Genealogy

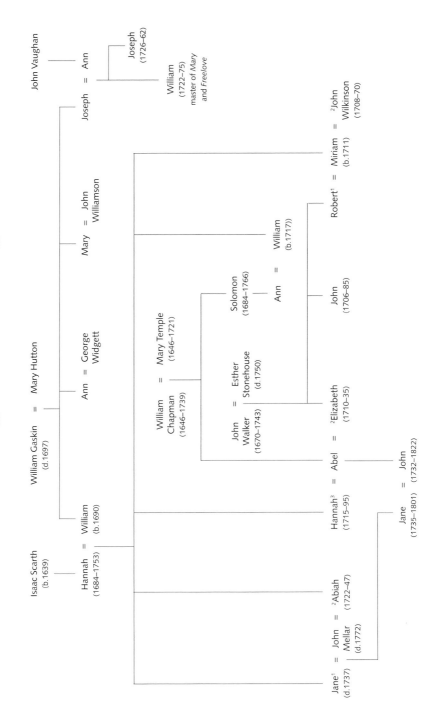

8 June for London and *Three Brothers* left Whitby on 14 June. They managed to swap masters *at sea* on 17 July.

The rest of the year for *Freelove* was apparently another series of coal runs between Shields and London, ending on 9 December, with a crew of sixteen. The mate, James Dunn, was replaced by the 30-year-old Isaac Gofton in October. Interestingly, there was no cook appointed until 8 September when the 62-year-old Thomas Johnson filled the post. This does not mean that no cooking was done; just that no one was officially assigned to the task. The cook was paid more than an able seaman, so it was a privileged position, often reserved for a long-serving sailor whose age and sometimes disability made it difficult to perform the arduous tasks that seamen had to do on a daily basis. He was a member of the crew and as such would have to turn out when required or in emergencies, but would not be required – nor possibly able – to climb up the masts on the ratlines. It would be an added bonus if he could cook.

The rest of 1748 and all of 1749 were steady work for *Freelove* with Watson as master and Gofton as mate. There were regular trips taking coal to London from Shields and timber from Norway to Gravesend. Occasionally there is a triangular voyage from Shields to London then sailing to Norway and back to Newcastle.

In 1750, Gofton was replaced by Joseph Robinson, then by Matthew Bryant, who didn't stay long either. In 1751, Robert Watson became master of *Three Brothers*, and William Gaskin, previously master of *Mary*, took over as master of *Freelove*. The mate on *Freelove* in 1752 was Nathaniel Fatkin of Newcastle. In his first year as master of *Freelove* Gaskin took her to Riga at least once. The Baltic was becoming more popular as a trading destination, providing timber, flax, tar and iron. The drawback was that the Baltic froze in winter, when shipping would revert to Norway and the coal trade.

We have a glimpse of *Freelove* as a collier in the diaries of Ralph Jackson, apprentice to William Jefferson, hostman of Newcastle. His entry for 9 July 1753 includes: 'a Boy from the *Freelove* came to the Door, Nathl Jatkin Master, Mr Jno Walker Owner'. Probably the boy was William Lishman (the oldest apprentice) who told Ralph to tell his master that Nathaniel Fatkin would be on the quay the following morning. Ralph not only got the name wrong, but also assumed that Fatkin was the master as it was customary for hostmen to deal with masters concerning the purchase of coals. The next morning Ralph was up before six. He 'went upon the Key [quay]' and fetched 'Mr Nathaniel Jatkin Master of the *Freelove*' who 'fixed to load Tanfield' coals.

Three Brothers

If we survey a ship, what an exalted idea we must form of the ingenuity of the carpenter who framed so complicated, useful and beautiful machine?

(David Hume, *Dialogues Concerning Natural Religion*)

In 1747, John Walker had commissioned a new ship which he named *Three Brothers* after himself and his brothers Henry and Robert. She was built by Benjamin Coates,[1] was larger than *Freelove* and was launched early in 1748. She set out on her maiden voyage from Whitby to London on 14 June 1748, with John Walker as master. He had not captained a vessel for over ten years, but the designated master, John Jefferson, was not yet available; and Walker had plans.

Having tested his new ship and been pleased with her, Walker went to the Navy Board to tender her for a transport. It is possible that Walker had the transport business in mind when he decided to have a new ship built.

This done, Walker would have renewed his contacts in the nautical suburbs of London, Shadwell, Wapping and Ratcliff.

St John's Church, Wapping, 1755.

Quakers naturally sought out other Quakers, and it is not surprising that many of John Walker's business contacts were also Friends. He did regular trade with the Sheppard family of shipwrights and mast-makers in Wapping who were importers of timber from Norway, using – amongst others – Walker's ships, in which they part shares.[2]

Sheppard also used Walker ships to send goods from their yard to supply Whitby shipbuilders; for example, six months after Walker arrived in London, *Freelove*, Robert Watson, sailed to Whitby from London with a cargo of James Sheppard's which comprised: '1 Suit of Masts & Yards, 26 Deals, 1000 Treenails, 8 Loads Eng[lish] Oak Plank & 3 barrels Pitch & Tar.'

Three months later another Walker ship, *Friendship*, John Waller [sic], arrived in Whitby from London with a cargo in the name of Joseph Sheppard which included a 'Suit of Masts Yards & Bowsprit for a Ship, 14 Iron Guns of abt [about] 7 Tons, 8 Iron Anchors of 4 Tons, 4 barrells gunpowder' as well as a hundredweight of 'Deals' and a parcel of 'Rammers, Spunges & Laddles'.[3]

Walker knew the Sheppards through Zachariah Cockfield, master mariner of Whitby, who had married Sarah Sheppard in 1735. Zachariah was master of the 238-ton Whitby ship *Industry* and had been a witness at the marriage of John Walker's brother Robert to Miriam Gaskin in 1737. Other ships used by the Sheppards to take cargoes in 1748 included *Friend's Adventure*, Solomon Chapman; *Prince of Wales*, John Holt; and *Sea Adventure*, Robert Clark. They were all carrying a suit of masts and yards to Whitby, and all colliers were so very pleased to have some cargo to take north before fetching their next cargo of Newcastle coals. The Sheppards' brisk business is indicative evidence of the success of shipbuilding in Whitby.

On 14 October 1748, *Three Brothers* entered into service as a transport ship. John Jefferson was master; John Wood, mate; John Newton, second mate; John Atkinson, cook; and John Wilson, carpenter. The seamen were new to the ship, but the servants were as before, namely James Cook, Donald McDonald, Ralph

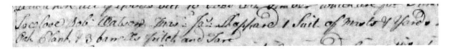

Freelove, Robert Watson, delivered cargo for James Sheppard at Whitby, 9 December 1748.

Friendship, John Waller, delivered cargo for Joseph Sheppard at Whitby, 24 March 1749.

Newby, Edward Smith, Richard Sanderson, William Beilby, Walker Chandler and Luke Collingwood.

Walker Chandler had been a servant in *Freelove* in 1747 at the same time as his twin brother Robert had been a servant in *Friendship*. The fact that he was given Walker as a Christian name implies that John Walker was a friend of his parents and probably a godparent to the young child; it also suggests that he was the smaller of the twin babies and that his parents did not expect him to live.

Three Brothers was ordered by the Navy Board to be part of the convoy of twenty-five transports to fetch troops, both infantry and cavalry, from Williamstadt to Ireland. The Victualling Board was providing two months' supply of food and started loading it on to each ship. By 17 October, *Three Brothers* had already been provided with '190 Baggs of bread, 3040lbs of cheese and of butter, 1520 pieces of beef and of pork, and 1330 gallons of spirits' – needing only the ration of 'pease' to be completely victualled.[4] The convoy arrived in Ireland safely.

It is interesting that John Walker, and others of the Whitby Quaker community tendered their ships as armed transports and accepted cargoes which included cannon and gunpowder. The evangelical zeal of the early Quakers seems to have faded over the intervening years as they settled into a less austere lifestyle. The old-style Quakers, like the Richardsons of Great Ayton, were known as 'plain' and the newer, more worldly were known as 'gay'. The Walkers were clearly going gay.

The rise of Methodism stole some of the Quakers' thunder with the fearless evangelising and preaching to outdoor crowds which had become rare among the Society of Friends. The Quaker message that there was good in everyone was losing out to the message that everyone had evil in them. The Methodists also had congregational worship with rousing hymns, and combined their preaching with practical advice about saving money and household management. Wesley wrote a cookery manual, and a guide to common ailments and the easily accessible medicinal herbs used to cure them. Methodism appealed to the poor, despised and marginalised more than the Quakers who in turn had put to shame the Established Church of England for its similar neglect.

There seems to have been difficulties in the Whitby Society of Friends. Samuel Bownas, an itinerant Quaker preacher, recorded his travels in the north. He found the Scarborough meetings as 'large and comfortable'. Then he moved to Whitby, and saw quite a different spirit; the meetings there were 'laborious, being pretty hard to get through'.[5]

After the *Three Brothers'* transport contract ended at London on 14 October 1748, James Cook never sailed again as an apprentice. When her next voyage started, on 20 April 1749, he was listed as a seaman, so his three-year apprenticeship must have ended between these two dates. He stayed on board to 8 December, when the crew was discharged at Shields.

Genealogy 18: Whitby Shipbuilders

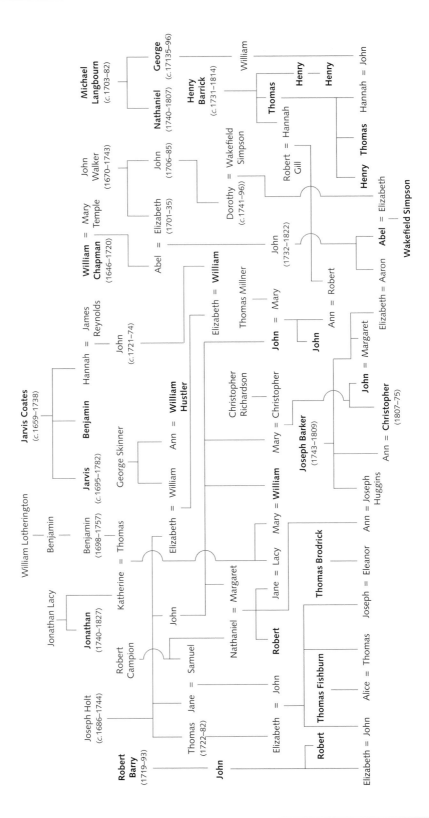

In 1750, Robert Watson, who had been mate on *Freelove* and then (briefly) on *Three Brothers* followed by eighteen months or so as master of *Freelove*, returned to *Three Brothers* as master. She started the year early with a voyage to Guernsey and then to Southampton, arriving on 13 January, departing on 8 February to London.

In 1751, James Cook was back on *Three Brothers* as a seaman; her season started at Shields, and it is possible that she over-wintered there. It could also be that she over-wintered at Whitby and sailed with the basic crew of master (Robert Watson), mate (John Swainston), carpenter (John Gofton), and the servants (Ralph Newby, Richard Sanderson, Luke Collingwood, William Bielby, Edward Smith and John Brooks) to Shields to collect the seamen. This would be eminently safe as the servants, apart from John Brooks, were all experienced sailors. Intriguingly, three of the seamen, Robert Clarke, James Cook, Robert Storpe, and the cook Henry Pearson all listed their abode as Sunderland. Maybe *Three Brothers* visited Sunderland first and picked up some of the cheaper coals there before moving on to Shields. Speculations are intriguing, but as Beaglehole made clear, the muster rolls are not always very accurate.

John Walker the elder died in April 1743 and his widow Esther died in January 1751. His brother Henry died in December 1751, a year after his wife Ann, leaving John as the sole survivor of the three brothers.

There must have been fairly mild weather in the early winter, as *Three Brothers* went on trading until 8 January 1752, and was back in business again on 23 February, but without seaman James Cook. After a coal journey, *Three Brothers* sailed from Newcastle to Riga. There was at least one other voyage to Riga before the season finished surprisingly early on 8 November which, because of the calendar change, was really late October. It was on 25 September that *Three Brothers* had its only recorded casualty. It was William Beilby who had been a servant on *Three Brothers* from her first voyage until 16 August 1752 when he was first entered as a seaman. The muster roll gives little information, recording neither the place, the cause nor the severity – only that he was 'wounded unfit for action'.

On 27 February 1753, Ralph Jackson records going out with his friends and cousins Billy Hudsbeth and John Campion together with 'one Watson, Master of one of Walkers ships of Whitby', whom they were entertaining while the lading of coals in *Three Brothers* was concluded. They went 'down to the Fort and went on board the Peggy, Man of War'. There they gawped at the French smugglers that had been captured by *Peggy* the week before.

Three Brothers did another coal run after which she returned from London to Newcastle, then to Norway and back to London, perhaps with timber for the Sheppards. What happened after that is not known, but the probability is that there were more coal voyages. What is known is that on 4 November 1753

Genealogy 19: Sheppard and Cockfield

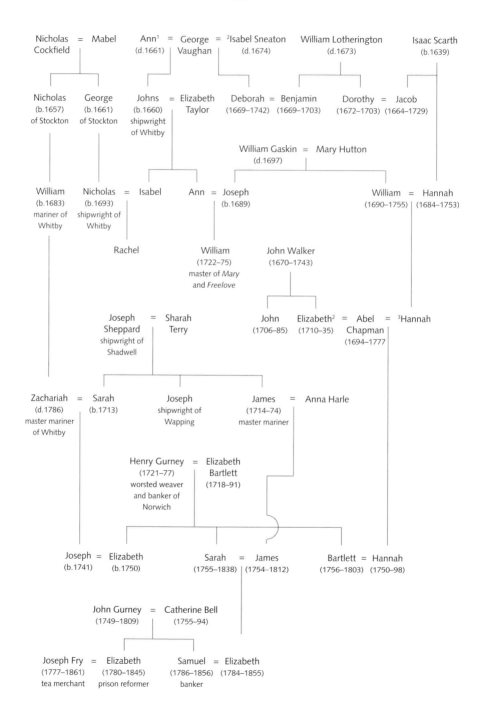

Three Brothers was 'Lost'. Where and how are not recorded; there were many ways in which a ship was lost but a main reason was that she was lost – in the sense that the master simply did not know exactly where they were and the ship foundered in rough weather or poor visibility on hidden reefs or rocks. For all the sophistication of the mid-eighteenth century, ships still navigated by 'dead reckoning', using little more than a logline, a sandglass, compass, a telescope, a sextant and knowledge of the unerring motion of the sun, moon and stars.

12

Flora

I made it my business to search most countries and corners of this land with severall of promontories, islands and peninsulas thereof in order to observe the variety of plants there described or nondescript.

(Thomas Lawson)[1]

Geoge Fox was very keen that Quaker children should learn useful information, which included 'the nature of herbs, roots, plants and trees', and not just in theory. William Penn had given him a piece of property near Philadelphia which Fox dedicated to the building of a meeting house, with a parking lot for horses, and a school which would have a garden, to be planted 'with all sorts of physical [medicinal] plants for lads and lasses to learn simples there, and the uses to convert them to distilled waters, oils, ointments, etc.'.[2]

He was not alone. The seventeenth century saw a boom in the study of botany, often inspired by a religious belief that the physical world was the beautiful creation of a loving and all-powerful God, who had endowed the wide variety of plants with properties that were of benefit to mankind.

John Ray (1627–1705), the Essex clergyman, botanist and Fellow of the Royal Society, was inspired by 'the varied beauty of plants … the cunning craftsmanship of Nature and the rich spectacle of the meadows in spring-time, so often thoughtlessly trodden underfoot'.[3] Wishing to know more, he turned to Cambridge University where he had studied, only to find that there was no one there who had the expert knowledge he craved, so he set out to teach himself. He described and catalogued the plants of Britain, and then of much of western continental Europe. He pioneered the classification of plants – 'the well-ordered arrangement into classes, primary and subordinate' – insisting that the basis of distinguishing species had to be shape and structure. Ray was not just a botanist: he collected fossils at Whitby, which he realised were of creatures 'lost out of this world'; he did not believe that such fossils of sea creatures were embedded in rocks as a result of Noah's Flood – an opinion which he claimed was not 'easily reconciled with the Scripture' as 'that Deluge proceeded from the Rain, which was more likely to carry Shells down to the Sea, than bring any up from it'.[4] Ray's friend and botanist Thomas Lawson (1630–91) was also an Anglican clergyman, but became a Quaker after meeting Fox and hearing him preach.

Another important Quaker botanist was Philip Miller (1691–1771), son of a market gardener in Deptford. Deptford in the eighteenth century was not just a squalid cluster of seedy inns and sailors' lodgings, but much was given over to orchards and farming; indeed, all down the Thames estuary land was used for providing food for the growing metropolis. However, the sailors and the seedsmen were not always friends: the *Farmers and Gardeners of the Parish of Northfleet* complained to the Commissioners of the Navy that the seamen from the transport ships moored near Gravesend came ashore 'in bodies' rampaging over hedges, treading down crops, going 'into Gardens and Orchards' and taking 'what Greens and Fruit they please'.[5] Miller set up as a florist at St George's Fields. His knowledge not only of plant biology but also of how to grow plants brought him to the attention of Hans Sloane and his circle, and enabled him to be appointed superintendent of the Society of Apothecaries' Physic Garden at Chelsea for almost fifty years. He was very much aware of the usefulness of plants, not just for their medicinal properties, but also as a way of generating wealth and prosperity. In 1735, he was the first to send cotton seeds to the British colony of Georgia. His exceptional and useful skill was in working out how to grow plants from other countries and climates in Britain, and in sharing his knowledge – especially in his enduringly popular *The Gardener's Dictionary*. Additionally he researched the function of insects in plant fertilisation, a little-studied area at the time, and was made a Fellow of the Royal Society. He also collated information and illustrations of plants in his care, compiling an impressive herbarium which was later bought by Joseph Banks.

Swedish botanist Carl Linnaeus (1707–78), the son of a gardening Lutheran pastor, published his massively influential and constantly revised *Systema Naturae* in 1735. This book introduced to the world his system of classifying all living things by fitting them into a broad category, a 'kingdom', and then into a series of increasingly narrow categories: 'class', 'order', 'genus' and 'species'. The last two would comprise the 'binomial' by which every species could be identified, and which helped transform biology into a 'real' science. Plants he classified them according to their sexual reproduction, often becoming quite sensual in his descriptions of flowers. His binomial taxonomy, although continually amended, not only enabled his contemporary biologists to impose some order on the plethora of new species that were being discovered in almost overwhelming profusion, but also has provided the overall structure of classification to this day. He was appointed Professor at Uppsala University in Sweden where he reorganised the botanical garden according to his taxonomy, and founded a new breed of students whom he would encourage to travel on botanical expeditions. His massive *Species Plantarum* (1753) contained a description of all plants that he was aware of, identified by their binomials. He regarded species as fixed, but he was aware of hybridisation.

John Bartram (1699–1777) was an interesting American Quaker botanist. He was a farmer in Pennsylvania with a keen eye for nature. He was fascinated with the world of plants, even noticing 'the admirable system of war which the great author of the universe had established throughout their various tribes'[6] – an early insight into natural selection. He collected new plants, growing them in an 8-acre plot of land which he bought near Philadelphia, thus establishing the first botanical garden in America. He was also the first American biologist to adopt the Linnaean classification. Bartram's house, garden and greenhouse survive.

Botanists and Quakers both had an international network, so it is hardly surprising that Bartram would meet Peter Collinson (1693–1768), who was both. Collinson acquired wealth from the flourishing family business which exported cloth to America. For Peter, America was a whole world full of new plants, interesting, strange, beautiful, useful and valuable; and he was ready to pay good money to have them. Bartram had the plants and Collinson had the money. Collinson's friends included Hans Sloane, John Fothergill and Benjamin Franklin; he became a Fellow of the Royal Society and was instrumental in Franklin being elected as a Fellow in 1753. Additionally, he was in regular correspondence with Linnaeus and his pupil Daniel Solander. Bartram's plant business flourished; he became the official royal botanist for America and a founder member, along with Benjamin Franklin, of the American Philosophical Society. Among Bartram's clients were Hans Sloane, Philip Miller, and the Royal Gardens at Kew. Sadly, Bertram was ejected from the Quaker community for denying both the divinity of Jesus and the existence of miracles, which broke the divinely established laws of nature.

John Fothergill (1712–80) was a Yorkshireman, an apothecary, a doctor, a biologist with a special interest in botany, a Quaker, a Fellow of the Royal Society, and a friend of Collinson, Franklin and Banks. As a doctor, he started his practice among the poor of London but his successful treatments (rejecting the medical profession's obsessive use of bloodletting and purgatives) especially during the outbreak of scarlet fever in 1746–48, ensured his reputation and he soon became the most popular and richest doctor in London. He always dedicated time in his busy schedule to treat those who could not afford to pay. He effected cures for malarial fever with cinchona bark, which was of vital importance as Britain extended its empire into areas where that disease was endemic. Fothergill's particular interest was in collecting useful exotic plants, and growing them in Britain and her colonies. He bought Upton House, near Stratford in Essex, of which Joseph Banks remarked that 'no other garden in Europe … had nearly so many scarce and valuable plants'. Fothergill had built immense heated greenhouses, several hundred feet in length, in which he successfully grew plants which had been sent to him from John Bartram and many other collectors. He managed to grow a Chinese tea plant successfully at Upton, sending specimens to southern America for cultivation. He encouraged the growing of coffee in the British West Indies and the drinking of it in Britain, as he understood that botany could benefit trade. Linnaeus also understood this, but his attempts to grow coffee, rice and bananas in Sweden were unsurprisingly unsuccessful.

Fothergill's *Directions of the taking up Plants and Shrubs, and conveying them by Sea* was enormously influential in later botanical maritime voyages. He was also a philanthropist, being active in prison reform and the abolition of slavery, and he founded and funded Ackworth School in Yorkshire for Quaker children who were 'not in affluent circumstances', which was run on similar lines to those George Fox had suggested.

Hans Sloane (1660–1753) was a botanist and a doctor. In 1687, he went to Jamaica as the physician to Christopher Monck, 2nd Duke of Albermarle who had been appointed governor there. It was a perfect time and place for an enthusiast like Sloane, as Jamaica had a rich and varied flora which had not previously been botanised. He noted some 800 new species even though he was there for less than two years, as Monck died in October 1688. On his return, he wrote the expected tome in Latin (Latin still being the *lingua franca* of all educated men in Europe),

Ackworth School.

though the public had to wait until 1725 for the English-language two-volume illustrated account of his discoveries. Sloane's interest was also in finding uses for various plants which included *Theobroma cacao* beans which the Jamaicans ground, roasted and stirred into water with other spices, especially chilli peppers. It was called *chocolatl* (meaning warm liquid) and Sloane didn't like it, adding that it was 'nauseous in large quantities'. However, he was the first to mix it with hot milk and sugar to make a drink which became very popular in Europe – and from which he made a lot of money.[7] Sloane was a friend of John Ray and Robert Boyle, and of Henry Compton bishop of London who, when overlooked for the post of Archbishop of Canterbury, had turned to making the grounds at Fulham Palace into a magnificent botanic garden. He never gained an archbishopric, but he was appointed Deputy Superintendent of the Royal Gardens, which must have been something of a consolation.

The passion for botany crossed many boundaries; including those who were interested in medicinal plants, those who wished to make profits, those who were

Botanical watercolour of a strawberry plant (*fragaria x ananassa*) by Miss Elizabeth Plant, 1836.

fascinated by anything new, those who saw divine benevolence and purpose in the natural world, those who wished to understand and classify plants, and those who simply enjoyed gardens and flowers. It crossed all barriers; Joseph Banks and John Wesley sought information from cottagers and herb-women, learning the folk names and the properties of plants, while gardeners learned their Linnaean names from their employers.[8] Country women had always been seen as repositories of ancient and practical knowledge, and as the eighteenth century progressed genteel ladies took to the study of botany as a stimulating pastime which combined indoor study with outdoor cultivation and accurate painting of plants (a tradition which lasted well into the twentieth century), though some of the 'coarser names' for plants, such as 'black maidenhair, naked ladies, priests bollocks and horse pistle'[9] had to be replaced with more decorous nomenclature.

With all this enthusiasm it comes as little surprise that 'the number of plants cultivated in Britain saw a fivefold increase in the Georgian period, from 1,000 to 5,000'.[10] Botany had become fashionable. It had also become big business of interest to merchants, and to both the merchant and the royal navies.

13

Mary

All Nature is but Art, unknown to thee;
All Chance, Direction which thou canst not see;
All Discord, Harmony not understood;
All partial Evil, universal Good;
And, spite of Pride, in erring Reason's spite
One truth is clear, Whatever is, is RIGHT.

(Alexander Pope, *Essay on Man*)

On 15 December 1736, at Sneaton, a village a couple of miles to the south of Whitby, Dorothy Chapman, the 26-year-old Quaker and daughter of Ingram, committed a shocking offence in the church, and soon the officials were knocking on her door. She had 'married out', her chosen husband being William Benson, a master mariner and an Anglican. Some of the leaders of the Whitby meeting would have visited her to admonish her 'in love and tenderness' and see if she would repent of this unacceptable deed, but she did not – and was 'disowned'.

Another similar December marriage at Sneaton church took place seven years later when Miriam (née Gaskin), the widow of Robert Walker, married John Wilkinson, master mariner and Anglican, whose aunt was Esther (née Stonehouse), wife of John Walker Senior.

It was becoming increasingly difficult for Quakers to find acceptable partners within their comparatively small community. Those in master mariner families were more inclined to seek out partners in their own line of business than in the Society of Friends; believing that all people are equal in the sight of God, did not mean that a wealthy Quaker wished to marry a poor one. When John Walker married Elizabeth Newton it was an Anglican and not a Quaker marriage; John Walker had also married out.

John Wilkinson was master of the ship *Buck* from its maiden voyage in 1729. Robert Walker owned a ⅟₆₄ share, and later John Walker invested in a ⅟₃₂ share. By 1743, the captaincy of *Buck* had passed to Henry Wilkinson; John Wilkinson had married and was master and husband of the 326-ton Whitby-built ship *Mary*, which was launched that year. She was immediately submitted to, measured and accepted by the Navy Board as a transport. During the war she carried troops between London, Leith and Ostend, with the occasional visit to Stockholm when not required as a transport. Her last troop voyage was to replace the Dutch troops with Hessians, by which time John Coverdale was the master, followed in 1746 by John Walker's younger brother Henry. In 1747, John Wilkinson returned as master for a few months before handing *Mary* back to John Coverdale for the repatriation of 486 soldiers from Williamstadt, alongside *Three Brothers*, after the peace of 1748. In the following year Coverdale continued as commander, sailing to Stockholm.

John Walker had come to like James Cook and certainly perceived he was a man of promise, and he wanted those skills nurtured so he would become a ship's master – ideally in one of Walker's own ships. Cook had finished his apprenticeship in April 1749, which meant he worked on board ship as an ordinary sailor; at sea he would sleep 'before the mast' with the other seamen in the wettest and smelliest part of the vessel.

John Walker perhaps thought it would be good experience for Cook to sail in a ship that wasn't part of the Walker fleet, suggesting that for 1750 he should sign on to *Mary*, William Gaskin, owned by John Wilkinson – which he did. *Mary's* sailing season began on 8 February from Shields and she was at Newcastle on 26 May, perhaps being to London twice beforehand, then a voyage to Petersburg, possibly two, before passing Gravesend on 2 October, and mooring in the Pool of London shortly after. James Cook was discharged on 5 October along with all the other seamen and the cook. They were not replaced until 30 November. What was happening in the meantime is intriguing; too long just to unload the cargo. Possibly she had moved down river and was undergoing repairs – maybe at the Sheppards' Yard. Wilkinson knew the family, for the same reasons as Walker did, and the James Sheppards, Senior and Junior, were to be witnesses to Wilkinson's will. John Hutchinson, *Mary's* carpenter, 'cut two of his Fingers' and had to be sent to 'St Thomas Hospitall' on 20 November so presumably he had been working on repairing the ship.

Seaman James Cook, no longer an apprentice, left John Walker's elegant house in Haggersgate to find his own accommodation.

He would have received advice about where to stay when ashore and there were enough people to advise him: John Walker, John Jefferson, Robert Watson, John Wilkinson, William Gaskin and Zachariah Cockfield among others. It is likely that The Bell at Wapping, run by the widow Mary Batts, was given a good rating. It is open to question whether Cook stayed there for long in 1750 as *Mary* was recruiting sailors (and a new carpenter) for a departure on 30 November for Whitby, and one would expect Cook to have signed on if he was still in Wapping.

A Georgian building in
Haggersgate. John Walker's house
no longer exists, but may have
looked something like this.

Mary started the new season on 18 February 1751, but the muster roll does
not say where. Her new master was Martin Kildill, who had been mate of *Buck* in
1732 when John Wilkinson was master. Martin's brother John was a part owner of
the Dock Company. The voyages in 1751 and 1752 were the triangular trade to
Newcastle, Stockholm and London, continuing for the next few years. On at least
one voyage *Mary* stopped at Great Yarmouth on the way back from Stockholm,
probably bringing timber and iron; *Mary* could then have carried another cargo
(probably corn) on to London. In 1754, although John Hoggart remained the
carpenter and Robert Hutchinson, who had been the cook since 1751, also

stayed on; there was a new mate in Thomas Galilee. *Mary*'s voyages to Shields, Stockholm and London continued; but Thomas Galilee had an accident and 'brok his arm' on 14 March 1755 when the ship was at London. Later that year worse was to follow: Joseph Elmgren, who had been taken aboard as a 'servant' at Stockholm on 24 June, fell from the fore-yard on 27 September – also at London – and was killed.

A greater tragedy happened in the morning of 31 November which, although it occurred a long way away from Britain, was to have significant consequences throughout Europe; this was the disaster which is generally known as the Great Lisbon Earthquake. There were three tremors in increasing intensity, the final of such violent strength that it destroyed an estimated 12,000 buildings including several churches which, as it was All Saints' Day, were packed with worshippers who had come to hear mass.

About half an hour after the last tremor subsided, a tsunami swept into the city, the first of three massive waves, the greatest reaching 6m in height. In those areas not doused by the sea, fires broke out and quickly spread, taking several days to extinguish. The city was devastated, and probably more than 50,000 people were dead. Henry Taylor was on board ship anchored in Portsmouth harbour at the time:

The Carmo convent church, Lisbon, destroyed in the earthquake.

when on a sudden the ship began to bounce so that whole crew were alarmed, they were afraid she would break all her moorings; although it was nearly calm, the water in the bason ran about six feet up the sides; and the ships building near us trembled like leaves shaken with the wind.[1]

In terms of mortalities and casualties it was one of the worst earthquakes ever recorded. It was also possibly the only earthquake ever to have had such a dramatic theological aftershock. Traditionally, the Christian view was that suffering was either a punishment for wickedness, or a test of one's fortitude and inner strength – a kind of spiritual *no pain no gain* situation. Not surprisingly, some suggested that the city must have deserved this divine punishment; but Lisbon was not Sodom, just a city like many another city – no more or less wicked than London, Paris or Vienna. And if God was punishing sin, why did he kill all those devout Christians by letting their churches collapse and crush them while the city's red-light district remained virtually intact? John Milton in *Paradise Lost* had stated his aim was to:

> … assert Eternal Providence,
> And justify the ways of God to men.

How effectively he achieved this goal is a matter of debate; but certainly after the Lisbon earthquake justifying the ways of God to man became much more difficult.

Leibnitz (1646–1716) was a mathematician, physicist, philosopher and Fellow of the Royal Society. He made important advancements in calculus, binary numbers, and mechanical calculation and thus was one of many ancestors in the family tree of computers. He also became court philosopher to the Electorate of Hanover. At that time a court philosopher was every Enlightenment ruler's must-have: Queen Christina of Sweden had employed Descartes, Catherine the Great was patron of Diderot, and Frederick of Prussia's court philosopher was Voltaire. Today, Leibnitz is generally known for his belief that when God created the universe he had made 'the best of all possible worlds'. Leibnitz's view was axiomatic to most deists and rational Christian thinkers at the time; it was Joseph Addison's view, and it was the view put forward by Alexander Pope in his *Essay on Man* in which he too sought to 'vindicate the ways of God to Man'.

When Voltaire heard of the Lisbon earthquake, he wrote an angry poem about it; angry with God, and angry with those who could believe in the face of such a terrifying example of natural evil that they lived in 'the best of all possible worlds'. Four years later Voltaire followed this up with his novel *Candide*. The eponymous hero, who had led a sheltered life, travels with his tutor Pangloss, a believer in Leibnitz's optimism, and sees that the world is full of terrible evils. Candide's ultimate conclusion on how to live in such a godforsaken world is that 'we must cultivate our garden'.

Leibnitz's reputation was destroyed, and God's reputation was not undamaged. Newtonian science, with its unalterable laws of nature, had resulted in many seeing the universe as the complex, beautiful and ordered creation of a rational and beneficent God. But if these laws are unalterable, then God cannot break them. If they are alterable, and God can interfere in cause and effect, making the sun and moon stand still at his divine whim,[2] then there is no science, and mariners cannot rely upon the unchangeable movement of the sun, moon and stars to navigate their fragile vessels 'upon the waves of the sea'.[3]

David Hume (1711–76), historian, philosopher and luminary of the Scottish Enlightenment, had already written a critique of miracles.[4] Though he did not actually state that he believed that miracles did not happen, he raised a number of doubts. His destruction of the Design Argument (i.e. that the existence of God is the only rational solution to explain the existence of the order of the natural world) he dared not publish in his lifetime, even though it was written as a discussion between four characters with differing views, so Hume's own opinions were (in theory and law) not clear.

James Boswell, Dr Johnson's biographer, visited Hume, a fellow Scot, shortly before he died. They discussed religion and the afterlife; Hume said that 'he never entertained any belief in religion since he began to read Locke and [Samuel] Clarke'★ adding that 'when he heard a man was religious, he concluded he was a rascal, though he had known some instances of very good men being religious'. Boswell, who was a serial user of women and riddled with gonorrhoea, was duly shocked and disturbed.

The Enlightenment left the world a more explicable but, in some ways, a darker place. In 1756, the darkness of war broke out again; the Treaty of Utrecht had solved nothing. There was unfinished business between France and Britain concerning who would rule the waves and thus command the trade, wealth and power of the world. Spain and Holland waited in the periphery like hungry dogs to see what morsels they could snatch while France and Britain weakened and impoverished each other.

In America there had been a number of incidents between Britain and France, but none significant enough to light the fuse of war until Colonel Braddock's

---

★ Samuel Clarke (1675–1729) was a rationalist philosopher and Anglican cleric. He sought to prove the existence of God by using the 'first cause argument', namely that everything in the world has a cause and logically this complex chain of causes and effects must have had an 'uncaused causer' to bring it into being, and this must be God. He also attempted to justify all the tenets of (Protestant) Christian belief and ethics by reason alone. His contemporary, Anthony Collins, philosopher and deist, commented in a witty put-down that no one had doubted the existence of God until Clarke attempted to prove it (Porter (2000), p.104).

defeat by French and indigenous American fighters in the summer of 1755. Although the British were the aggressors, there was outrage when the news reached London. The government was in some disarray: the Prime Minister, Henry Pelham, had died in March 1754 and his brother Thomas Pelham-Holles, 1st Duke of Newcastle had been appointed as his successor, amply aided by Lord Hardwicke. But they found it difficult to form a stable government, as there was a lot of jockeying for power, with the added complexity that King George II still refused to accept William Pitt into any significant post.

The French were much better prepared for war than the British: their army was larger and their system of manning the navy in time of conflict was more speedy and efficient. There were rumours of invasion, and worries that sending troops abroad might leave the country vulnerable – memories of the Pretender's Rebellion were still painfully fresh. A militia act, which proposed a territorial reserve force and was strongly supported by Pitt, had been rejected by the Lords; now that war had been declared there was panic.

The French realised that invading England was not a realistic strategy and moved their forces to invade Minorca. The British were taken off guard. Admiral Byng fought a French fleet in the Mediterranean but, greatly outnumbered, he made a tactical withdrawal to Gibraltar. This was probably a wise decision as the navy could not afford to lose more ships, but it meant the sacrifice of Minorca, whose small garrison was soon overwhelmed by the French. Minorca was strategically important to the British who wished to maintain a presence in the Mediterranean.

The harbour at Mahón.

The popular response to the loss of Minorca was seismic; mobs chanted 'Hang Byng!' and he was burned in effigy. Newcastle and Hardwicke desperately hoped for news of a victory to raise public morale, erase the shame of the defeat of Braddock and of the surrender of Minorca, and thereby make the government less unpopular.

But the people were with Pitt, and there was no good news. The French General Montcalm captured British forts in Canada, and a French army defeated the Duke of Cumberland in a battle near Hamelin and occupied King George's beloved Hanover. In India, Calcutta was taken by Surajah Dowlah, Nawab of Bengal, who incarcerated Europeans in the so-called 'Black Hole' where over 100 died.

Things were so bad that the king realised that he had to allow Pitt an important place in the government, but not quite bad enough for him to call Pitt to be Prime Minister. In this new coalition, formed in July 1757, Newcastle headed the administration, but Pitt was to have total responsibility and a free hand to organise the war.

The new government did not start well; the news from Canada and India was not encouraging, and the passing of the Militia Act caused riots. The hasty impressment of large numbers into the navy ('hot press') happened at the beginning of each war. Impressment was unpopular for the same reason that the Militia Act was: it was contrary to personal liberty, on which Enlightened Britain prided itself.

Trade had to continue, but suffering the dangers and difficulties of war. On 5 February 1755 *Mary*, Martin Kildill, with a crew of eighteen men, received an exemption of press by virtue of being in the coal and coasting business. The following year *Mary* arrived at the Nore on 10 March; it seems likely that she had arrived in convoy with other vessels and was awaiting her turn to go upriver to sell her coal. Ships gathered there at anchor were easy prey for the press to help themselves to 'recruits' for the navy. From *Mary* they took John Seaton, the mate, Henry Adamson, the carpenter, and three seamen. There were clear rules about who could and could not be pressed from merchant ships into the Royal Navy:[5] mates were exempt from impressment, but clearly what was laid down in the rules and what happened when the navy required experienced seamen were often very different.

One suggestion as to why James Cook, mate of *Friendship*, volunteered for the Royal Navy rather than stay to be master of a Walker ship is that he feared he might be pressed, and thought that it would be more advantageous, indeed a sound career move, to volunteer rather than be taken. He knew that although in theory he had exemption from press, the reality was that mates, such as John Seaton and himself, had the very skills that were needed in the navy, and whatever the navy wanted the navy (usually) got. Carpenters were also technically exempt, but that was of little consolation to Henry Adamson.

Contrary to the traditional caricature of the press gang capturing drunks in pubs, what the navy needed were men of sailing experience, and sea carpenters were particularly valued. Carpenters were valuable to the merchant ships too, and *Mary* was without a one until John Hoggart was signed on again at London on 20 April 1756; he did not last long, being 'sent ashor [sic] at Whitby', to be replaced by William Gales. In autumn there was a trip to Stockholm, and *Mary* finally arrived at Whitby on 14 December. In 1757 and 1758 were similarly voyages to Shields, Stockholm and London.

In 1759, Wilkinson once more succumbed to the lures of the Navy Board and *Mary* became a transport ship, but with a new master, Joseph Hornsby. Thomas Brocket as cook, Thomas Pearson continued as carpenter, and seven servants, including John Brocket (in at least his sixth year on *Mary*), were again on board.

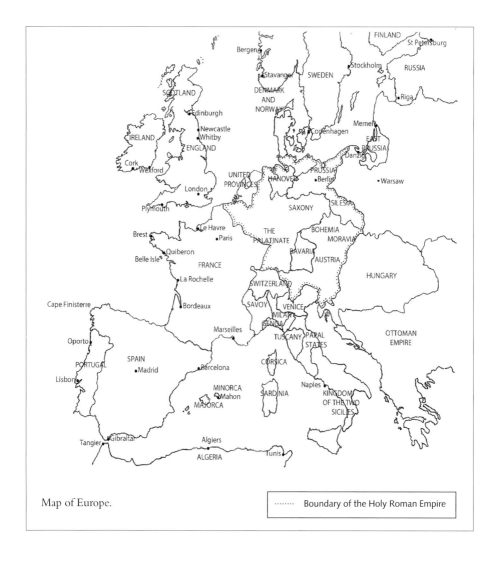

Map of Europe.

┈┈┈┈ Boundary of the Holy Roman Empire

Joseph Hart, seaman in 1758, was upgraded to second mate. As a transport ship, the crew, which had been between fourteen and eighteen in number, was now twenty-one, as required by the charter party. Another change was that *Mary* was now called *Maria*. This explains the mention of *Maria* in a biographical reference to Cook's early years: 'In the Spring, 1750, Mr Cook shipped himself as a seaman, on board the *Maria*, belonging to Mr John Wilkinson of Whitby, under the command of Captain Gaskin.'[6]

Changing his ship's name was a wise move, as *Mary* was one of the commonest ship names and there were already a large number of transports called *Mary*. Transports with the same name were given a number to distinguish them but this was not always reliable. In 1758, Deptford Yard had clearly been confused by transports named *Hopewell*, as their letter of explanation[7] makes (moderately) clear:

We have at last found out Four Ships named *Hopewell*, the *Amity* being called by that Name we have alterd agreeable to your Letter of the 23d instant to *Hopewell No 2, Hopewell No 3* we find to be the same as *No 2* mentioned on the Boards Order of the 18th instant the Masters Name George Watson, and the 4th *Hopewell*, Robert Westell Master is mentioned in their Order of the 20th, by the Name of *Hopewell 2d*.

The fortified Georges Island at the entry to Halifax harbour.

If it was possible to get this entangled with four ships with the same name, the confusion potential with numerous *Marys* would be enormous. Changing the names of ships was not uncommon and was not generally considered to be bad luck.

Maria, Joseph Hornsby, carrying supplies and probably troops, sailed from England to Halifax, Nova Scotia. Halifax, which commands a large natural harbour, had been established only ten years previously as a British stronghold, much to the anger of the native inhabitants. However, as Louisbourg had been handed back to the French in the treaty of Aix-la-Chapelle in 1748, the British desperately needed a fortified settlement near the strategically important mouth of the St Lawrence, and the financially important fishing grounds. *Maria* was about to play a part in one of the most significant, dramatic and memorable campaigns of the war.

14

Friendship

The all searching eye … looks to every quarter of the world, in which can be found an object either of acquisition or plunder. Nothing is too great for the temerity of its ambition, nothing too small or insignificant for its grasp of rapacity.

(William Pitt the Younger)[1]

*F*riendship of Whitby is documented from 1729, master Newark Waller, sailing between London, Newcastle and Norway until 1739. Newark Waller was a Quaker and was linked to John Walker by a confusing concatenation of Quaker marriages.

James Hill took over as master of *Friendship* between 1744 and 1746, voyaging to Ostend and Holland, possibly as a transport. On the 1747 muster roll the commander was John Waller, son of Newark, with John Walker as the chief owner;* the ship was again a troopship. John Waller continued as master in 1748, with Christopher Pearson as mate. The servants were Newark Headlam, Walker Chandler, James Dobson, Thomas Scrafton, Thomas Woodill, Luke Collingwood and John Asleby. The muster roll indicates that *Friendship* was engaged in the Newcastle to London coal run. In April, Walker Chandler had moved to *Three Brothers*, but otherwise the servants stayed the same that year. In 1749, John Blackburn was master, John Harland as mate, sailing to Cork and then to Newcastle, Norway and London. Blackburn left *Friendship* on 28 October 1750 and Francis Dunn, previously in *Liddell*, became master in his stead.

In 1751, the carpenter was John Hardick [Hardwick], the brother of Mary Prowd, John Walker's housekeeper. He was discharged on 2 July, and he was buried on the 29 October. For 1752, there were more changes: Richard Ellerton was

---

* Also on this voyage was the 17-year-old Thomas Pindar. In 1756, he was briefly a seaman on the Whitby ship *John & Elizabeth*, Thomas Holt, and in 1766 he sailed in *Dolphin*, Samuel Wallis, on her voyage to the Pacific.

master and James Cook was mate. Richard had previously been master of *Walker* of Whitby which had sailed from Newcastle for London with coals in 1742 but was lost on Yarmouth Sands. The crew was saved by a Great Yarmouth ship called *Freelove*. Losing a ship was always bad for a master's résumé, and Ellerton had subsequently served as mate for some years. There are Quaker connections with the Ellertons, which could be the reason that Richard regained his position as a master.

The year 1752 was a straightforward one for John Walker's *Friendship* in that it seems to have continued with the coal trade; the following year Richard Ellerton was replaced by John Swainston, previously mate of *Three Brothers*, James Cook remaining as mate. *Friendship* collected coals from Shields and Sunderland then sailed to London, Norway, London, Dram (Drammen in Norway), London and then probably two or more loads of Newcastle coal to London, the crew being signed off at Whitby where *Friendship* over-wintered. John Swainston took command of *Freelove* on 22 February, and Richard Ellerton (after a year as master of *Lark*) returned to *Friendship*.

Cook would have been pleased to see Ellerton again, as they worked well together and became friends; the last months of Cook's service in the merchant marine were spent in *Friendship* with Ellerton. When twenty years later Cook

The outer harbour at Sunderland, early nineteenth century. Notice the shipbuilding, centre and right; the pier would be for easy loading of coal.

returned from his second voyage in 1775 he sent an account of it to John Walker in Whitby, adding that he would like his compliments to be passed on to 'Mr. Ellerton if he is yet living'.[2] Ellerton was still living; indeed he lived for another fifteen years, and was buried at Whitby in 1790, aged 84.

Later in 1754, a year that was largely involved in coal trading between Shields and London, *Friendship* received another previous occupant – Walker Chandler, who had been a servant in her (1747–48, and probably earlier) before moving to *Three Brothers* (1748–49); he was now 24, an able seaman, and would have been a familiar face for James Cook. In July 1754, John Prowd became carpenter in *Friendship*, a post he would keep for five years.

By the beginning of 1755, the rumours of war gave way to expectation of war. On 5 February, Walker had secured a 'Protection from Press' for *Friendship* on the ground that she was engaged in the coal trade. Ten days later the ship left Whitby to pursue its declared business.

Some three months after sailing with the protection, Francis Sutton, servant, was 'Prest'. He had been on board *Friendship* in 1753 as a servant aged 21, so it looks as if he was a 'three-year man' like James Cook. Less than a month after Francis Sutton was pressed, James Cook left the ship at Wapping and, armed with a letter of recommendation from John Walker, volunteered for service in the Royal Navy. The wartime demand meant that mates were vulnerable to being impressed and were difficult to replace: *Friendship*'s next three mates lasted less than five months in total, and for a time she had no mate. Carpenters were similarly in demand.

Two of *Friendship*'s servants 'ran' (deserted) in 1755; Charles Rought (or Ross) had been an apprentice since May 1749 on *Freelove*, and although he had not finished his training, he was old enough to be pressed into the navy, and jumped ship on 28 August. Obadiah Towers was apparently new to the sea and didn't like it; he embarked on 23 July and left on 11 September.

In 1756, *Friendship* had a new mate, Thomas Preston. War with France, the 'Seven Years War', officially began in May. The Receivers of Sixpences accounts register *Friendship* as being in London on 21 July, having arrived from Chatham,

Friendship, Richard Ellerton, exemption from press. The last two columns are (approx.) tonnage, and number of men. (TNA ADM 7/370)

Chatham dockyard.

which indicates that she was working in some capacity for the Royal Navy. Moses May, another fresh servant, enrolled on 13 February and was drowned on 12 July, possibly while at Chatham. No age is given; he could have been only 11. Thomas Preston lasted until 20 August, and then *Friendship* was devoid of an official mate until John Hardwick, who served for the final ten days of the year's sailing, from 12 November.

In 1757, *Friendship* had a new master, William Marshall, and mate, Henry Boynton; and Britain had a new government with William Pitt as Secretary of State. The main focus of the war had tended to be Europe, where Britain's ally Prussia had been attempting to curb France's territorial ambitions. In June, a cluster of transports had been assembled to ferry reinforcements to Stade; *Friendship*, William Marshall, was one of them.

Pitt became Prime Minister in July; he passionately believed that the future for Britain was in commanding the seas, developing colonies, and benefitting from the ensuing boost in trade. He thought that the British army should not expend its strength fighting in Europe where there was so much to lose and so little to gain. Pitt was popular; he had the rare gift of understanding the mood of the people. He was also an excellent orator which was important in politics; he spoke his mind without toning down his extremity of passion and self-belief, and the House listened. He was compelling, and he raised the morale of the troops and sailors. A mood of belligerent patriotism was sparked: Britain stood for liberty and property and she was going to fight hard and win.

Politicians coming to power have not always been able to deliver what they promised, and Pitt as Prime Minister found himself having to compromise. The Duke of Cumberland, leader of the British forces serving in the Army of Observation,⋆ had been defeated by the French who had seized Hanover in 1757.

⋆ An allied army of Prussians, Hessians, Hanoverians and British.

They also captured Emden, a strategically placed port in north-west Saxony across the estuary of the River Ems from Holland, which was an important line of supply to the Allied army. Emden was recaptured in 1758 and Pitt, contrary to his plans not to commit troops to the European front, sent 9,000 British soldiers to Emden, which they held as a British territory for the remainder of the war.

In November and December of 1757, the Prussians had achieved victories over the French army, which reassured Pitt that Prussia was the only army which could match the French on land. In early 1758, Britain and Prussia agreed to be firm allies and that neither would make a separate peace with France. Britain gave Prussia £670,000 (*c.* £ 1,300 million) per annum to help maintain a strong front against France, while the main focus of the British forces turned to North America and the West Indies.

Pitt's strategy worked. Prussia defeated France in a series of victories culminating in the Battle of Minden in 1759. The Prussians were doing very well, though Britain did retain a military presence in mainland Europe. John Manners, Marquis of Granby, colonel of the Royal Horse Guards was in charge of the British forces in mainland Europe, a part of the Allied Army of Observation. Granby had fought in the Battle of Minden and, in the ensuing victory at Warburg the following year, led his cavalry into battle with such speed and panache that, like John Gilpin, 'away went hat and wig',[3] after which he made it a matter of pride to go bald-headed, which further endeared him to his troops, as well as being excellent publicity.

Likeness of the bald-headed Marquis of Granby on The Marquis pub in Colchester.

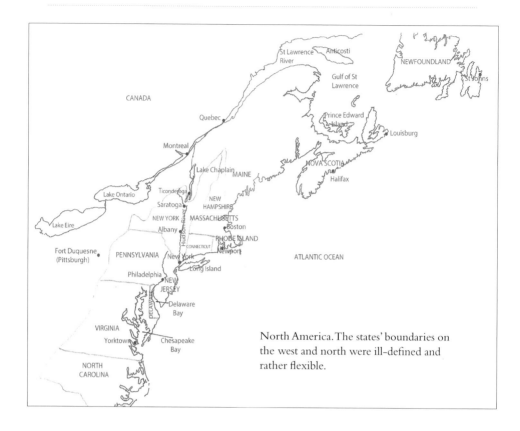

North America. The states' boundaries on the west and north were ill-defined and rather flexible.

Pitt was planning a massive and coordinated series of amphibious landings to recapture Louisbourg and to drive the French from Canada. Fortunately, the Admiralty was one of the largest and most efficient organisations in Europe, and it had learnt how to coordinate effectively with the army. That expertise, and the additional troops and ships that Pitt could divert to defeating the French in Northern America, changed the balance of the war. Fort Duquesne, which Colonel Braddock had so spectacularly failed to take in 1755, was captured.

Troops and supplies were carried across the Atlantic to Halifax. Louisbourg fell to the British in a dramatically effective amphibious attack. Edward Boscawen, Vice Admiral of the Blue, had chosen the ninety-gun HMS *Namur* as his flagship, and General James Wolfe sailed in her from England to Louisbourg. Also in the ship was the 6th lieutenant Michael Henry Pascal, whose slave and servant, Olaudah Equiano (renamed Gustavus Vasser by Pascal), was to be very influential in the anti-slavery movement.

Equiano described the ceremony of surrender as 'the most beautiful procession on the water I ever saw', in which:

The entries of Michael Pascal and Gustavus
Vasser in *Namur*'s muster for January–June
1758. (TNA ADM 36/6252)

The rebuilt fortifications at Louisbourg.

All the admirals and captains of the men of war, full dressed, and in their barges,
well ornamented with pendants, came alongside of the *Namur*. The Vice-admiral
[Edward Boscawen] then went on shore in his barge, followed by the other
officers in order of seniority, to take possession, as I suppose, of the town and
fort. Some time after this the French governor and his lady, and other persons of
note, came on board our ship to dine. On this occasion our ships were dressed
with colours of all kinds, from the topgallant head to the deck; and this with the
firing of guns, formed a most grand and magnificent spectacle.[4]

After the capture of Louisbourg, Boscawen sailed back to Britain in *Namur*.

With secure bases at Louisbourg on Cape Breton Island and Halifax on Nova
Scotia, the British moved down the St Lawrence to capture Québec. This would
have been hazardous had not James Cook in *Pembroke*, and others, previously

sailed up the river expertly correcting the existing charts. Numerous transports were required to carry troops and horses, including food for both, as well as the multifarious supplies needed to support an army in the field. When Québec was captured in September 1759 it was indeed a splendid victory, but it was also a triumph of logistics and cooperation. Seventeen Whitby ships can be identified as transports for this campaign, including John Wilkinson's *Mary/Maria*, master John Hornsby; *Two Brothers*, Scarth Stockton; and *Three Sisters*, Samuel Millner – which was lost at Québec. In the following year the British captured Montreal. Canada ceased to be French.

Among the many vessels tendered for horse transport in 1758 was *Freelove*, John Swainston, John Walker's ship. She was approved by the commissioners of the navy subject to a report by the Navy Board at Deptford.

The subsequent assessment accepted *Freelove* as a horse transport; she was calculated to be 318.68 tons and was described as 'roomly'. She was 30 years old, and had undergone a 'large Repair' two years previously. The Yard would then have set to and build forty-six stalls. She was 'ready' the next day, which probably meant that this was the first day that she was taken into paid service. Transport ships were armed; the Whitby ship *Porpoise*, Richard Woodhouse, had been delayed by Deptford Yard as not being 'ready' because she only had '5 Carriage Guns' and she 'should have six to be agreeable to the Conditions we have received for equipping Transports'.[5]

It is not clear when John Walker decided to tender *Freelove* as a transport. The beginning of the year, judging by the not always accurate muster rolls, was taken up with carrying coals from Newcastle: she is listed as being in Shields on 28 January, 24 February, 10 March, 12 April and 28 April. These coal journeys

From the Deptford Yard Letter Book, 19 July 1758. *Liberty*, Richard Watkins, and *Love and Unity*, Francis Easterby, were also Whitby-owned ships; this suggests that they were all being handled by the same agent. (TNA ADM 106/3312)

would have been to London and that is probably where Swainston heard of the need for transports. He would then have passed this information on to Walker who either came in person or briefed an agent to discuss terms and when to bring the ship to Deptford for assessment. Not all these coal journeys were non-stop between Shields and London, as on 7 June she was at Lowestoft where the 17-year-old servant William Blaney had to be sent ashore as he had 'Brok his Thy' (broken his thigh). At Lowestoft, *Freelove* was probably unloading coals and taking on board a cargo of wheat for London.

How long it was after 20 July, when she was pronounced as ready, that *Freelove* sailed is not known, but she was back in London in September, having been to Emden (possibly more than once) ferrying the horses for cavalry units that were part of the 9,000 strong garrison. She then was resurveyed on 23 September, presumably for a new contract. On this occasion she was assessed as a transport for 'foreign service' which would mean that the charter party would have included a rate of pay of 11*s* per ton per month. Sailing to Emden would have counted as 'home service' and would have been cheaper.

In November 1758, a sizeable task force of ships-of-the-line and accompanying transports set sail from England for the West Indies with the intention of capturing French territories and diverting enemy troops from the European front. Arriving at Barbados, they were joined by more ships, and attempted to capture the French-held island of Martinique. When this seemed too difficult, attention moved to Guadeloupe, arriving there in January. There followed a furious battle in which the invaders struggled with strong French resistance and the terrible ravages of disease; the French surrendered in May, but the sickness continued.

Eleven Whitby ships are known to have been involved in this expedition; what part *Freelove* played is not clear; but we know she was at Grand-Terre, Guadeloupe, on 10 June when Stephen Bovens, second mate and steward, ceased to be on the roll, possibly 'discharged dead', but no details are given.

Freelove was back at Deptford on 24 August 1759, where the crew were discharged and the ship no doubt was repaired after the ravages of the Caribbean. On 9 September, a largely different crew was enrolled, and *Freelove* returned to the coal trade, which had its own dangers and tragedies – John Prowd was drowned on 14 October. He was only 26. He had been the ship's carpenter since July 1754, and was the only surviving child of Mary, John Walker's housekeeper, who had done so much to look after not only his children but also his live-in apprentices.

On 31 January 1760, John Swainston with a crew of fourteen other men and boys sailed out of Shields in *Freelove* on the first voyage of the season. But that voyage lasted only a few days; *Freelove* was lost on 15 February. There was no loss of life; the only casualty seems to have been that the seaman Henry Anderson bruised his hand. This information is recorded in the muster roll, which was completed on 29 May. Six months later (on 14 July) *Freelove*, John Swainston,

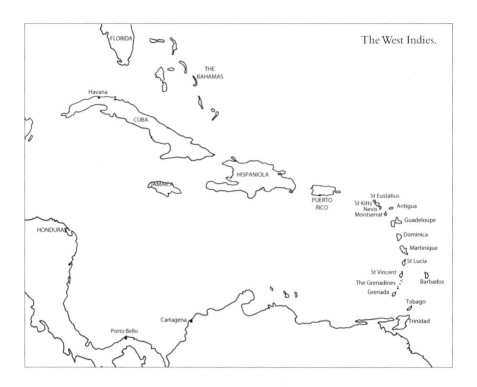

The West Indies.

owned by John Walker, sailed out of Whitby. Five of the servants and one of the seamen who had sailed with Swainston before were on board.

All this presents problems. It seems clear that the ship *Freelove* which James Cook sailed in was built at Whitby in or about 1728, and which was recorded as lost in 1760. But what ship was the *Freelove* which sailed on 14 July? It could have been a new ship altogether, but its launching and naming would have had to fit into the lacuna between news reaching Walker that the first *Freelove* had sunk or been damaged beyond repair and the naming of the second one, which means either he already had a ship virtually completed, or else had bought a ship and decided to rename it *Freelove*, but there is no evidence of a new ship.

A Whitby-owned ship *Freelove* survived until compulsory registration and was recorded, in January 1787, as being of 341.38 tons, owned mainly by John Walker's children, and built at Great Yarmouth in 1746; *Lloyd's Register* (of 1780) agrees she was built at Yarmouth, but in 1742 . This has generally been accepted as the ship which Cook sailed on, and is identified by such by Weatherill and the great Cook scholar Beaglehole.[6] However, it seems clear that Cook's *Freelove* was not built in Yarmouth in 1746; it is possible that the 'second *Freelove*' could have been, but then it would not have been Cook's ship.

Although there is no clear answer to all this, at present it seems most likely that the second *Freelove* was the same as the one which was reported lost and which was later rescued and perhaps rebuilt. Interestingly, there was another *Freelove*, James Norfar master, which was believed to have been lost in 1742 and later arrived in Yarmouth where she was repaired. It looks as if something similar happened to Walker's *Freelove* in 1760, and later there was perhaps some confusion between the two ships. If *Freelove* had been seriously repaired at Yarmouth in 1746, then the owners clearly felt justified in registering her in 1787 as a 41-year-old ship rather than a 59-year-old one.

In July 1759, Admiral Rodney had bombarded Le Havre where flat-bottomed boats were assembled for a massive invasion of Britain. In August the French Mediterranean fleet which was to take part in the invasion was defeated by a squadron led by Admiral Boscawen, in his flagship *Namur*[*] at the Battle of Lagos. Three months later, Admiral Edward Hawke achieved an even greater victory at the Battle of Quiberon Bay. All this was a serious setback for the French, who abandoned (yet again) the idea of invading Britain.

Charles Edward, the Young Pretender and now a member of the Church of England, hoped that France would defeat the British, which would be to his advantage; but Louis XV considered Charles more of a liability than an asset, and did not intend to restore the Anglican James Stuart, by this time quite an elderly pretender, to the throne of Britain. Charles had become a habitual drinker, and was not as bonnie as he once had been. James Stuart died in 1766 and was buried in St Peter's, Rome, by the Pope; his son Charles died in 1788 and was buried next to his father.

In terms of trading wealth, the small islands of the West Indies were far more valuable than wide and massive Canada, largely because of their exports of sugar and rum. British victories in the West Indies continued: in June 1761, Dominica was captured from the French. In October of that year a massive force was assembled in order to capture the impressively defended island of Martinique, the military hub of French possessions in the West Indies. Admiral Rodney sailed from Portsmouth with forty fighting ships, including Captain Augustus John Hervey and his young nephew Constantine John Phipps in the seventy-four-gun *Dragon*. Among the many accompanying transport ships was John Wilkinson's *Mary/Maria*, William Swales. The attack on Martinique was fiercely defended, but the French finally surrendered on 12 February 1762. St Lucia and St Vincent followed before the end of the

---

[*] Olaudah Equiano was still aboard. *Namur*, launched in 1756, served for many years; between 1811 and 1814 her commander was Charles (later Admiral) Austen, brother of the writer Jane. Charles was later involved in policing the Abolition of the Slave Trade Act. His final post was *Bellerophon*, famously the ship on which Napoleon came aboard to surrender in 1815.

Rome, showing St Peter's and Castel Sant'Angelo, 1823.

month and Granada on 4 March. On 12 March, William Swales died 'at Granadye [Granada]'. The mate Joseph Hart took over command of the ship and successfully brought her home with no further casualties. Thomas Pearson (carpenter), Thomas Brocket (cook), Robert Blair and Robert Jackson – all previous members of the crew of *Mary/Maria* – were also on this voyage. Constantine John Phipps, for his part in the capture of Martinique, was made up to lieutenant; he was 17.

The wealth of France became the wealth of Britain, as the latter captured island after island from the former; a wealth generated by the labour of slaves. If it was not clear that these campaigns were largely about slave-generated prosperity, in 1758 the British seized the French fort of St Louis and the whole of Senegal with its flourishing slave trading post, and later captured the offshore island of Gorée with its splendid harbour. These successes gave the British a larger section of the lucrative slave market at the expense of France.

Granada, when under the domination of France, had few slaves and did not produce much of the wealth-bearing commodities of sugar, rum etc. The British saw the island had financial 'capabilities' and introduced a large influx of slave labour which made the plantation owners and Britain rich.

Senegal and Gorée provided Britain with greater control over the shipping in the south Atlantic (mainly slaves), as illustrated in the newspaper report in 1762: 'On board the 14 vessels lately taken on the windward coast of Africa, there were 1333 slaves' – who were no doubt duly sold. A more acceptable benefit of these new West African possessions was access to gum Arabic which was a high-price, low-volume cargo with a regular market among the fabric printing industry.

The transport *Liberty*, Richard Watkins, which had been assessed with *Freelove*, participated in this attack on Senegal, perhaps unaware of the irony of the ship's name. Britain seemed unstoppable. In June 1761, Belle Isle, an island off Brittany near Quiberon Bay, was taken and occupied. One of the ships involved was HM fireship *Ætna* on which was Equiano, still a slave. The capture of Belle Isle was not only an impressive propaganda coup, but also was a good bargaining chip for the peace which everyone knew had to come soon.

The news from India was similarly heartening for the British; from 1757 Robert Clive of the Honourable East India Company, reinforced by British troops and naval support, had enjoyed a number of successes, culminating in the surrender of Pondicherry in 1761 after a lengthy siege. The French attempt to gain sizeable territory and influence in India was at an end.

In 1759, Ferdinand V, King of Spain, died and was succeeded by his brother Charles III who was much more ambitious that Spain should be an important power and trading nation, and he realised that if Britain won the war that was unlikely to happen. So in 1761 Spain formed an alliance with France, known as the Family Compact because Louis XV of France and Charles III of Spain were first cousins. This was exactly the situation which the War of the Spanish Succession was intended to prevent.

In 1750, John V of Portugal died and the throne passed to his son Joseph I who was married to the Infanta Mariana Victoria, daughter of Philip V and half-sister to Charles III of Spain. It looked as if this marriage would cement the alliance between Spain and Portugal. Joseph I was known as 'The Reformer', but left his chief minister Pombal to put reforms into practice while he concentrated on opera and hunting. Pombal effectively ran the country, and his skills were needed after the earthquake of 1755. He instituted an impressive programme of civil reconstruction, rebuilding cities, repairing roads and harbours, and restoring trade. Pombal believed, as did the country at large, that it would be peace in his time – so spending on the military had been virtually ignored. The country was unprepared when Spain, in 1762, turned on Portugal, capturing Almeida and invading from Galicia in the north, as well as seizing Portuguese territory in Latin America – roughly modern Uruguay.

Portugal appealed to Britain, her long-standing ally and trading partner, and help was promised. Portugal and Spain were now in the war. This was exactly what Spain had hoped for: with fewer British troops fighting the French they hoped that tide of the war would be turned, and the French would defeat the British, while the Spanish would plunder Portugal's colonial wealth.

The British army had to assemble 8,000 soldiers to go to Portugal's aid, and the Navy Board had to find 6,250 tons of transports to carry them. The first tranche of troops destined for Lisbon assembled at Cork, sailed on 24 April 1762 in convoy (with several Whitby-owned transports), and arrived at Lisbon on 8 May.

Statue of King Joseph in Praça da Comércio, Lisbon (known in Britain as Blackhorse Square). Part of Pombal's renovation of the city.

The soldiers were camped about 4 miles out of town, and the transport ships were back at Plymouth in June.

Spain's plan did not work. The Spanish invasion of Portugal was repulsed by the British task force. Less successful was the protection of Portuguese-held colonies in South America, where an allied army was defeated.

With Spain now an enemy, Rodney's amphibious fighting fleet was diverted from the business of capturing French-owned islands in the West Indies to an assault on Havana, capital of Spanish-held Cuba. This was not an easy place to capture, as the English had discovered in 1748; but after five months of mutual slaughter the town surrendered in August 1762. Manila, another Spanish-held target, was captured in the following month.

All these military exploits required an enormous number of transport ships; during the course of the war over a thousand merchant ships were chartered as transports, though a number of the contracts were for specific, and comparatively

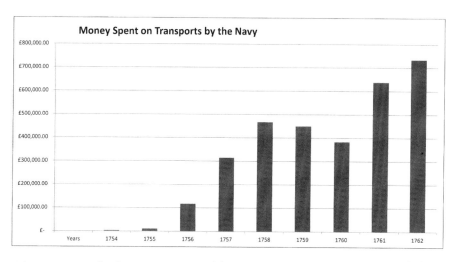

The money spent by the Commissioners of the Navy on transports (1754–63), not including victuals for troops while on board ship. (Data from TNA ADM 106/3524, listed in Syrett (2008), pp.153–4)

short, periods of time. The hire of transports cost fabulous sums of money, particularly after Pitt's strategy for the war was instituted, as this chart reveals:

To have some idea of how expensive these policies were, £500,000 would be about the equivalent of £1,000 million today.

The Commissioners of the Navy were fortunate that the 'British merchant marine in the mid-eighteenth century was the largest in western Europe'.[7] This meant that (most of the time) there were sufficient vessels to continue British trade and to supply transport and victualling needs, so it was not difficult for the Navy Board to find shipowners to tender vessels. When ships were required, there were no advertisements in the newspapers as was the case with seeking tenders for food and drink. The Navy Board put up posters in London, contacted agents and shipowners, and generally put the word about concerning what they were looking for, and they received sufficient tenders. Although payment was by Navy Bonds, which could not be exchanged at full value for some time, there was money to be made – and there was security in that if a ship was lost while fulfilling its function in accordance with the charter party then its value was paid by the Navy Board.

It is not surprising that shipowners, combining profit with patriotism, were sucked into the transport business, and Whitby was no exception. Indeed, a list of transports which were 'ready for service' between 25 June and 27 July at Deptford[8] contains ninety-seven transports for horse, fifteen for infantry and seventeen for forage, a total of 129 ships, of which forty-four can be identified with some certainty as Whitby-owned. Although this is a small sample and is not therefore representative, it is impressive that these figures show Whitby as providing over a third of the transports. If only the figures for horse transports are taken into account Whitby ships contributed 39 per cent of the total.

The specifications for a horse transport were more demanding than those for infantry. The horses were kept in specially built stalls in the hold and the requirement was that there was at least 9ft from the floor of the hold to below the lower deck beams. The horses' stalls were on either side of a central gangway, so the ship would have to be wide enough to accommodate this arrangement. Whitby ships tended to make good horse transports, as they were mainly full-built, with little tumblehome,* and of sufficient size to be roomy. There would also have to be space for food and water for the horses, and for the men who looked after them, who would be accommodated on the lower deck in 'cabbins'. In addition, the Navy Board provided the slings and ship halters which aimed to keep the animals safe from damage in an ever-moving, ever-rolling ship, and other essential items for looking after horses, such as pails and dung rakes. The Navy Board provided the food and water for the horses; the Victualling Board paid for the victuals of the men, and the ship owners paid for the crew's sustenance.

Thomas Linskill, a Quaker, also owned a vessel called *Mary* which was 'taken into the service of government'. The master was Henry Taylor of North Shields. Taylor was a man of religious disposition, an Anglican, but sympathetic to Methodism. As captain, he felt he had a duty to maintain a high moral standard aboard ship; he remarked that, 'I discouraged drunkenness, quarrelling, and swearing; so that those disorders, so common in most ships, were rarely seen or heard of in that which I commanded'.[9] Taylor had small respect for Quakers who tendered their ships as transports; he wrote, 'It must give pain to a reflecting mind to know that this ship belonged to one of the people who in their society capacity have always borne an uniform testimony against war, defensive as well as offensive, for which many individuals have experienced deep suffering; but the owner of this ship entered freely into the business of war, from motives of temporal interest'. It is always a risky business to infer people's motives from their actions, but it cannot be denied that the Quaker owners who profited from hiring out their ships as armed transports were acting against the publicly proclaimed and privately valued pacifism of the Quakers. This might make them bad Quakers, but not necessarily bad people; it almost certainly made them responsible ship's husbands.

The main Whitby Quaker owners who hired transports to the navy were Abel and Aaron Chapman, Thomas Linskill, Isaac Stockton and John Walker. They were all reproved, and refused to repent their actions. They all thought of themselves

---

* Narrowing of the sides of the ship from the main deck downwards.

Genealogy 20: Quakers who owned armed transport ships (Seven Years War)

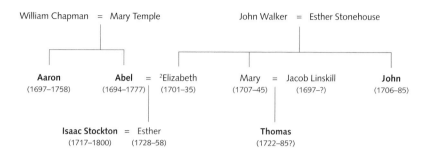

as Quakers, probably went to meetings (which were open to all) and were all buried as Quakers.* They were also related, and no doubt supported each other when they were shunned, slighted or – worse – patronised by members of the Whitby meeting.

These are only the main owners; part owners are more difficult to trace, but we know from his will that Solomon Chapman (nephew to Aaron and Abel) owned a sixteenth share of the armed transport *Liberty*. Quaker masters also sailed in armed transports; for example, Scarth Stockton was master of Henry Wilkinson's ship *Two Brothers* which was at Halifax (1757), Louisbourg (1759) and Québec (1760).

The British navy's blockades of France's ships, keeping her Atlantic and Mediterranean fleets apart, and the largely Prussian forces keeping much of her army busy in Germany, ensured that Britain could plunder the French colonies with some success. However, committing such a large section of the army on the other side of the Atlantic meant that Britain could be vulnerable if French ships escaped from their blockades. If France could control the Channel long enough for a sizeable army to be ferried across to England they would have little more than the local militias to stand in their way, and – in the words of Adam Smith – 'A militia, however, in whatever manner it may be either disciplined or exercised, must always be much inferior to a well disciplined and well exercised standing army'.[10] Naval supremacy in the Channel was as crucial for the future of Britain as air supremacy over the Channel was during the Second World War.

---

* The records of the burial of John Walker and Thomas Linskill are annotated with the phrase 'not in membership'. This would no doubt have been the case with Abel Chapman but he died in 1777 and the practice was not begun until 1790.

There were worries about the cost of the war. Many suggested that enough victories had been won, and that to acquire too much wealth and power only invited coalitions of enemies to unite against Britain in the future. Pitt argued that France's military and naval forces must be totally destroyed so she could never be a danger in the future. When Pitt, who had been given the responsibility of running the war, found his plans opposed he was angry and frustrated. He was further frustrated after George III came to the throne in 1760. George disliked Pitt and wished to promote the career of his tutor and protégé, John Stuart, Earl of Bute. Pitt resigned in October 1761 and Newcastle stayed in power in a coalition with Bute which lasted only seven months before Newcastle himself resigned, leaving Bute as Prime Minister and George Grenville as Secretary of State.

From August 1758, Walker's *Friendship* had a new master, Samuel Bartis of Shields. Bartis remained as commander of *Friendship* for two years, during which she continued with the Newcastle–London coal trade. He was succeeded as master by Thomas Porter in 1761. The last muster roll of Walker's *Friendship* ends on 14 December 1761 at Whitby; she is heard of no more. Weatherill, who rarely mentions his sources, simply states that *Friendship* was 'Lost, 1762–3'.

John Wilkinson's ship *Maria* reverted to the coal trade with Martin Kildill once again master. She was at London from Stockton on 5 September 1763. Soon after that she seems to have been lost.

Earl of Pembroke

Why seek ye Fire in some exalted Sphere?
Earth's Fruitful Bosom will supply you here.

(Henry Bourne, *Newcastle*, 1736)

George III became king on the death of his grandfather George II on 25 October 1760; he was 22. He chose his wife, Charlotte of Mecklenburg-Strelitz, from a selection of eligible German Protestant princesses and, though he never met her until 7 September 1761, the day before they were married, they proved to be a very happy couple. His coronation was held on 22 September 1761 to much popular acclaim. He was born in England and spoke English, a proper English monarch.

After the initial excitement of the coronation, enthusiasm for the new king waned. Politically, George's reign had started badly. He had ensured that Bute was Prime Minister, and there was a Tory government for the first time since 1714; but there was a feeling that the king had overstepped his authority in so doing. For Bute, and the king, ending the war was a priority.

Coat of arms of George III. Quarterly: 1, English lions halved with Scottish lion; 2, French *fleur de lys*; 3, Irish harp; 4, Electorate of Hanover.

After negotiations which smacked of marketplace bargaining, the Treaty of Paris was signed on 10 February 1763 by France, Spain and Great Britain. Portugal was involved, but was not a signatory; Prussia and Austria were excluded from the negotiations in spite of the agreement made with Prussia. Canada, including Cape Breton, was ceded to Britain, provided that the Catholic colonists were allowed to practice their religion; the Canadian islands of Miquelon and St Pierre were retained by France together with some fishing rights off Newfoundland (as had been agreed in the Treaty of Utrecht). France was allowed some trading posts in British-held India in return for submitting to British authority there. St Lucia, Martinique and Guadeloupe were given back to France, as was Gorée. The French agreed that British colonists could settle on the American territory east of the Mississippi, and the Spanish on the West. The French agreed to reduce the fortifications of Dunkirk, which had been the base for many planned invasions of England. France returned the strategically important island of Minorca, and the British reciprocally returned Belle Isle. Britain kept the recently captured islands of Granada and the Grenadines, St Vincent, Tobago and Dominica. Spain restored most of the territories captured from Portugal, and Britain returned Manila and Havana to Spain, which granted Britain rights to fell the valuable logwood trees in Honduras.

Many in Britain objected that too much had been given away, especially to France. Bute, who had attempted to ensure that this treaty was the basis for a lasting peace with France, came in for much abuse. There was no way that the French were going to be happy about the terms, but the repossession of the profitable Newfoundland fishing rights and the even more profitable islands of St Lucia, Martinique and Guadeloupe, together with the ending of the expense of garrisoning Canada, ensured that the French economy, so sadly depleted by the war, would recover to fight another day. The menace of the French had been scotched, not killed.

The treaty left Britain with no friends. She had alienated her allies: Prussia resented the early stoppage of the payments, and the humiliation of being excluded from the peace negotiations. The Portuguese were annoyed that not all her colonial territories had been returned by Spain. The Dutch, who had fought with the Allied army, were largely ignored, as they had been in the Treaty of Utrecht. Nearer to home England had issues with Scotland and Ireland. France and Spain had not been pacified by the peace, and sought every opportunity to strike at Britain – to destroy her supremacy and wealth and to regain their national pride.

King George had the best interests of the country at heart, and although he could be immovably stubborn and stubbornly patriotic, he was no fool. His father, Frederick Lewis, Prince of Wales, had died in 1751 when young George was only 13. John Stuart, Earl of Bute, a keen amateur botanist, had been appointed tutor to the young prince – a role he performed excellently. George's education was similar to that recommended by Isaac Watts (1674–1748), the Nonconformist logician and hymn writer, which included the study of 'the nobler inventions of Sir Isaac Newton, in his hypothesis of the heavenly bodies and their motions, in his doctrine of light and colours, and other parts of his physiology' as well as the 'natural history of birds, beasts, and fishes, of insects, trees and plants'. Naturally, Bute ensured that George learned Latin, which Watts described as 'the living language of the learned world'. In many ways, the educated people of Europe shared a common culture; paintings and music could be widely understood and could cross language barriers, but for ideas to cross language barriers they had to be in Latin, which is why (for example) Newton's *Principia Mathematica* was in Latin. Such books were eventually translated into vernacular languages, but with science it was (and is) important to know *exactly* what was being described. This was particularly important with classification and agreed terminology without which, especially in the nascent sciences of botany and zoology, there could not be clear and sound progression. Linnaeus naturally chose Latin, which is why plants and animals have Latinate names.

George was educated in physics, chemistry and maths as well as an understanding farming and commerce. Like Charles II, George had a fascination with astronomy, but perhaps his greatest interest was in botany – an enthusiasm he shared with his wife. His interest in horticulture and agriculture was to earn him the nickname 'Farmer George', a classical pun as the name 'George' derives from the Latin *georgicus* meaning 'an agricultural man'. George would have read the Roman writer Virgil's *Georgics*, a lengthy poem which gave specific instruction on a variety of agricultural topics including growing crops, the uses of dung, grafting fruit trees, weather forecasting, farming livestock, breeding horses and beekeeping. George would probably have read it in Latin – though Dryden, who referred to the *Georgics* as 'the best poem by the best poet', had translated it into English in 1697, reviving an interest in agriculture and arboriculture. In the eighteenth century, Virgil's first-century BC *Georgics* could still be used as a helpful manual.

Agriculture in Britain was developing, struggling to feed the increasing population: for many, a good harvest meant the difference between living to work or starving to death.

Arboriculture for a maritime nation in times of war was of crucial importance. Ships were captured, destroyed or 'lost', so the Royal Navy and the merchant marine were constantly in need of replacement ships; less obviously, the existing ships were constantly in need of repairs. Wooden ships suffered from wear and tear: masts, yards and spars regularly fractured with stress or were damaged in stormy weather; the hulls (particularly 'betwixt wind and water') needed regular inspection and repair even when sailing in temperate seas; vessels in tropical

Harvesting at Hadleigh, Essex, overlooking the Thames estuary.

waters were also prey to the wood-boring mollusc *Teredo navalis*. In the best conditions, ships needed to have a thorough repair every twelve to twenty years; vessels that had been involved in sea fights or major battles needed serious repairs immediately. Also, both the royal and merchant navies needed to expand, by building new ships. Timber, along with hemp (for ropes) and flax (for sails) were crucial commodities to keep ships in operation.

The building and maintenance of the Royal Navy ships and the hired transports, victuallers, hospital and cartel vessels, was an enormous task, rapidly becoming 'the largest industrial complex in a pre-industrial world'.[1] That it worked as efficiently as it did was largely due to the work of Samuel Pepys, who had set up an efficient body of professional administrators. They were answerable to the Admiralty Board which consisted of seven commissioners, led by the First Lord of the Admiralty, who were all political appointees, usually members of Parliament. As such, they changed as the government changed but this caused minimal disruption because the day-to-day management was run by professional, and not political, employees.

There was also a significant decline in the life expectancy of the Royal Navy ships built between 1730 and 1745. Clive Wilkinson has identified two causes for this phenomenon: firstly, a series of warm winters which meant that trees, even if winter-felled, would have been more sappy, and secondly, 'the poor management of timber stocks at the Yards', with the exception of Deptford and Chatham, 'which did not soak their timber in water to season them sufficiently (as was the practice in France and Holland), but allowed them to suffer being alternately dry and damp – conditions that encourage rot'. This inferior timber had been used to build ships which consequently needed to be repaired more often and more completely and replaced sooner.

The result was that the dockyards could not keep up with demand. The Seven Years War following swiftly after the War of the Austrian Succession meant that there was little time or money even to repair their own dry docks and other structures, let alone for expansion and improvement. There seems to have been no attempt to enlarge Deptford Yard since July 1741 when there is mention in the Yard's Letter Book of the acquisition of some 'Ground Purchas'd of Sr John Evelyn'.[2] Sir John Evelyn was the grandson of John, the diarist, and the land was part of the Sayes Court Estate.

Timber was needed by the Admiralty and was being brought into the country in vast amounts; the turnover was swift, but the sheer quantity often led to stockpiles growing so large that there was not time or space to treat the timber properly. The Sheppard's yard at Wapping had just such a backlog in 1750 when their imported timber was stacked so high against the adjacent premises of Charles Hiller that the latter's chimneys collapsed – an industrial accident which resulted in prosecution and imprisonment.[3] Sheppard did much business with the Navy Board. On 7 January 1760, John Cull, master mast-maker at Deptford Yard, claimed his expenses for 'surveying Transps, Arm'd Ships & Tenders, masts, yards and sea Stores' which required dealing with, among others, 'Mr James Sheppard', a contractor 'for making Masts, Yards, &ca for His Majtis Service'. But because Sheppard was across the Thames from Deptford, Cull had 'been oblig'd to cross the water, to and from him on his Majtis Service, which was Attended with a great expence'.[4]

Without timber, no ships; without ships, no command of the sea; without command of the sea (according to the contemporary mercantilist belief), less trade, less wealth, less liberty and property, less happiness. Timber was too valuable to burn, hence the demand for coal.

As coal pits had to be dug deeper and deeper, so pumping water out the mines became more problematic. The first steam pumping engine, invented by Thomas Newcomen, was installed in 1712. James Watt's 'atmospheric' steam engine of 1769 was faster, more powerful, cheaper to run and able to drive any kind of machinery. In partnership with Matthew Boulton, Watt constantly upgraded his coal-fuelled steam engines, which were not only used in coal mines and the profitable Cornish tin and copper mines, but were increasingly used for manufactures, and were already poised to fuel the incipient Industrial Revolution.

Some waggonways to ensure easy transport of heavily loaded coal trucks from the mine to the Tyne had been laid by the end of the seventeenth century,

George III. This penny coin of 1797 was stamped by Boulton and Watt using steam power.

Tanfield being one of the first, as it was also one of the first to make coal trucks with cast-iron flanged wheels, which ran on straight wooden rails. All was set for the invention of a steam railway engine.★

Coal was a valuable commodity, and was being mined at an impressive rate – some 15.5 million tons in 1750.[5] The miners and keelmen of the Tyne benefitted little from all this generated wealth. For the miners, those 'wretches who work in unwholesome Mines … [whose] senses are corrupted in the operation of their Trade',[6] disasters were common and wages were low. The keelmen, who lived in their own area of Newcastle, had their own community, their own uniform and their own boats (*keels*), but were only ever on a year's contract. Although trade unions ('combinations') were illegal, the keelmen were an integrated community and were prepared to look after each other in hard times, and go on strike if need be. Militancy and strikes were to become common among keelmen and miners in the nineteenth century.

The real winners were the coal barons who accrued unimaginable wealth. A few mine-owning families (Liddell, Lyon, Bowes, Wortley-Montagu) controlled a significant proportion of the most valuable mines near Tyneside. Their 'Grand

---

★ One of the first working steam railway engines was *Elephant*, built in 1815 for the Wallsend, Washington & Hetton colliery. She was designed by John Buddle and William Chapman, the latter being the great-grandson of William Chapman (shipbuilder) and Mary Temple and the great nephew of Abel Chapman, who married Elizabeth Walker. There is a working replica of *Elephant* at Beamish open air museum.

Newcastle, 1830. Only boats could sail under the bridge, so the ships were clustered below.

Alliance', reinforced by intermarriage, enabled them to control prices and maximise profits.

Good money could also be made by shipowners. There were so many varying elements that a single unlucky coal voyage could make a significant loss for its owners, but over time it was a profitable trade. Later, the Committee of Whitby Shipowners was formed to protect their interests, which largely consisted of lobbying the Yorkshire MPs. Shipowners and coal barons could form groups which were, in effect, 'combinations'.*

Thomas Millner [Milner] was a Whitby shipowner. In 1728, when he was not yet 21, Thomas was master, and probably the owner, of the collier *Mary Ann*. By 1740, he was master of a larger vessel, *Triton*, sailing between Newcastle, Norway and London. In 1747, he was master of the 390-ton *Friends Glory* just for a season, probably testing the new ship before passing command to his younger brother Samuel, who was master and owner of this ship from 1748 to 1755. From 1750, Thomas was master and possibly owner of *Neptune*, importing timber from Norway and the Baltic. In October 1760, she arrived at Plymouth Yard with 'masts, yards &c' from Riga, which implies a contract with the Navy Board. Later, she had become a transport ship (possibly a victualler) being at Belle Isle in 1761

---

* Tom Paine: 'The House of Peers … amounts to a combination of persons in one common interest. No reason can be given why a house of legislation should be composed entirely of men whose occupation consists in letting landed property, than it should be composed of those who hire, or of brewers, or bakers …' (*Rights of Man*, Part II, Ch. 5, p.268).

and 1762. The following year she was carrying troops back from Williamstadt when the war was over.

By this time, Thomas had amassed sufficient money to commission a new ship. This was the *Earl of Pembroke*, built by Thomas Fishburn, and launched in 1764, probably in the spring. Fishburn was described as 'a gentleman of considerable professional reputation, and highly meritorious for his unimpeached integrity and benevolent disposition'.[7] This ship, later to be Cook's *Endeavour*, was named for Henry Herbert of Wilton House, 10th Earl of Pembroke. He was a real horse enthusiast; he joined the 1st Regiment of Dragoons when he was 18, and three years later he established a riding school at Wilton. He rose to be a general in command of the cavalry in the Army of Observation. In 1761, he wrote *Military Equitation: or A Method of Breaking Horses and Teaching Soldiers to Ride*. It was a detailed and practical book which ran into several editions and became the handbook for the cavalry.

One hopes that it is for his military and equine talents that Thomas Millner named his ship after the earl, who was also rather prone to what 'men call gallantry and gods adultery'.[8] In 1756, he had married Elizabeth, daughter of Charles Spencer, but less than six years later he eloped with a woman called Kitty Hunter.* Having fathered an illegitimate child, he returned to his wife. It was not the last time that Henry slid into temporary extramarital relationships, and Kitty herself seems to have erred in favour of variety.

The 368-ton *Earl of Pembroke*, Thomas Millner as master and owner, was a roomly and sturdy collier, which carried between 214 and 220 chaldrons of coal. She sailed between Newcastle and London at least three times between July and December of 1764. In 1765, she started from Shields on 8 March with John Brown as mate, William Gibson as carpenter, Robert Cuthbertson as cook, six seamen and four servants. It seems that she over-wintered at Shields, and it is possible that most of the sailors came from there; but the muster rolls are unhelpful. There was a fairly rapid turnover of crew members; the mate John Brown was replaced in May 1765 by Robert Boasman who lasted a year. The next mate, Francis Alleley, was possibly appointed because he was married to Sarah Kitchingman, sister of Thomas Millner's wife Mary (and of Samuel Millner's wife Ann); the second mate at this time was Charles Kitchingman, brother of Sarah. Both stayed on board for less than six months. Nepotism does not seem to have served Thomas Millner well.

The coal trade was becoming increasingly unpopular with Whitby shipowners. In the early years of the century, an enterprising master mariner sailing in his

---

* As can be imagined, Henry Herbert came in for a lot of rather dubious puns about riding a hunter.

Genealogy 21: Millner Family Tree

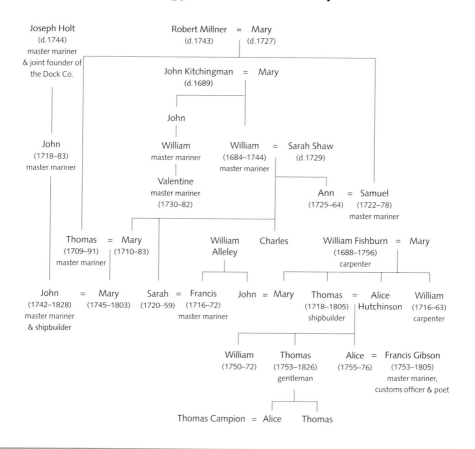

own vessel could become wealthy. It might involve pushing the ship to its limits in the storm-fraught North Sea with its shifting sandbanks in order to fit ten or more voyages into the season, driving himself and his crew to do more and work harder, and skimping on expenses, repairs and even insurance. Larger ships with several owners were not able to take such risks.

Most colliers returned from London in ballast with no cargo, and therefore no profit on the return journey. It is an indication of Millner's enterprise that he returned to Shields from London on 3 July 1767 with 'Rye, Chalk, Dung and Goods'.[9]

But once the money had been made, the owner-master sought to become a gentleman, living off the profits of his ships, investments in land and the 3 per cents. The coal trade required the master to buy the coal in Newcastle and then to sell it in London or the southern and eastern ports; consequently, the shipowners needed to employ masters who were not only able to guide their precious ships and cargo safely and speedily, but had the business acumen to get the best prices for the coal and to be alert enough to snatch up an opportune cargo of dung. Such masters were not easy to find.

The Port of London was becoming congested, accidents were common, and theft was on the increase – John Holt of Whitby had a boat of over 17ft cut from his ship *Margaret and Ann* in 1742. There were no river police. Violence was rife among rival gangs of stevedores, who were controlled, and frequently exploited, by coal undertakers and inn-holders; there was also a deep antagonism between the sailors and the, largely Irish (and Catholic), coal-heavers. An incident happened to John Walker's ship *Freelove* in 1768, James Tayler master and Richard Ellerton mate, which resulted in the death of John Beattie, 'a Mariner, belonging to the *Freelove* of Whitby'. *Freelove* had moored the previous day, and as there were so many colliers seeking to discharge their cargoes no coal-heavers were to be got, so the crew started the unloading. The next day (24 May) they continued to do so, but were interrupted by a gang who came aboard, hindering the sailors – who suspected them of being troublemakers rather than coal-heavers. Antagonisms escalated, sailors were thrown into the water and Beattie 'received a blow … from a broomstick' which broke his nose. He was then struck with a cutlass by James Murphy who was the protagonist of this violent affray, making a wound which 'reached from the temple to the back part of the head, and went through the skull to the brain'. He was left for dead; but when he was seen to be struggling, another man 'gave him a cut across the shoulder, which went into the joint'. Mr Grindal,

The Custom House, London.

Tower Wharf, London, on a quiet day.

the surgeon to the London hospital where Beattie was taken, 'imputed his death to the wound on his head, but gave it as his opinion, that either of the wounds was sufficient to have killed him'. James Beattie 'languished ten or twelve days' before he died.

After a preliminary examination, Sir John Fielding committed James Murphy to Newgate for murder, and James Duggan for 'aiding, assisting, and abetting'. The event was widely reported in the press, one comment being that 'some prejudices still subsisting between the Seamen and the Irish Coal-heavers … prevent, for the present, perfect peace amongst them; but it will be difficult to find men so adapted from strength, &c. to execute this laborious task of coal-heaving as the Irish are'.

The trial, which lasted all day, was on 18 June and the Court found both guilty, and they were condemned to death. At Tyburn, on 11 July, Murphy and Duggan admitted to being rioters but 'declared themselves innocent of murder', and were hanged. At that moment, a pickpocket was detected, and was 'severely ducked by the mob'. Before Murphy was cut down, 'a well-dressed woman with a child about 3 years old in her arms' came forward and, taking Murphy's right hand, rubbed it over her daughter's scrofulous left hand. She departed 'well pleased and satisfied' – no doubt certain that her daughter would be cured.[10]

By that time, the *Freelove* had long since continued on her collier duties. The relevant muster roll, scrappily and cursorily submitted on 25 June 1769, names only the master, mate, carpenter and servants; the rest of the crew were included in the phrase 'Five Men & Cook Names Unknown'.

The *Endeavour* replica sailing through Tower Bridge. There was no bridge here in the eighteenth century, and ships could sail all the way up to London Bridge.

While Thomas Millner and the *Earl of Pembroke* were regularly sailing up and down the North Sea coast, other more dramatic voyages were taking place. John Byron (grandfather of the poet) who had sailed round the world in Anson's voyage of 1740–41, did his own circumnavigation between 1764 and 1766 in HMS *Dolphin* with Philip Carteret as a midshipman. No sooner had he returned than *Dolphin* set out once more, with Samuel Wallis as captain, accompanied by Carteret, now a lieutenant, in HMS *Swallow*. Early into the voyage the two ships were separated. Carteret discovered Pitcairn's Island, but having no chronometer on board made an error in longitude and charted the island some 200 nautical miles from its true position, so future voyagers had difficulty finding it. Wallis discovered Tahiti, which he claimed for Britain, giving it the new and rather clumsy name 'King George the Third's Island'. Wallis's reception there had at first been hostile, but he managed to establish good relationships with the inhabitants, which made life easier for subsequent British visits.

On one of his many coal voyages, Millner heard that the Navy Board was looking to buy a ship for 'foreign service'. It clearly seemed a good opportunity, so he offered to sell on 28 March 1768.[11] Two other ships were surveyed, but *Earl of Pembroke* was the one purchased.

There were some issues: there were delays in removing her rigging and stores, and later several of the masts and yards were found to be 'sprung and defective' rendering them 'unfit for a Foreign Voyage', but finally the metamorphosis of *Earl of Pembroke* into HM Bark *Endeavour* was completed.

Thomas Millner retired from being an active master mariner to become a gentleman.

Marquis of Rockingham and Marquis of Granby

History is a necessary study … for gentlemen who deal in politics. The government of nations, and distressful and desolating events which have in all ages attended the mistakes of politicians, should be ever present on their minds, to warn them to avoid the like conduct.

(Isaac Watts, *On The Mind*)

The 336-ton *Marquis of Rockingham*, launched in 1769, and the 462-ton *Marquis of Granby*, launched a year later, were both built by Thomas Fishburn for William Hammond of Hull and his partner John Wilkinson.★

Charles Watson-Wentworth, 2nd Marquis of Rockingham, was a wealthy man whose massive stately home, Wentworth Woodhouse, was built, literally and metaphorically, upon coal mines. He was a reforming Whig, and after the resignation of George Grenville in 1765 he became Prime Minister. At the end of the Seven Years War it was clear that the American colonists were not happy, and they were not backward in expressing their bitterness now that the French were no longer a threat. They resented the patronising attitudes of the British army during the war, and of the British government after the war – particularly when it was clear that Grenville's regime thought the colonies should pay their share of the war deficit and passed the deeply unpopular Stamp Act and Sugar Act. The Rockingham administration repealed both these acts before its brief time in office ended when Pitt was called to form a government the following year. Rockingham

---

★ Possibly the same man as the owner of *Mary/Maria*. It is a common name, and no hard evidence to make the connection has yet surfaced. However, it is likely that Cook knew Hammond, as he was planning to go to Hull to meet him in January 1772, and John Wilkinson could be the link.

was a Yorkshire-based Whig who was keen on religious tolerance and parliamentary reform, and was popular among the merchant and commercial interests.

It is easy to see why Hammond was happy to name one of his new ships after him, along with the ever-popular bald-headed Marquis of Granby – who was appointed Master-General of Ordnance in the new government. The Earl of Egmont became Lord High Admiral, with Charles Townshend as Paymaster-General.

Francis Stennett was a master mariner from Hull in whom Hammond had considerable confidence. Stennett was an experienced commander: he had been master of several ships owned at Hull, mainly in the Baltic trade – the *Neptune* from 1758 to 1762, *St George* in 1765 and *Rockingham* from 1766 to 1768. He had sailed in the last two of these when they were new ships, and this was clearly his special area of expertise, as he was master on their maiden voyages of both *Marquis of Rockingham* in 1769 to Leghorn [Livorno], and of *Marquis of Granby* in 1770 to Petersburg.

Endeavour's voyage was a great event. The transit of Venus had been accurately measured, a significant improvement on the 1761 sightings, which pleased the Royal Society. The existence of *Terra Australis*, a southern continent with an abundance of mineral and vegetable wealth (and therefore perfect for colonising before the French, Spanish or Dutch did) had been shown to be rather doubtful, which was a disappointment to many. Cook had accurately charted several islands in the Pacific, New Zealand and the east coast of Australia, an achievement which was of real advantage to the navy and to the government; he had noted information about their peoples and their societies, and had claimed many of these territories for Britain. Cook had circled the earth and guided *Endeavour* safely back to Britain with most of the crew healthy (until they reached feverous Batavia), which was an impressive feat of seamanship, leadership and navigational skills. Drawings, seeds and specimens of flora and fauna, previously unknown to Europe, had been brought back in their hundreds – a major enterprise – largely due to the expertise and wealth of Joseph Banks, which appealed to all who enjoyed botany or novelty.

On 17 July 1771, *Endeavour* docked at Greenwich. The next day Cook attended the Admiralty, and then went home to his wife and family after three years' absence. He prepared an account of the Transit of Venus which he sent to the Royal Society. He was promoted to commander and collected his commission from the king.

Then he sat down and composed letters to John Walker, giving him an account of his voyages. Much has been written about the influence Walker had on Cook. Clearly, he trained him well and certainly he did not impose Quakerly beliefs; perhaps the most appropriate words are those which Hilary Mantel gave to Thomas Cromwell: 'A good master gives more than he takes and his benevolence guides you through your life.'[1]

Genealogy 22: The Marquis of Rockingham Genealogy

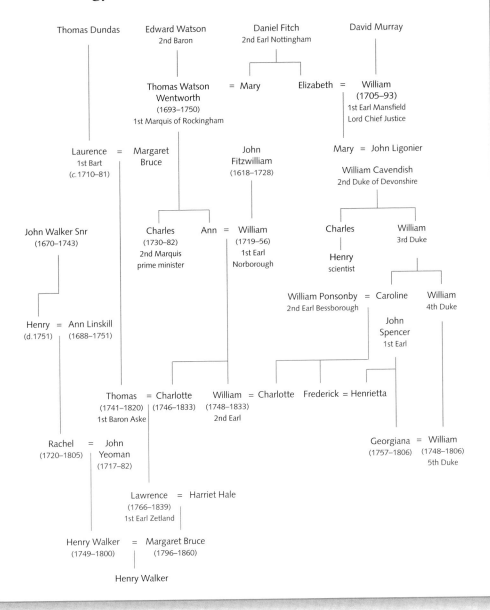

On 10 December, Cook wrote to Mr Joseph Cockfield who had expressed an interest in 'seeing some of Mr Banks's rare Plants &ca'. Cook said he would be happy to arrange such a visit, adding, 'let me know on what morng you can go to Mr Banks's and I will engage that gentleman or Dr Solander to be at home and will at the same time attend you my self. I can meet you anywhere between

Upton House (later Ham House) and garden, *c.* 1765. Owned by Dr Fothergill, later by Samuel Gurney.

Mile end and Newburlington Street.' This last sentence means that Cook would be setting out from his home in Mile End and walking to Banks' house at 14 New Burlington Street, and would be happy for Cockfield to come to his house, or meet at Banks', or anywhere in between. Cockfield had not visited Cook at home before, as he had to be given directions as how to get there: 'Next Door to Curtis's Wine Vaults'.

Beaglehole, who quotes this letter, remarks that Mr Joseph Cockfield was 'not a man, evidently, interested in voyages to remote parts'. It is not clear what he means by this, as Joseph came from a family of Whitby master mariners and would be intrigued by voyages afar. It is possible that Cockfield was also interested in botany, as his cousin James Sheppard later bought Upton House from the Quaker botanist Dr Fothergill with all its variety of plant life and its massive greenhouses.

Cockfield did not leave an account of his experience, but a few days previously the Rev W. Sheffield, Keeper of the Ashmolean Museum in Oxford, had made just such a visit to Banks' house, which he described in a letter to Gilbert White:

His house is a perfect museum; every room contains an inestimable treasure. I passed almost a whole day there in the utmost astonishment, could scarce credit my senses …

[In the second room is] a compleat hortus siccus [herbarium] of all the plants collected in the course of the voyage. The number of the plants is about 3000, 110 of which are new genera, and 1300 new species which were never seen or heard of before in Europe. What raptures they must have felt to land upon countries where every thing was new to them! Whole forests of nondescript [not previously described] trees clothed with the most beautiful flowers and foliage ...[2]

The *Endeavour* voyage had been successful, and a number of voices were calling for a similar journey, only bigger and better. The Royal Society and the government were both keen that the existence or non-existence of *Terra Australis* should be finally settled. Cook agreed to lead such an expedition, and then went north to visit his family and friends in Yorkshire. First, he went to Great Ayton to see his father. Cook stayed at Ayton Hall, previously the residence of the recently deceased Thomas Scottowe, but then the home of William Wilson, an 'early patron and friend'[3] of Cook. Wilson, like Thomas Scottowe's son Nicholas, had served as a captain working for the East India Company.★ Wilson was brother-in-law to Ralph Jackson, the diarist, who recorded meeting Cook on this occasion: 'Spent all day at Ayton, this afternoon came Capt. Jas. Cook (& his wife) whose father lives in that Town, this Gentleman lately commanded the Kings Bark *Endeavour* on her voyage round the World and made many discoveries in the South Seas and in high Southern Latitudes ... he and his wife lay'd at Br. Wilson's.'[4] On the last day of 1771, Cook rode over to Whitby to meet John Walker, who was then living at Grape Lane in Whitby. The account of the enthusiastic welcome given to Cook by Mary Prowd, who was 65, has been much repeated.

By the time that a second voyage was decided upon, *Endeavour* had been repaired and was being used elsewhere. It was also determined that two ships should be sent. William Hammond wasted little time in proffering *Marquis of Granby* and *Marquis of Rockingham* – which were the chosen two.

In 1771, *Marquis of Granby* sailed to Leghorn where she took on board, among other things, some marble blocks. It is possible that they were from the famous marble quarries at Carrara, only some 50km north of Leghorn. Then she went to Barcelona before returning to London, passing Gravesend on 8 October. In preparation for her survey by the Navy Board, which was in early November her cargo, was unloaded into the premises of the shipbroker firm of Henry Chapman and William Elyard who were presumably acting for William Hammond in the sale of the two *Marquises*. Unaccountably, nine blocks of marble were not collected and were still unclaimed in the agents' yard in June 1773.[5]

★ *The Neptune of Europe* (1782) recorded all the ships in the service of the East India Company. It listed Nicholas Scottowe, Esq. as ship husband of the 804-ton *Bridgewater*, and George Wilson, Esq. as husband of the 758-ton *Earl of Dartmouth*. Also on the list was the 538-ton *Chapman*, master Thomas Walker, husband Abel Chapman, Esq. and built by Thomas Fishburn. Her acceptance by the East India Company, which had a policy of only using 'River-built' ships, was unusual.

The river end of John Walker's Grape Lane house (right, with flagpoles in the yard), now the Captain Cook Memorial Museum.

The *Marquis of Granby* was bought for £4,151 (*c.* £7.6 million) and *Marquis of Rockingham* for £2,103. They were renamed, respectively, *Drake* and *Raleigh*. These names were soon changed to *Resolution* and *Adventure* for fear they might offend the Spanish – which was possibly the very reason why they had been chosen in the first place, but Anglo-Spanish relations had become very sensitive.

It was all to do with the Falkland Islands. The first known European to land there acquisitively was Captain John Strong who came ashore, in 1690, to find fresh water. He claimed the island for England, naming it Falkland's Island after the First Lord of the Admiralty. The name suggests that he was unaware that there was more than one significant island. In 1764, the French landed on East Falkland and set up a colony, called Port St Louis, funded by Bougainville. In 1765, *Dolphin*, Captain John Byron, accompanied by *Tamar*, Captain Anthony Hunt, on their circumnavigation of the world, landed on the West Island. Byron discovered a fine harbour, which he named Port Egmont after the First Lord of the Admiralty, and described as: 'one of the finest harbours in the world. In every part of Port Egmont there is fresh water in the greatest plenty, and geese, duck, snipe and other birds so numerous that our people grew tired of them'.[6] Byron raised the British flag on the adjacent Saunders Island and claimed all the islands for the king. Based on Byron's panegyric on their return to Britain, *Tamar* was sent back to the Falklands, with Anthony Hunt as commander, to set up a colony there, accompanied by *Favourite*, Maltby.

Hunt set about his task with enthusiasm; soon there were twenty gardens to help feed the garrison. And he clearly took an interest in the islands' wildlife. Oliver Goldsmith (1728–74), playwright, poet, novelist and natural historian, wrote in his *History of the Earth and Animated Nature* that 'Captain Hunt, who for some time commanded at our settlement upon Falkland Islands' had informed him that the 'albatross seems to have a peculiar affection for the penguin, and a pleasure in its society. They always seem to choose the same places for breeding … their nests are seen together, as if they stood in need of mutual assistance and protection.'[7]

In 1766, under the Family Compact, France agreed to surrender her interest in the Falklands to Spain which believed it had the right of ownership as the colonial power in Argentina. Port St Louis became Port Solidad. As soon as the Spanish realised that the British had a settlement on the Islands, a letter was sent telling them to leave as soon as possible, as they were on Spanish territory. Hunt replied that 'the said islands belong to his Britannic Majesty, my master, by right of discovery as well as settlement; and that the subjects of no other power whatever can have any right to be settled in the said island.'[8]

On 20 February 1770, ships arrived in Port Egmont from the Spanish governor in Buenos Aires with a letter demanding the British settlement be removed. Captain Hunt's reply was similar to his previous letter, after which the Spanish ships sailed away. Realising that they could be planning more drastic measures, Hunt returned to England to inform the Admiralty of the situation.

On 7 June, five Spanish frigates and a sizeable force of marines arrived in Port Egmont, demanding of Captain Maltby (the senior officer in Hunt's absence) that the British settlement must leave or be driven out by military force. Maltby replied that he refused to believe that they would take such an action 'in a time of profound peace'. The Spanish marines disembarked and shots were fired; Maltby – massively outnumbered – surrendered. The British left, having been given a meticulous inventory of the property left behind (which included the gardens), and sailed back to Britain.

The common albatross.

When the news broke in London the reaction was speedy and belligerent; the Admiralty set about assembling a task force, readying ships and impressing sailors. One of the ships put on standby was HMS *Raisonable*, Captain Maurice Suckling. The 12-year-old Horatio Nelson begged his father to allow him to sail on his Uncle Maurice's ship; it was agreed, and on 24 April 1771 young Horatio joined the crew of *Raisonable*.

Negotiations were lengthy, involving much posturing and face-saving. Britain would not even consider discussing Spain's putative rights until their forces were withdrawn, and Port Egmont returned to the British. It looked as if the incident would spark a full-scale war with Spain and perhaps with France as well. When Louis XV made it clear that France would not go to war over the Falklands, the Spanish became more amenable and a solution was reached in which Spain would return Port Egmont to the British. The crew of *Raisonable* was paid off, and Nelson's first experience of life at sea was not in *Raisonable*, but in *Mary Ann*, a merchant ship.

The agreement was a return to the *status quo*, which left the Spanish on East Falkland and the British on the West, each insisting that they had the right to total sovereignty of both. It was a precarious peace. Hence the need to respect Spanish sensitivities, and change the names of *Drake* and *Raleigh*.

Meanwhile, Banks was making plans for the next voyage, deciding what and whom he would take. In addition to Dr Solander and a group of collectors and draughtsmen, he recruited the society painter Zoffany. He proposed that the Board of Longitude should sponsor the scientist Joseph Priestley★ for the expedition – but this idea was rejected on the grounds that, as a Unitarian, Priestley was unsuitable. Banks' insistence that *Resolution* should be converted into his own floating academy involved the carpenters adding extra height. As the Navy Board was later to comment, 'Mr Banks seems throughout to consider the Ships as fitted out wholly for his use; the whole undertaking to depend on him and his People; and himself as the Director and Conductor of the whole'.[9] Cook had misgivings, but Banks had influence, and on 2 May Banks entertained Lord Sandwich and the French ambassador on board ship. On 10 May, *Resolution* sailed to the Nore; but it became painfully clear that Banks' additions had rendered the ship top-heavy and unseaworthy.

Changes were initiated which made the ship safe, but Banks angry. Banks withdrew from the expedition in a petulant tantrum; but Palliser (Comptroller of the Navy, and Cook's patron) and Sandwich both approved of the alterations.

Finally, on 13 July 1772, with a new selection of scientists, *Resolution* and *Adventure* set sail from Plymouth, leaving England for the second voyage. Among

---

★ Priestley discovered oxygen in 1774; but it was named and understood by Lavoisier.

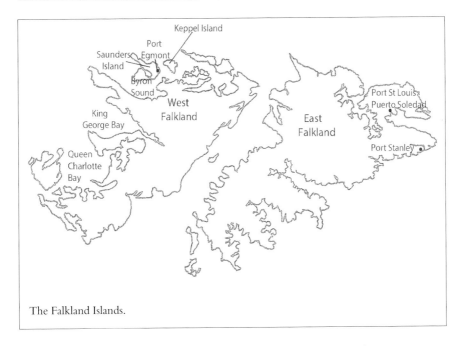

The Falkland Islands.

the scientific instruments taken aboard was a state-of-the-art chronometer – a copy (now known as K1) made by Larcum Kendal of John Harrison's fourth and wonderful watch (H4) which was so consistently accurate even in stormy weather that it would make the finding of a ship's longitude more simple and reliable. In addition, they took three other watches made by John Arnold,[10] which proved less successful.

To save face and to add to scientific knowledge, Banks chartered the 190-ton brig *Sir Lawrence* and sailed to Iceland on 12 July 1772 with his group of sponsored colleagues including Solander. He also took John Gore, who had sailed round the world with Byron, then with Wallis and latterly with Cook on *Endeavour*.*

In one way, the voyage to Iceland was a great success. Banks returned with 121 books and thirty-one manuscripts which covered a wide range of Icelandic culture from history and poetry to contemporary manuals. The majority were religious books, including a sixteenth-century printed copy of the Bible in Icelandic. Most of these he donated in 1773 to the British Museum (now the British Library). He also returned with information about the country, which was ruled and neglected by Denmark; Banks considered the Icelanders as 'the poorest people in the European world'.[11]

The Icelandic trip was sparse in botanical terms. These lines from the eighteenth-century poet and landscape gardener William Shenstone seem appropriate:

---

* He was later to sail on *Resolution* as 1st lieutenant on Cook's third voyage.

> Bleak, joyless regions! where, by Science fired,
> Some prying sage his lonely step may bend;
> There, by the love of novel plants inspired.[12]

Iceland is precariously balanced at the junction of two tectonic plates; its scenery contains large areas which are virtually barren, steaming like a somnolent dragon before its next unpredictable volcanic awakening. There had been one such in 1765, Banks recorded, which had desolated 'a tract of country about as large as an English county'.[13]

Sir Lawrence sailed for home on 18 October.

In spite of his pique over the issue of *Resolution*, Banks was not a self-centred, over-rich amateur. He was a serious and rigorous – indeed obsessive – scientist. Solander, who had been the professional botanist on *Endeavour*, worked well with Banks and respected him. Banks could be charming, and never forgot a friend. John Pringle, the president of the Royal Society in 1772, described him as a 'genteel young man [he was 29] … and of an agreeable countenance, easy and communicative, without any affectation or appearance of assuming'.[14] The influence of the *Endeavour* voyage on science, and especially botany, was immense – and that was unquestionably mainly due to Banks' skill, knowledge, enthusiasm and money. Many plants were first brought to Europe by Banks; and a genus of plants (*Banksia*) was named for him.

Joseph Banks had not totally cut himself off from the voyage of *Resolution*. Francis Masson, botanist and gardener from Kew, had sailed with the sloop to Cape Town where he disembarked to do plant hunting on Banks' behalf.

Icelandic scenery.

Above: 'Old Man Banksia', *Banksia serrata*.

Above right: 'Lantern Banksia', *Banksia ericifolia*.

Right: 'Bird of paradise flower', *Strelizia reginae*.

Princess Augusta, the mother of George III, had established a botanic garden at Kew with the help of John Stuart, Earl of Bute. When she died in 1772 ownership of Kew passed to the king, who was to take a particular interest in developing the garden. One of his first steps was to appoint Joseph Banks as his advisor at Kew which, under his management, was directed towards 'serious scientific and economic botanical purposes'.[15]

Masson had sent back a plant from South Africa which had a beautiful flower. Banks grew it on, and named it *Strelizia reginae*, in honour of Queen Charlotte of Mecklenburg-Strelitz (*reginae* being the Latin for 'of the queen').

17

Endeavour

Sea he had searched …
Downward as far antarctic …
… Thus the orb he roamed
With narrow search, and with inspection deep.

(John Milton, *Paradise Lost*)

After *Endeavour* had returned from her epic voyage round the world she went to Woolwich to be repaired, resheathed, supplied with new sails and made ready for her next voyage. She was to be a store ship to carry provisions and stores to the Falklands, with a crew of forty-five, and armed with six carriage guns and four swivel guns.[1] She was ready on 23 August 1771.

Lieutenant James Gordon was in command with Joseph Irving as the sailing master. The first problem was assembling and maintaining a crew; this was not an easy matter, as some were transferred to other ships, and several ran at Woolwich before the voyage even began. The next task was loading 'sufficient provisions to serve 350 men [the garrison at the Falkland Islands] to the end of the year 1772'.[2] These included beef, pork, suet, bread (ship's biscuits), flour, pease, oatmeal, mustard, vinegar, malt, butter, oil, cheese, sugar and rice. She also carried wine, rum, brandy, arrack, beer and water, and 45 chaldrons of coal.

There were also the provisions for the journey itself which included, besides the food and essential spirits, 'Sea Beer for the Ships use and some Ayle'; but all these had to be stored between decks as the ship was 'much lumbered'.[3]

Endeavour sailed down the Thames coming to Galleon's Reach on 15 October. Her first port of call was to be Portsmouth, and on board were some sixteen sailors who were to be taken to the recently opened Hasler Naval Hospital at Gosport. The chief physician there was James Lind, whose *Treatise of the Scurvy* had been published, and largely ignored, in 1753.

Endeavour rounded the Kentish Coast in good weather, but was beset by 'strong gales' on the night of the 26th and all the following day. Joseph Irving, the master,

Portsmouth.

'being near Drounded was Taken Bad with a Fever' and when *Endeavour* reached Portsmouth he was 'sent on Shore to Sick Quarters at Gosport.' John Dykes, previously master's mate, was appointed master.

Endeavour sailed from Portsmouth on 8 November, heading for Madeira. The following day John Lancaster a 22-year old able seaman from Guinea was punished with twelve lashes for theft.[4] On the 10th the two Yorkshiremen in the crew John Beadland (aged 39) of Whitby and Robert Wild (37) of Boroughbridge received twelve lashes for 'Drunkenness and Neglect'. *Endeavour* anchored in Funchal Road, Madeira on 5 December, and took on water and wine for the ship's use. The next day she sailed for St Jago (Santiago in the Cape Verde Islands).

The journey passed without incident, the crew being 'Imploy'd About the Rigging', 'making spun yarns', assembling for regular readings of the Articles of War, practising the use of 'the Great Guns & small Armes', and other essential activities. Another regular activity was broaching a puncheon of beer.

As they neared the Equator an awning was made for the quarter deck. On 14 December *Endeavour* reached St Jago and moored in the Praia Road. Here they bought fresh food and water, and took the opportunity to maintain the ship, varnishing the lower masts and rubbing tallow onto the top masts and the top-gallant masts (and then doing the same with the spares), and using the longboat for watering, and for tarring the sides of the ship. The 15th was a Sunday and the crew were treated to pork and wine.

On the 17th December *Endeavour* left the Cape Verde Islands. On the 19th the ship's company were issued with 'Fishing Hooks and lines' which would not only

Funchal,
Madeira.

keep them busy but also add fresh fish to a diet that would otherwise become less and less exciting the further they went.

On 22 December two seamen were punished with twelve lashes: John Cochrane (26) of Ireland for theft, and Anthony Vansack (22) of Oporto for broaching the water without permission (a serious matter as *Endeavour* was not making another landfall until the Falklands, so water had to be carefully rationed). On Christmas Day a cask of wine was opened, but the mate's log mentions no festive feasting. However, on 2 January 1772 a 46-gallon cask of wine was opened to celebrate the New Year.★ Slops and tobacco were 'served' on 6 January. These were sold to the crew and could be a lucrative sideline for the Purser, and

---

★ At sea, the day started at noon, so an entry on the second hour of 2 January was – on land time - two o'clock in the afternoon of 1 January.

Lieutenant James Gordon was both 'Commander & Purser' – as Cook had been. A list[4] of all his tobacco sales to the crew amounted to £11 1s 10d (c. £1,350 / £20,300), his best customer being John Bartlett (21) of Bristol who spent a lavish 15s 10d (c. £83, retail price index). With so much that was combustible on board ship (including gunpowder), there were limited times and places where sailors could smoke; though chewing tobacco was safe.

Some time in the first week or so of January *Endeavour* must have crossed the Equator; but there is no mention in the master's log of the 'Ceremony… practised by all Nations' which, Cook recorded, 'was not omitted' on 26 October 1768 when *Endeavour* crossed the line for the first time and anyone aboard who had not previously crossed the Equator had 'either to pay a bottle of Rum or be ducked in the sea'.

Being at sea for so long, the water becoming putrid, the casks of meat no longer a pleasure to eat (if they ever were) and cheese infested with weevils was clearly having an effect on the morale of the depleted crew. On 9 February Thomas Foster, a 20-year-old youth from Dumfries, was punished with twelve lashes and being put in irons for forty-five hours because he had made 'Mutinous Expressions'.

On 11 February the master recorded that he had 'Seed a Great maney Birds & a Deal of sea Weed with broad leaves'. The ship was passing Capo Blanco on the Argentinian Coast, which meant that the Falklands were not many days away. This must have raised morale somewhat as pork and wine were on the menu on the 13th. On the 18th the lead sounded 57 fathoms and 'fine brown sand with Mudd', and a cask of beef was broached. The ever-observant master saw 'Severall Penguins' and a 'great maney Whails & young sea Lyons' on the 21st. Three days later the Ship's company were served Grog, 'the Wine being all Expended'. On the 27th they thought they had arrived at the Falklands but the fog was so thick that they had no idea where they were; they fired guns and sent men out in the longboat to no avail. The following day the fog lifted somewhat and they discovered they were in Byron's Sound. It took them until 1 March to arrive at Port Egmont, where they came across HM Sloop *Hound*, John Burr commander, at anchor.

The next few days were spent in 'Landing Cargo & Overhalling the Rigging'. On the 10th, with much of the unloading done, they 'Scrubt Ship between wind & water' and 'brotched a Cask of Rum'. The weather was rainy, overcast and miserable and all the stacked stores were a temptation. On the 12th John Cochrane and John Lancaster were given twelve lashes for theft; clearly (for these two at least) whipping was not an effective deterrent. The weather grew worse with strong gales, squalls of hail, thunder and lightning; and unloading cargo in those circumstances after all those months at sea bred despondency at the best. Edward Critchett (26) of Exeter clearly found it all too much: he received twelve lashes on the 25th for 'Neglect of Duty'. Other faults escaped detection – the master found that the quantity of rum was deficient.

The crew a *Endeavour* prepared to sail home; ballast and fresh water were taken aboard, Isaac Suckey the carpenter was busy caulking, and other members of the crew were cleaning and preparing the masts and yards. While doing this Thomas White (21) from Scotland fell from the main yard and broke his left arm. Food was put aboard the ship, but the weather still continued to be vile. Everyone felt irritable. On 30 April John Cochrane was again in trouble, this time for 'Drunkenness & Disobedience to Orders', as a repeat offender he received twenty-four lashes.

It was undoubtedly with feelings of great relief that James Gordon and the ship's company sailed from Port Egmont on 4 May. The return journey was not particularly remarkable, time passed with the regular cleaning of the ship, opening of barrels of meat (which were nearly always pieces short), broaching casks of alcoholic beverage, reading of the Articles of War and the almost routine administration of twelve lashes.

Endeavour sailed to England non-stop, sighting the Scillies on 30 July. On the same day was the first real tragedy of the voyage: seaman John Ward (24) fell from the maintop into the sea; the master 'Hove the Ship in the wind' and threw overboard 'a Hencoop, the Deep sea line & Reel … But Could not save him'. Then, on 4 August while *Endeavour* was at anchor off Portsmouth Thomas Foster, the 20-year-old from Dumfries, fell overboard and was drowned. The ship was taking on new supplies of water, beer (the crew had been making do with grog) and beef which must have been most welcome. On the 9th the ship moved on up the Channel, and was at Gallions on the 14th where the guns and gunpowder were unloaded, and the ship cleaned. The beer taken on board at Portsmouth had all been drunk, and more was taken on board at Gallions, the empties being duly returned.

On 18 August John Montagu, 4th Earl of Sandwich and First Lord of the Admiralty, together with Sir Hugh Palliser, Lord Commissioner of the Admiralty came aboard *Endeavour*. There were new plans afoot for the Falklands and they were checking *Endeavour* to see if she was suitable. The garrison of the Falklands was the 350-strong ship's company of the fourteen-gun sloop *Hound*. The plan was to reduce the number of men and to replace *Hound*, which spent most of its time idling at anchor at Port Egmont, with a much smaller vessel. This was the 36-ton shallop *Penguin*, armed with ten swivel guns, and built at Woolwich specially for this enterprise. It was a collapsible vessel, and she was carefully taken to pieces, which were stowed on board *Endeavour*. The *Penguin*'s master and commander was Lieutenant Samuel Clayton, and the crew comprised a master's mate, two midshipmen, two surgeon's mates and eighteen seamen, plus twenty-three marines and a marine lieutenant, all of whom sailed with their deconstructed ship in *Endeavour*. One of the surgeon's mates was Bernard Penrose who wrote an account of the *Penguin* and her crew, from which much that follows has been taken.

Hugh Kirkland had replaced John Dykes as master of *Endeavour*, there were four shipwrights whose function was mainly to reassemble *Penguin* once they reached Port Egmont, and several new able seamen including the 29-year-old Thomas Taylor from Rhode Island.

On 15 November *Endeavour* was at Gallions Reach where she took on board guns and powder. She then moored off Sheerness where the marines and *Penguin*'s crew came aboard and the two ships' crews were paid two months wages in advance. Then the voyage began. On 10 December were the first punishments. On 21st *Endeavour* moored in Santa Cruz Road at Tenerife, where water and 653 gallons of wine, which Penrose called 'a sufficient quantity of wine', were taken aboard.

Endeavour sailed from Tenerife on the 25th. The next port of call was St Jago which James Gordon planned would be the last stop before Port Egmont, and consequently they took on board not only fresh fruit, but also a variety of livestock. Suitably provisioned, *Endeavour* sailed from St Jago on the 5 January 1773. The weather was favourable for most of the rest of the journey until they were near the Falklands when they sailed into a 'furious storm' which lasted four days. It was the 28th by the time they anchored at Port Egmont.

Stores were unloaded and *Penguin* was reassembled by the supernumerary ship's carpenters who had accompanied her. She was put into commission and

Santa Cruz, Tenerife.

The *Endeavour* replica in the Thames.

launched on April 8, after which she was dragged up onto the land to keep her safe from storms. The incoming residents gained useful information from the 'Hound's people' about 'the haunts of sea-lions, birds, bays for fishing' and other helpful survival tips.

On the 17th *Hound* and *Endeavour* set sail together for England, leaving the crew of the *Penguin* as the only human residents on West Falkland, keeping it for Britain. The sloop and the storeship arrived at Ascension Island on 23 May where they stayed four days. The next, and last, stopping-off place (10–14 July) was Fayal [Faial] in the Azores. Punishments had been meted out for the usual offences during the voyage with horrible regularity. On 3 August the two ships were anchored off Spithead. *Endeavour* was at Gallions Reach on the 18th and at Deptford on the 23rd. The next few weeks were passed in unloading the various stores, and on 15 September *Endeavour*'s crew were paid. It was intended that the storeship *Endeavour* would return to the Falkland Islands to take the next year's provisions for the *Penguin*'s crew; but changes in politics change the fates of ships.

The government was worried about the increasing troubles in America which, if they turned from a revolt into a revolution, would absorb a great number of ships and men. Spain had seized the Falkland Islands before and would wish to do so again; if they did so while Britain's forces were otherwise engaged it would be impossible to divert sufficient naval and military strength to retake them. And if any of *Penguin*'s men were killed or captured there would be a tremendous popular outcry which could topple the government. The easiest way out of this problem would be to evacuate the islands altogether. And that is what *Endeavour* was commissioned to do.

Endeavour's departure in January 1774 was hampered by a storm – when she should have been anchored safely off Sheerness for the crew to receive their prepaid wages she had been driven ashore. Fortunately she was got off without damage, the crew was paid and the ship sailed to the Falklands.

The crew of *Penguin* had been busy settling in. They had no idea how long they may have to stay in the Falklands, so they had to assume they were there for the long haul. They made more gardens which they manured with 'decayed seaweed'. In this way they managed to grow successfully a variety of vegetables including potatoes, broccoli, cabbages, carrots, turnips, spinach, parsley and lettuce. There were also wild plants which were useful, especially a tasty wild celery which they ate all the year round. Penrose mentions a plant whose leaves made a good tea which they generally had with breakfast.

The commanding officer, S. W. Clayton, also left a description of the islands,[5] in which he identified Penrose's tea plant as a wild myrtle. He went into clear and knowledgeable detail of plants and animals, identifying four kinds of penguin. He also mentioned a 'Beautyfull little bird like a goldfinch with its pretty Notes' adding that it was 'very troublesome in the Seed time'.

He told of when birds lay their eggs: the albatrosses first, then penguins and after them the sea hens and gulls. And when the egg-eating season was over

King penguins, *Aptendytes patagonicus.*

the wild geese were 'grown fit food & their young large enough to eat'. His description can at times be charming, as when, in his description of albatrosses, he wrote that they 'breathe hard through 2 small holes in the upper part of the Bill and frequently make a sound exactly like the little toy trumpets sold to Children at fairs'.

Clayton also provided detail about the weather. All this could be important information, which is why he requested that his account be laid, 'before their Lordships [i.e. of the Admiralty], if proper'. He concluded, 'this Climate is very agreeable to European Constitutions and with temperance and good exercise health is easily preserved … it is a good port to touch at for Refreshment in the Passage round Cape Horn.'

Penrose, fortunately not writing for the Lords of the Admiralty, recorded the activities of the members of the crew: 'We contrived to enjoy ourselves with cheerfulness and frequently with festivity', admitting there was a 'wide disparity' between their antics and those deemed acceptable for young men 'at home under the care and protection of a lady mother'.

Not everything was rosy for the *Penguin* crew. One of them had his leg bitten off by a sea lion which he was trying to kill; his colleagues carried him nearly 20 miles to the settlement, but he 'only lived to undergo an amputation'. Potentially worse was to follow when a fire broke out and threatened to consume their settlement and all their stores. They tried to launch *Penguin*, but there was not sufficient depth of water. The only time they needed her was not a success. Eventually the fire was brought under control, mainly due to the elements.

Endeavour arrived at Port Egmont on 23 April, by which time most of the islanders had given up hope that she would ever come. They were very pleased to see her, thinking she only brought provisions and news from Britain, but when they learnt that they were to be evacuated their 'sensations were beyond description'. The next month was very busy, the crews of *Penguin* and *Endeavour* working together 'clearing the storehouses, and getting everything valuable on board'. *Penguin* was taken apart, but 'most of the plank and timbers, being slight, were so damaged in the operation, that they were fit for nothing more than the fire.' So ended one of the strangest of the ships of the Royal Navy.

The *King George*, a whaler from Rhode Island, sailed into Port Egmont on 19 May. She had been much battered in a storm and had come to seek shelter. Unfortunately, as *Endeavour* was sailing the next day, there was not much help the departing residents could provide, apart from information. Everything of value was on board, apart from two boats for which there was not sufficient room on deck. *King George* had a year's supply of food, so her crew were not going to starve, and in addition the *Penguin* people gave them their thirty-eight gardens stocked with vegetables. Also left behind were a ram, a pregnant ewe and a pair of fairly tame pigeons with the hope that they would create a breeding population; Penrose recorded that the Rhode Islanders were made a 'solemn promise not to molest them', but in spite of that, Clayton suspected they would probably eat the pigeons.

The next day the seamen and the marines were all on parade for their departing ceremony. A leaden plaque was fixed to the door of the blockhouse, which read:

> Be it known to all nations, That Falkland's Island, with this fort, the storehouses, wharfs, harbours, bays and creeks thereunto, are the sole right and property of His most Sacred Majesty George the Third, King of Great Britain, France and Ireland, Defender of the Faith, &c In witness whereof this plate is set up, and his Britannic Majesty's colours left flying as a mark of possession by S. W. Clayton, commanding officer at Falkland's Island. A.D. 1774.

The Union Flag was then raised and those assembled gave three cheers. They then embarked on *Endeavour* which sailed with the next fair wind. The entire British presence in the Falkland Islands had set sail in *Endeavour* on 20 May 1774 in fine weather. Unfortunately they sailed into a terrible storm which raged for twelve days. It was so rough that they were unable to light a fire and the crew had to manage with uncooked meals. The silver lining was that, although they were perforce driven by the wind, the wind was taking them in the right direction. But that was not the end of their problems. A course was set for Ascension Island, but they missed it; the next plan was to sail to the Cape Verde Islands, but they missed them as well, by which time the water supply was getting very low and was rationed to four pints a day. *Endeavour* then sailed towards the Azores which, in spite of bad weather, she reached successfully – mooring on 30 August. Here the crew took on much-appreciated fresh water together with 'eight large hogs, one live cow, and vegetables in abundance'. Two days later they left the Azores and had, at last, an uneventful voyage home.

Endeavour was at Spithead on 19 September, and arrived at Woolwich on the 30th. She remained in ordinary over winter. On 2 February 1775 she was surveyed and found wanting; she would need considerable repairs which would take six weeks. It was recommended that she should be put up for sale immediately, avoiding the time and expense of repairs. She had been bought from Thomas Millner for £2,840 10s 11d (c. £5.4 million); she sold for £645 (c. £1.2 million).

For the next few years, British whalers used Port Egmont as a useful staging post. In 1780 the Spaniards, no doubt believing that King George had as much right to claim the Falkland Islands as he had to claim to be King of France, destroyed the British Settlement buildings, and once again claimed the Falklands, which they called Islas Malvinas.

18

Diligence

Let Holland, France or Haughty Spain
Boast their Discoveries o'er the Main
And sing their Heroes' Mighty Fame
Which now with time Decays
Britannia's Isle at length hath found
A man who Saild the Globe around
Discovering Isles 'till now unfound
And well deserves the Bays.

(R. Richardson)[1]

Among the plethora of voyages of discovery, the desire to discover a means of sailing from the Atlantic to the Pacific by a route north of Canada (the North-West Passage) was a recurring theme. Finding such a route would make far-reaching changes to trade and politics, as well as making the discoverer very rich.

One proposed solution was that there might be less ice in the north polar ocean than on water close to land, working on the assumptions that, as icebergs are not salty, they are made from fresh water and therefore are more likely to form at the estuaries of rivers, and also that ice forms more readily in tranquil water, 'but in the wide ocean, where the waves tumble at their full convenience it is imagined that the frost does not take effect'.[2] If this were the case, then it could be possible to find the North-West Passage by going close to the North Pole. Constantine Phipps was appointed to organise and lead the expedition. He was assigned two ships: *Racehorse* (in which he sailed) and *Carcass* (Captain Lutwidge); both were bomb ships and thus sturdy and more resistant to being crushed by ice. The Admiralty wisely appointed two Greenland whaler masters as pilots.

Aboard *Racehorse* was Dr Charles Irving with his 'apparatus for distilling fresh water from the sea'.[3] Working with Irving was Olaudah Equiano, freed slave, who was 'daily employed in reducing old Neptune's dominions by purifying the briny element, and making it fresh'.[4]

Equiano was responsible for an incident which 'was near blowing up the ship and destroying the crew'. He slept in the doctor's storeroom which was 'stuffed with all manner of combustibles'. While he was writing his journal by candlelight 'a spark … touched a single thread of the tow, all the rest caught the flame, and immediately the whole was in a blaze'. Fortunately there were many people nearby who helped extinguish the fire. Equiano was not much hurt: his clothes were burnt and he suffered from smoke inhalation.

Also on this voyage (in *Carcass*) was the 14-year-old Horatio Nelson, thanks to the patronage of his uncle, Maurice Suckling, Comptroller of the Navy. Nelson allegedly attempted to kill a polar bear with his rifle butt in a dramatic feat of teenage foolhardiness; in fact, the bear was frightened away when a gun was fired from the ship. Equiano did not mention this, simply recording that during the voyage nine bears were killed and, although many thought that they were very tasty, he considered polar bear meat was 'coarse eating'.

Phipps' voyage disproved the theory that there was a virtually ice-free zone near to the Pole and showed that a polar north-west passage was an unlikely proposition. He gave the first scientific description and classification of the polar bear, and also was the first person to identify and classify that beautiful scavenger, the ivory gull.

They had experienced poor weather in the North Sea on the outward journey, spending time at anchor in Robin Hood's Bay and Whitby Roads. On the return, near the Shetlands, the ships ran into an immensely ferocious storm: *Racehorse* and

Polar bear,
Thalarctos
maritimus.

Carcass were separated, and Equiano's account describes how the waves crashed over the ship sweeping everything moveable on deck into the sea – including the boats and 'many curious things of different kinds' which had been collected during the voyage. The storm followed them down the coast, and the two ships did not meet up again until they reached Orfordness. The voyage ended peacefully with the arrival at Deptford on 30 September 1773.

In the following July, *Adventure*, Furneaux, arrived at Spithead. On their voyage *Resolution* and *Adventure* had lost contact twice, the second time on 30 October 1773. On board *Adventure* was Omai, from Tahiti's near neighbour Ulaietea (Ra'iatea). Banks had encouraged another Ulaietian called Tupia to sail homewards in *Endeavour*, but he had died in Batavia. Bougainville had taken a Tahitian called Aoutourou back to France, which was not a success as he had venereal disease, and was troublesome during the voyage, making advances to the only woman on the ship, Baré, who had enlisted disguised as a boy. Once in Paris, Aoutourou sparked a moment of interest; but soon it was clear that he was not *un bon sauvage* ('a noble savage') but just a rather ordinary, rather stupid, rather uninteresting human being of which there were already so many in civilised Europe that there seemed little point in importing an extra one. Aoutourou was to be repatriated, but he died of smallpox on his way home.[5]

Omai was different. He was intelligent, personable and he had charm and a sense of humour. Banks took charge of him, guaranteeing all expenses incurred. Banks brought him into society (including an audience with the king), his manner being a mixture of someone introducing a friend, a scientist revealing a new anthropological specimen, a romantic philosopher displaying a noble savage, and a fairground showman displaying a novelty.

Cook arrived at Spithead in a rather battered *Resolution*, on 30 July 1775, after more than three years away. He had shown that there was no *Terra Australis* flowing with milk and honey; if there was a polar land mass (and Cook thought there probably was) it was a terrain of barren ice which would generate no trading profit. There had been much surveying and discovering new islands. There had also been much botanising by Reinhold and Johann Forster, the father and son replacements for Banks and Solander, and Cook took a pragmatic interest in the fine tall trees in New Caledonia (*Araucaria columnaris*, Cook pine) and on Norfolk Island (*Auracaria heterophylla*, Norfolk Island pine) which he thought – erroneously – would make fine masts and spars.

There was also a lengthy stay at Tahiti; evidence of cannibalism there damaged the idea of the noble savage, and was later to encourage waves of missionaries. Cook had discovered South Georgia, which he named the 'Isle of Georgia'. *Resolution* also stayed briefly at St Helena where Cook met John Scottowe, son of Thomas of Great Ayton.

Norfolk Island
pine.

After Cook had reported to the Admiralty he went home. He requested a post at Greenwich Hospital, conditional upon his being released if a suitable active opportunity arose. He was nearly 47.

From home, Cook wrote letters to John Walker at Whitby.

Meanwhile, Banks was taking Omai to Yorkshire to meet Constantine Phipps at York, and then they were to travel on to Mulgrave Castle, near Whitby, the ancestral home of the Phippses. Accompanying them was Constantine's brother Augustus, George Colman (owner of Covent Garden Opera House) and his son, also George, who was 12 at the time and wrote his account of the voyage some decades later. In it he records that they 'never saw a tree with an unusual branch, or a strange weed, or anything singular in the vegetable world, but … out jump'd Sir Joseph … [and plants] which would have not sold for a farthing in Covent Garden Market, were pull'd up by the roots, and stow'd carefully in the coach, as rarities'.

They spent time on Scarborough beach. Young George, who had only seen sea the day before, was about to take his first tentative dip from a bathing machine when Omai indicated that if George climbed onto his back he would carry him out to sea. With the unthinking enthusiasm of youth, George agreed. Omai walked out with the boy on his back until the water reached his chin, and then he swam out some distance, much to George's increasing fear, but they both returned safely to shore.

Greenwich, 1796, showing the Royal Hospital for Seamen.

The fashionable resort of Scarborough, c.1784, with bathing machines.

There had always been some rivalry between Scarborough and Whitby. Scarborough was *the* fashionable spa resort on the East Coast, but Whitby exceeded Scarborough as a shipowning and shipbuilding port. William Coulson had moved to Whitby to begin his shipbuilding business by renting a Dock Company shipyard, and so did the brothers George and Nathaniel Langbourn. The Langbourns were certainly based on a Dock Company shipyard in 1764 when they launched *Henrietta* for Nicholas Piper of Scarborough, and were probably still there in 1774 when they built the 295-ton *Diligence* for William Herbert of Scarborough.

Diligence sailed on her maiden voyage, with William Herbert as master, to Memel (Klaipėda), returning to Hull with fir timber, lathwood, five large masts, and undressed flax.[6] Her next port of call was Newcastle, before sailing to the Baltic, passing Elsineur on the return in November. In 1775, she sailed from Hull to the Baltic, returning to London. This would suggest that either Herbert was dealing with London timber merchants, such as the Sheppards, or was fulfilling a contract with the navy.

The Admiralty was planning a new voyage ostensibly to return Omai, but the big intention was to aim at discovering the North-West Passage by starting in the Pacific, offering a bounty of £20,000 (*c.* £30 million) for discovering such a trade route.

It looked as if James Cook had retired from such perilous travels, and was going to settle down to family life as a husband and father with a comfortable job at Greenwich Hospital. But in January 1776 he put himself forward as a candidate for leading this voyage, and was accepted. *Resolution* was chosen for this next voyage, and she was taken in for repairs which, sadly, Cook did not supervise. *Adventure* could not accompany her as she was employed elsewhere, so the Navy Board let it be known that they wished to purchase a ship.

In December 1775, Francis Easterby submitted his ship *Minerva*, built at Whitby in 1773, which was assessed on 22 December at Deptford in the presence of Captain Cook.[7]

The surveyors concluded that they were 'of the Opinion with Captain Cook who was on the Survey, [that] she appears to be a fit Ship for the Service in remote parts with the following alterations, as he proposes …' The estimate for these alterations was for £580 (*c.* £1 million). But clearly *Minerva* was not perfect, as further ships were assessed.

A fortnight later, *Diligence* was submitted, and surveyed by the Navy Board along with a similar ship, *Priscilla*, built in North Shields. The report was sent on 5 January 1776:

In Obedience to your Warrant of the 2nd & 3rd inst we have (with Captain Cook) Surveyed the Brig *Diligence*, to accompany the *Resolution* Sloop to

Assessment of *Minerva*. (TNA ADM 106/3318)

remote parts, and have inspected in the best manner we could the *Priscilla* Brig, which has most of her Loading of Coals onboard; and send you an estimate of the alterations & fitting for them for the intended Service also the Value of their Hulls.

Diligence was larger and longer but older. *Diligence* was 298.85 tons and *Priscilla* computed as 280 tons. Both were 'Bottom Single, full built, very roomly'. Indeed both were very similar, including their estimates for repairs (both £550, cheaper than *Minerva*). *Priscilla*'s concluding evaluation was, 'in our opinion, she appears a fit Ship for the Service'; that of *Diligence* was similar, but with a significant difference: 'we are of opinion, with Captain Cook who was on the Survey, that she appears a fit Ship for the Service'. Which is to say, there was nothing much between them – except that Cook wanted *Diligence*, possibly because he trusted Whitby ships. Cook got *Diligence*, which was renamed *Discovery*.

There was still much to do; as is shown by a letter from Deptford Yard to the Navy Board a few days later: 'We pray leave to Acquaint you that We have Breemd the Bottom of the *Diligence* in the Single Dock, & are in hand trying and Caulking the same.' They also wished to have 'directions relating to fitting her for remote parts', particularly 'whether she is to be Sheath'd & the same fill'd, & to have a Capstan … & whether she is to remain a Brigg or made a Ship'. It seems that these questions were prompted by the fact that 'Captain Cook wishes to have her fitted similar to the *Resolution*'.

On 7 October 1776, under the heading 'Wear & Tear', Deptford Yard tabulated figures for the amount spent on repairs and replacements of all vessels owned by the Admiralty from the beginning of the year to the end of September.

The figures (in pounds) for the sloops *Resolution* and *Discovery* are tabulated below. The latter had to have many changes; but there was surprisingly little spent, especially for 'Hull, Masts and Yards' on the larger ship, *Resolution*, a money-saving decision that was to have dire consequences:

Ship names	Hull, masts & yards			Furniture & stores			Grand total
	Materials	Workmanship	Total	Materials	Workmanship	Total	
Resolution	457.11.3	346.16.0	801.7.3	2453.16.11	6.18.10	2442.14.11	3244.2.2
Discovery	1519.14.10	902.2.10	2427.17.8	3138.14.10	33.6.1	3172.0.11	5599.18.7

In March, Cook became a fellow of the Royal Society. James Boswell, who had expressed a desire to live in Tahiti for a few years to see 'what nature can do for man', was obviously fascinated by what he had heard about Cook's discoveries, though his ideas may have been influenced by Jean-Jacques Rousseau, whom he knew. Boswell had met Cook at a dinner hosted by the President of the Royal Society, and had dined with Cook, Solander and Banks shortly afterwards. Perhaps Boswell and Cook felt a common bond of Scottish ancestry; certainly Boswell took tea with Mr and Mrs James Cook at their home in Mile End on 22 April 1776.

Charles Clerke was appointed as commander of *Discovery*. He had sailed round the world with Byron in *Dolphin*, again as master's mate on *Endeavour* and again as second lieutenant on *Resolution*. Unfortunately, *Discovery*'s departure was delayed as Clerke was detained in Fleet Prison for a debt of his brother which he had underwritten. She caught up with *Resolution* in September at the Cape of Good Hope.

On July 1776, Cook had sailed from Plymouth in *Resolution* with John Gore as 1st lieutenant, William Bligh as sailing master, Omai, the rest of the crew and a great deal of livestock. King George had taken a scientific and agricultural interest in this voyage and had donated some useful domesticated animals to be given to the inhabitants of Otaheite or any other South Sea islands which had received his subjects with kindness and generosity. King George was not only a keen botanist he was also interested in stock breeding, especially of sheep, as was Banks. As landowners with extensive estates, this was not surprising; Britain's wealth was still heavily dependent on wool and cloth.

British wool could not be exported in its raw state, leading to a sizeable smuggling business (called 'owling'), but ironically the finest cloth which was

A farmer tends his small flock of sheep.

Herefordshire bull. The result of selective breeding.

exported relied upon the native wool being mixed with imported wool of a finer quality.

Banks was asked by the king to 'acquire' some Spanish merino sheep on his behalf, to help improve the British breeds.[8] Of course, selective breeding to improve desired qualities in animals and plants had been going on since prehistoric times, but was becoming more of a science, and horses, cows and sheep were being successfully genetically modified through systematic cross-breeding. The king's gifts of livestock were valuable presents, and a valuable investment for the future.

Cook added to the animals' number during *Resolution*'s stay at the Cape of Good Hope. This was in addition to the chickens, goats and pigs normally taken on long journeys to feed the crew. The result was something of a floating zoo with all the inconvenience, noise and smells; Cook himself likened it to Noah's Ark. The animals caused him serious problems with feeding and caring for them, and the crew cannot have been happy to have them all on board. In many ways, Cook was in a similar situation to that Bligh was to experience on his first breadfruit voyage in *Bounty*.

19

Freedom and *Adventure*

What we most insisted on was, to know the condition of New England, which appearing to be very independent as to their regard to Old England, or his Majesty, rich and strong as they now were, there were great debates in what style to write to them; for the condition of that Colony was such, that ... there was fear of their breaking from all dependence on this nation ... Some of the Council were for sending them a menacing letter, which those who better understood the peevish and touchy humour of that Colony, were utterly against.

(John Evelyn, *Diary*, 26 May 1671)

There were many in America who did not want independence, and many in Britain who sympathised with the American demand for representation and other freedoms that were seen as essential for civilised existence. Lord North had been Prime Minister since 1770, a Tory with the support of the king, and his administration's clumsy blundering exacerbated the situation from an insistence on change to a demand for independence. It can be said that it was largely the intransigence of the British government and of the king that managed to unify the thirteen separate colonies, each with their own agenda, into the inchoate United States.

From the beginning, the British government totally misread what was happening in America, at first believing that they were facing a localised bunch of unruly radicals based in Boston, and that a quick show of force and zero tolerance would suppress the troubles. A sizeable force, envisaged more as a policing exercise than as an invasion, was sent to occupy Boston. For this a number of transports had to be recruited.

In January 1775, the aged and infirm William Pitt tabled a motion in Parliament to withdraw troops from Boston, and to adopt a more comprehending and conciliating attitude towards America. The speech was one of his best:

Your vain declarations of the omnipotence of Parliament, and your imperious doctrines of the necessity of submission, will be found equally impotent to convince, or to enslave, your fellow-subjects in America … The spirit which now resists your taxation in America is … the same spirit which called all England on its legs, and by the Bill of Rights vindicated the English Constitution; the same spirit which established the great fundamental, essential maxim of your liberties – that no subject of England shall be taxed but by his own consent … But it is not repealing this Act of Parliament, it is not repealing a piece of parchment, that can restore America to our bosom; you must repeal her fears and her resentments; and you may then hope for her love and gratitude … I trust it is obvious to your lordships, that all attempts to impose servitude on such men, to establish despotism over such a mighty nation, must be vain, must be fatal. We shall be forced ultimately to retract …[1]

Pitt's motion was voted out. But there were many in Britain who agreed with Pitt, seeing the American's struggle for liberty as the same process which England had experienced between 1642 and 1688, and felt that Britain should nurture this desire for freedom rather than trying to destroy it by force.

The playwright and would-be politician, Richard Brinsley Sheridan, wrote a suitable prayer which was probably treasonable, but for the rather unconvincing last sentence:

O God most gracious, grant we most humbly beseech Thee, success and freedom, and all the glorious consequences of that freedom, to our fellow-men, our brethren in America. And may that people … be able, through all future ages, to afford an asylum to wretches … oppressed by the hand of power, and trodden in the dust by pride and insolence of unfeeling Despots … We pray also, O God, for the protection of our King and his family, and all his faithful subjects.[2]

But many supported the government's view that the American colonists were no longer 'faithful subjects' and needed to be taught a lesson, as the Highland Scots had been after Culloden. Trouble festered and escalated in America with the clash in April 1775 at Lexington and Concord, where the first British soldiers were shot.

More troops and ships were sent, one of the latter was *Adventure*, Furneaux's ship in Cook's second voyage but now a storeship commanded by Lieutenant Hallum. She sailed from the Nore on 16 June 1775, arriving at Halifax, Nova Scotia, on 28 August. Among the crew of (ideally) forty men, two had sailed on the ship previously under Furneaux: William Crispin, a carpenter's mate before, was now the sole carpenter, and the 32-year-old James Gibbs, previously boatswain's mate and now the boatswain. A third member of *Adventure*'s previous crew was Henry Pryor who had *Run* on 26 March 1775 at Deptford, several weeks before the ship sailed.

Halifax was chosen as a base for reinforcing the garrison: troops had been transported from there to Boston where they participated in the first real battle of

The Concord River,
from the North Bridge.

the war at Bunker Hill on 17 June 1775. The British won the battle, but it was a victory that smelled very like a defeat.

Typical of the mood of many was John Freeth's poem 'Bunker's Hill, or The Soldier's Lamentation':

> I am a jolly soldier,
>   Enlisted years ago,
> To serve my king and country,
>   Against the common foe.
> But when across th'Atlantic
>   My orders were to go,
> I griev'd to think that English hearts,
>   Should draw their swords on those
> Who fought and conquer'd by their side,
>   When Frenchmen were their foes.

War was officially declared in August 1775, and a large force in excess of 25,000 troops was assembled from all over British military outposts, together with her German allies, in an unparalleled logistical organisation of military and naval forces. In addition to the men, all their equipment, ammunition, horses and food had to be taken with them across the Atlantic. Large numbers of transports were needed, and Whitby shipowners were quick to make offers.

Between 23 December 1775 and 17 February 1776, sixty-one transports were passed as suitable by Deptford Yard on behalf of the Navy Board. The following chart shows the numbers that were built in each location. Although this is only for Deptford Yard, it does show the significance of Whitby-built ships, and the flourishing shipbuilding trade in America.

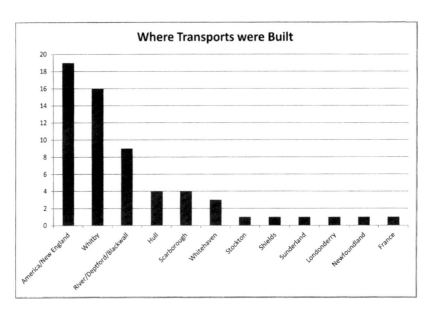

Where ships hired at Deptford for transports were built.

One of the many Whitby ships hired as transports 'for carrying troops to Boston' was the 319-ton *Jupiter* launched at Whitby in 1773, owned by Joseph Gibson and commanded by his son Francis, master mariner and poet. Francis had previously taken *Jupiter* to Norway and the Baltic, but declined being involved in a war he strongly believed was unjust. Additionally, he had recently married Alice, daughter of Thomas Fishburn (whose firm had built *Earl of Pembroke/Endeavour*), and did not wish to be away from home for too long. His father appointed William Richardson as master of *Jupiter* which was fitted with 159 beds and took troops to Boston; then she was commandeered to fetch cattle and hay from Nova Scotia and to return to Boston. She was only about 25 miles from Boston when the ship was struck by lightning. The transport agent Lieutenant James Dickinson was on board and described the event in a letter to his wife in Scarborough:[3]

> When the Lightning struck the Ship – And God preserv'd us, It rent the mainmast in pieces, split the Pumps Kill'd one seaman, Burnt a second most Dangerously [i.e. he was in risk of losing his life] and two Boys slightly – but to add to our misfortune it communicated [spread] to the Hay and the Ship was in Flames in less than five Minnets.

Although the crew tried their best to put out the flames, it was hopeless, and they had to abandon the ship, which was totally destroyed. Joseph Gibson sought to

Letter from some Whitby shipowners to the Lords of the Admiralty, 31 May 1776. (TNA ADM 49/125)

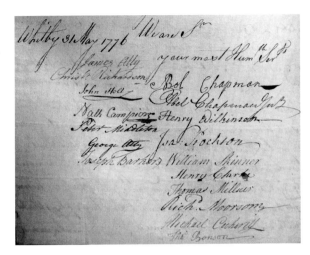

claim compensation, as *Jupiter* was on the king's business and as the conflagration was due to 'the dangerous Loading' of hay which Richardson had been 'obliged to take in' though the charter party only specified transport of troops. Gibson's assertion was that he should be paid what would have been be due had she been 'destroyed by the enemy'. He acknowledged that William Richardson was 'not yet quite of Age' but he was 'so promising that before he sail'd, Sir Hugh Palliser took particular note of him'. He also received a supportive letter from some of the most important shipowners of Whitby, including Christopher Richardson the father of William; Abel Chapman (in his 80s), erstwhile brother-in-law of John Walker; Henry Wilkinson, brother of John who was owner of *Mary/Maria*; John Holt and Joseph Barker, shipbuilders (and part owners of the Dock Company); and Thomas Millner, first owner of the *Earl of Pembroke*, later *Endeavour*.

And that very ship, Cook's *Endeavour*, had also been submitted as a potential transport. She was owned by James Mather, something of a second-hand ship dealer, who clearly had spent not much money on having her repaired since he bought her:

Deptford Yard to the Navy Board 6 Dec 1775

Honble Sirs

In obedience to your directions of Yesterday's date, We have Surveyed the *Endeavour* Bark, tendered for the Transport Service, and find her to be the same that was lately Sold from Woolwich Ordry [Ordinary], the Officers of which Yard having we apprehend, prior to her being Sold, reported her Defects such as to render her unfit for His Majesty's Service, and it appearing to us, that no Material Repair has been given her since, We cannot under those circumstances recommend her as a proper Ship, to be employed as a Transport.

Mather then changed the ship's name from *Endeavour* to *Lord Sandwich*, after the 1st Lord of the Admiralty, thinking that perhaps an influential name would help. It didn't. Deptford Yard's comment on 28 December was:

> *Lord Sandwich 2d*: unfit for Service. She was Sold out Service Called *Endeavour* Bark refused before.[4]

She was referred to as *Lord Sandwich 2nd* because another ship named *Lord Sandwich*, built at Shields, master William Deverson, 317.89 tons, had previously been accepted as a transport.*

Mather then decided that he would have to give her a serious overhaul with thorough repairs; duly noted by Deptford Yard:

> *Lord Sandwich*, Age uncertain, she is now under Repair, has many Timbers Rotten, and Mr Watson the Builder believes she was built somewhere to the Northwards, she appears to be Old and defective.

It is of interest that Watson was able to identify the style of shipbuilding practised in the north-east merchant shipyards. *Lord Sandwich/Endeavour* was, in fact, 11 years old, which was not a great age for a ship which was regularly serviced. However, her dramatic past had clearly aged her beyond her years. Watson must have done a good job, as when Mather again submitted her (with her age rounded down) she was accepted. She was entered into service, as transport *Lord Sandwich 2* on 7 February 1776.[5]

One of the many ships that the Navy Board accepted as transports was the 3-year-old, 359-ton Whitby-built *Marquis of Rockingham*, Thomas Hammond, which was built to replace the vessel of the same name which became Cook's *Adventure*. Commissioning Whitby-built ships and then selling or renting them to the government seems to have been a regular business of the Hammond family. On 10 October 1777, Thomas Hammond submitted the 385-ton, 2-month-old, Whitby-built *Countess of Scarborough* as a transport. She was passed as fit for a transport but was soon upgraded to an armed ship with twenty 6-pounder cannon and eight swivel guns. She helped in the capture of two French privateers, and on 23 September 1779 took part in the famous Battle of Flamborough Head when *Serapis* and *Countess of Scarborough*, which were convoying forty-one merchantmen, were attacked by John Paul Jones in *Bonhomme Richard* with three other French ships. The ensuing battle lasted over two hours, finally *Serapis* and

---

* Much of the narrative of *Lord Sandwich 2* in this book is dependent upon the research of Dr D.K. Abbass.

The bark *Lord Sandwich* assessed and accepted as a transport. (TNA ADM 106/3402)

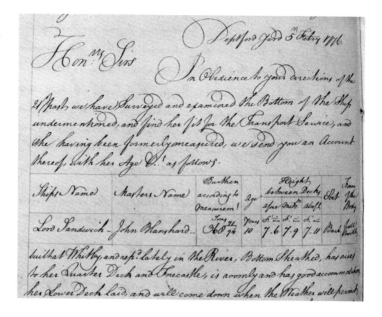

Countess of Scarborough surrendered, but all the merchant ships had been able to sail safely into harbour.

Weatherill mentioned the launch of the 650-ton ship *Yorkshire* at Whitby on 15 August 1776, quoting 'she is the largest ship yet built at that port, and is the property of Mr Hammond, of Hull, being the seventh of large tonnage this gentleman had had built at Whitby within the last few years'.[6] In August 1778, *Admiral Keppel*, a new armed ship commanded by Captain Thomas Hammond, was launched in Whitby. She sailed to London to be in the service of the government.

It seems that Mather was in a similar line of business as Hammond. While his ship *Lord Sandwich* was being guided through her qualifying stages by John Blanchard, James Mather was submitting another ship for a transport, the 361-ton American-built *Admiral Shuldam*, which was approved on 23 October 1775.

Some seventy-four Whitby-built ships were submitted for transports or armed ships and assessed at Deptford Yard between March 1773 and December 1777. They averaged 327 tons. Whitby shipbuilders were also providing for the town's own merchant fleet as well as selling to other ports. For example, eight Whitby ships built in 1775, averaging 318 tons, had been assessed at Deptford Yard and accepted as transports by the end of 1777. If Lionel Charlton is correct, a ship of this size would take about six months to build, so four of them would have been on the blocks at any one time. At a conservative estimate, this would have been half the town's output, so a new vessel would have been launched every three weeks or so, from some eight or more shipyards, each launching two sizeable

Flamborough
Head, 1842.

ships per year. The *London Chronicle* recorded that on 26 February 1778 three
ships were launched at Whitby, the smallest of which was 350 tons, and that 'nine
capital ships' were 'on the stocks at the above port' all of which would be 'ready in
two to three months'. Add to that the mast-makers, sailmakers and boatbuilders
and Whitby's harbour would have been seething with nautical manufactures.

The armada which sailed to America in 1776 was intended to strike the decisive
blow to the American rebellion. It was composed of two armies: one, under
General William Howe, was to capture New York and possibly Pennsylvania
before moving up the Hudson River to join forces with the northern army led by
General Burgoyne, which would sail to Canada to relieve the American siege of
Québec, and then move south, down Lake Champlain, capture Fort Ticonderoda
and then to meet Howe's army at Albany. This pincer movement would surround
and contain the (allegedly) more rebellious colonies, and ensure a safe supply
line from Canada. In theory the plan was sound, but it underestimated the time
that would be required to assemble sufficient troops and supplies, and (fatally)
there was no overall commander of the operation and the generals involved were
(understandably) allowed considerable leeway.

The storeship *Adventure*, sailing master Richard Passmore, had moved from
Halifax to Boston, arriving on 1 October 1775. The function of a storeship
was to have on board a range of spare parts, anchors, masts, yards and capstan
heads – indeed anything a ship may require. Other ships, or their boats, would
come alongside when they were in need. *Adventure* stayed at Boston through a
frozen New England winter; on 29 November the 'people' (crew) were employed

'Clearing a Passage thro' the Ice for Boats to come on board'. Richard Passmore was taken ill and was invalided out on 15 January, accompanied by Henry Passmore, his indentured servant, to be replaced the next day by Mr John Lamb (with his servant, William Jones). The Battle of Bunker Hill had revealed that Boston was not defensible, and for some time the British had planned to evacuate the city but it was not logistically possible until the Navy Board could provide sufficient transport ships. These arrived at Boston on the last day of the year.

It was the role of a storeship to stay out of the action where she would be an encumbrance, but to be accessibly near to the action where she could be a lifesaver. So on 15 March 1776 *Adventure* was moored off Nantucket, keeping in touch with Boston via her boat which brought news of 'ye Imbarkation of all our Troops' on 18 March. The next day eighteen boat-borne marines were 'Rec'd [received] on board', and the fleet of fifty ships then sailed to Halifax, which was reached on 30 March. Although the British sought to present the abandonment of Boston as a strategic *reculer pour mieux sauter*, it was clear the British had been driven out – and the Bostonians celebrated it as a victory.

There seems to have been discipline problems aboard *Adventure*, as even some of the warrant officers were unreliable. On 19 September 1775, Captain Edward le Cras of HMS *Somerset* came aboard and 'Ordered the Boatsn [the boatswain James Gibbs] … to be Confin'd for illegal Practices tending to Mutiny'. He was released on 24 November on the order of Admiral Graves. What Gibbs had done is not stated, but more than two months of confinement suggests a very serious offence, news of which had reached the highest levels. The following year the captain's entry in his log for 5 June states 'Mr Wm Crispin was Dismissed from being Carpr of this ship & to serve in ye Carprs Crew.' The ship's muster has:

Boston. The site of Castle William, which the British destroyed when they abandoned Boston. Rebuilt as Fort Independence.

'Dismissed pr Sentence of a Court Martl & Discharged into ye Niger per Order of Admiral Shuldham.' It would be interesting to know more, especially as Gibbs and Crispin were the only two seamen who had previously sailed in *Adventure* during Cook's second voyage.

Admiral Shuldham was commander-in-chief of the east coast of America. On 11 June 1776, he gave the order for the fleet of ships and transports to sail for New York, which at that time was held by the Americans. *Adventure* was part of this massive fleet, Hallum recording that on 20 June there were '126 sail in sight', which included numerous transports.

Back in England, on 22 March, in accordance with the 'Act to prohibit all Trade and Intercourse with the several Colonies in North America' over 200 transports were issued with licences to sail to America, including *Lord Sandwich 1*, William Deverson, which went to Canada, and *Lord Sandwich 2*, John Blanchard, which sailed to New York.

The fleet of vessels bound for New York set sail from Portsmouth on 6 May 1776; it consisted of 100 vessels, sixty-eight of which were transports carrying some 20,000 troops. More than half of which were Hessians – and it was two Hessians who have left us first-hand accounts of the voyage: Albert Pfister and Johann Seume.[7] The Admiralty documents list the transports;[8] *Lord Sandwich 2* carried 206 men mainly of the Hessian du Corps regiment, but the master was William Author (Arthur) and not Blanchard. A similar change happened with *Eolus* whose master was listed as Thomas Millner for the licence on 22 March, but when it came to sailing into action the master was Anthony McFarlane. Blanchard and Millner were wise to stay at home; the Atlantic crossing was terrible, with violent storms which scattered the ships and delayed the voyage. The accommodation was inadequate, with the soldiers 'pressed and packed like sardines'. Not only was it impossible to sit up in the tiered bunks, but six men were allocated per bunk which could only hold four in any degree of comfort, 'the remaining two could only find room by pressing in'. Seume, who was a poet as well as a soldier, recorded how the soldiers managed this crowded bunk problem: they all lay on their left side and then, on a given word, they all turned over in unison onto their right side. Seume also criticised the food, complaining that the monotonous diet of bacon and peas was varied only by peas and bacon. The ship's biscuits, 'often full of worms', had allegedly been captured from the French during the Seven Years War. Pfister was less Eeyorish in his descriptions, admiring 'the ever agile activity of the sailors' who, when storms had caused havoc among the sails and the rigging, 'were always ready with instant relief and reparation', remarking that, 'As a spider that moves about … in her web, so the sailors were going up and down the rope ladders of the masts and through the rigging, hanging on only at their feet, tieing the tackle and binding the sails.' Pfister recounted how the delay caused by the storms had resulted in the

Ships near New York, des Barres, 1777. (Sourced from the archives of the UK Hydrographic Office (UKHO))

supplies running low, and scurvy breaking out, and how rats, the sailors' constant shipmates, had nibbled through the cartridges.

Seume's conclusion was that, although 'many of the sufferings undergone by us on this voyage were no doubt unavoidable, nevertheless many of the things we endured were the result of an intentional deficiency of care taking and of a great greed'.

On 4 July 1776, representatives of the thirteen diverse colonies finally agreed on full independence and a form of words in which to proclaim it; the Declaration of Independence was signed, and America became a new country. The document owed much to the English Bill of Rights and to John Locke, with 'unalienable rights' of 'Life and Liberty', the addition of 'the pursuit of Happiness' instead of 'Property' revealing a change of thought over the century, exemplified in Bentham's *Utilitarianism* published a few years later. Perhaps the exclusion of 'Property' revealed a touch of reality in a country where the indigenous people were being progressively robbed of their property and the growing number of slaves *were* property. The document claimed that independence, when it becomes 'necessary', is an entitlement in accordance with 'the Laws of Nature and Nature's God'. The phrase would have had meaning to a range of religions and denominations, and reads as a deistic linking of God with the Laws of Science, but it is not clear exactly which laws were being invoked.

Most of the document is evidence of the political crimes of King George and his government which were listed as legitimising American independence; one of these was the support given by Britain to 'the inhabitants of our frontiers,

Rattus rattus; the black, or ship, rat.

the merciless Indian Savages, whose known rule of welfare is an undistinguished destruction of all ages, sexes and conditions'. Whatever the merits and short-comings of the Declaration of Independence, it did win the hearts and minds of the American people and provided a shared focus for their dreams and hopes for a free future.

On 4 July 1776, Hallum recorded in *Adventure*'s log that he had 'heard a Number of great Guns & small arms' and that 'our Troops landed on Staten Island'. *Adventure* was anchored off Staten Island to be available to receive and supply. George Washington reached New York by 9 July, and had ordered the reading of the Declaration of Independence, which was barely audible above the noise of a mob destroying the massive statue of George III, which was later melted down to make bullets.

On 21 July, Hallum again had cause to confine James Gibbs, the untrustworthy boatswain, this time for 'Breaking open one of ye Peoples Chests'.

Hotham's fleet had anchored off Halifax on 7 July just long enough for the ships to reassemble, before moving on to the next rendezvous at the Sandy Hook lighthouse; but their problems were not over. The sailors of the Whitby-owned transport *Spring*, William Dunn, mutinied on 8 July and they had to be replaced. And there were collisions among the crowded transports, one of which was between *Lord Sandwich 2* and *Hartley*.

Hotham's fleet arrived at Sandy Hook lighthouse on 12 August, but unfortunately many of the troops were not battle fit, which further delayed Howe's attack on New York. At about the same time, another fleet arrived. Sir Peter Parker was the fleet commodore, ferrying the troops under Generals Clinton and Cornwallis, who had endured the failure of the attempt to capture Charleston. The fleet consisted of four men-of-war, a fireship, a hospital ship, and the bomb *Carcass** accompanying 'a large Fleet of Transports'. One of the war ships, which Hallum recorded in his log on 15 August, was 'his Majesty's

Sandy Hook Lighthouse, des Barres, 1777. (UKHO)

ship *syron*'. This was the twenty-eight-gun frigate *Siren*, launched only two years previously, with Tobias Furneaux as captain. Furneaux, the first man who is known to have circumnavigated the world in both directions, was second lieutenant with Wallis in *Dolphin* (the first ship known to have circumnavigated the world twice), and then commander of *Adventure* on Cook's second voyage. Although there were numerous ship's assembling at New York at that time (finally some 300), if Hallum saw *Siren*, then it seems likely that Furneaux might have noticed his old ship *Adventure*.★★

So, on 15 August 1776, among the ships mustered at Sandy Hook was *Adventure* (which had sailed with *Resolution* on Cook's second voyage), Tobias Furneaux (who had commanded *Adventure* on that voyage) and *Lord Sandwich 2* (formerly Cook's *Endeavour*).

Howe's campaign was already behind schedule, so the main attack began within a week of the new troops arriving. In spite of 'Thunder, lightning and heavy rain', the British troops landed unopposed on the south of Long Island, outflanking the American defences. The colonists retreated, burning buildings as they went, defending themselves as best they could in an atmosphere of confused panic. Many prisoners were taken. On 30 August, Hallum recorded 'our Troops in sole possession of Long Island'.

★ The same ship that had sailed in the Arctic voyage of Constantine Phipps (recently 2nd Baron Mulgrave, since his father's death in 1775).

★★ On 6 November 1777, *Siren*, leading a convoy of transports on a wooding expedition on Long Island, 'by some strange Mismanagement' ran aground (one of a number of ships which find themselves in situations which render their names ironic), near Judith Point, Rhode Island, together with *Sisters*, William Trattles, of Whitby. The crew of *Sisters* were rescued; but 136 men from *Siren* were captured, though later released in an exchange of prisoners. Furneaux was exonerated of any blame.

General Howe was cautious, not wishing to capitalise on this success until the final troops and equipment arrived, as the Americans were in a strong defensive position in New York itself, on the southern tip of Manhattan Island. In the meantime, Hallum frequently reported there was much 'Cannonading up ye Harbour'. On 21 September, a disastrous fire broke out which rapidly spread among the wooden houses; Hallum, from his vantage point of *Adventure*, now anchored at Red Hook, tersely but movingly wrote that he 'saw New York on Fire'. By the time it was finally subdued, the conflagration had rendered some five hundred buildings into a large tract of smouldering cinders.

The rumour that Washington was to abandon New York emboldened Howe into action and there was a successful landing of troops in Kipps Bay on Manhattan Island north of New York; there the two opposing forces remained behind their respective defensive barriers, as week followed week, and the hoped-for reinforcements had not arrived. The Navy Board realised that it had sent many transports to America, and few had yet returned. It desperately needed more, so in June of 1776 it had raised the rate of payment for transports from 11*s* per ton per month to 12*s* 6*d* (the pre-war rate was 9*s*), which increased the number of owners tendering their ships.

Unable to wait longer, Howe inaugurated the next step of his plodding campaign, landing his army at Pell's Point [Pelham], marching them through La Rochelle [New Rochelle] to White Plains in the hope of destroying Washington's base camp and cutting his supply line and escape route. But Washington had had time to plan and prepare and had built a number of entrenchments with barrages of heavy guns. The resulting battle was fierce and bloody, the continuous bombardment of artillery making the ground tremble, flattening the landscape, and scattering the earth with the wounded and the mangled dead. The soldiers under Howe's command made steady progress through this smoke-filled nightmare.

The expected reinforcements arrived on 19 October in the form of 'several Transports with Hessian Troops'. Hearing of their arrival, Howe delayed delivering the final *coup de grâce* to Washington's depleted army until the Hessians could join him. Howe had waited too often and too long; during this next hiatus Washington's army silently slipped away.

In November 1776, Sir Peter Parker, who had fought at Charleston and had helped take New York, was deputed to capture Newport, Rhode Island, as it was considered that if it were to be occupied by enemy forces it would put New York in danger. He took most of Hotham's fleet with him, including *Lord Sandwich 2* which was carrying troops from the Hessian Du Corps Regiment (the same forces, and possibly many of the same men, whom she had carried from Portsmouth to New York). We know that *Lord Sandwich 2* 'carried one flat boat, and her identifying mark was a blue pennant with a white ball flying from the main mast'.[9] Newport was taken with little difficulty, and *Lord Sandwich 2*

Chart of New York, based on surveys by Lieutenants Knight and Hunter. (Published by des Barres, 1779. UKHO)

remained there as part of the occupying power, serving as a transport and later as a prison ship.[10] She was to stay there for a long time.

Despite the fact that everything was late, the British plans (apart from the failure to take Charlestown) had largely been fulfilled. New York had been taken, Rhode Island seemed secure, and all appeared to be going well for Burgoyne's northern army as well.

After sailing to Cuxhaven to collect troops from Brunswick and Hesse-Cassel, the fleet of ships and transports carrying Burgoyne's northern army had left Spithead on 4 April 1776 bound for Canada. After a rough crossing they entered the St Lawrence River on 20 May, and a few days later were told that Sir Guy Carleton, the Governor-General, had already raised the siege of Québec and driven the Americans back over the border. Burgoyne consolidated the defence of Canada, and prepared for the planned offensive in 1777.

Washington had retreated from New York with a small army, haemorrhaging deserters, through New Jersey, across the Delaware into Pennsylvania. Many (on both sides) thought the war was almost over, and that when the hibernating armies emerged for the following year's battle season the finishing touches would seal the deal.

But it was not to be. Washington's Continental Army emerged prematurely on Christmas Day, crossed the Delaware in freezing weather, and the following day marched into Trenton. The Hessian garrison, totally surprised and possibly only partially sober, were outfought, and surrendered. The national pride of the Americans was aroused. It was bad enough being occupied by the arrogant English, whose sole motive was to quench their right to live free, but for them to bring over foreign German hireling troops was intolerable. The local militia was stirred into action and, using the guerrilla tactics familiar to all liberation movements, they harried the army led by Cornwallis which was sent to relieve Trenton. When Cornwallis arrived at Trenton his army attacked three times and was thrice repulsed, though by then it looked as if the Americans could not withstand another assault. When the British attacked again, the American army was not there. In a typical Washington strategic move he had sidestepped Cornwallis and attacked Princeton which he captured in a near-run victory. It was enough, and a chastened British army abandoned New Jersey while Washington's army was inundated with new recruits.

The Americans then launched one of their most effective weapons – Benjamin Franklin, Fellow of the Royal Society and the 'most urbane of Americans', who reached Paris in December 'to use his charm and scientific progress to lure Louis XV and his ministers into the war.'[11] He was very successful, and the French sent armaments to America, which included the latest refinement in gunpowder manufacture, the brainchild of the chemist Antoine Lavoisier, who was also a Fellow of the Royal Society.

The nose of the British lion had been seriously tweaked, and it stirred angrily in the new year.

Burgoyne's army of the north, an agglomeration of British, Germans, Native Americans and Loyalists, moved into America and, struggling through difficult and unfamiliar terrain in unremitting rain, reached the north of Lake Champlain on 20 June 1777. They sailed down the length of the lake, disembarking within sight of the fort of Ticonderoga, which dominated the passage from Lake Champlain to Lake George and thus the route from Montreal to New York. The fort was impressively defended, but was overlooked by Sugarloaf Hill, an impossibly difficult, steep and unwelcoming natural feature. But if an artillery battery could be established on its summit by the British then Ticonderoga Fort would be helplessly vulnerable. This is exactly what happened. The American garrison slipped away on 4 July. When Burgoyne discovered this he left a body of

Plaque commemorating the defeat of the American army under General Montgomery by the British defenders of Québec under General Carleton.

men to secure the fort while the rest of the army pursued the Americans, killing many and taking several prisoners.

In September 1776, the *Adventure*'s sailing master, John Lamb, had been discharged, taking his servant, John Monday, with him. Lamb was not immediately replaced, as *Adventure*, moored in New York harbour, was going nowhere. She continued with her work throughout the acerbic winter, mainly taking supplies on board. The arrival on board of Mr James Colnett, with his servant William Hester, as *Adventure*'s new sailing master, was a sign that preparations were getting under way for the spring offensive.★

A fleet of transports with troops arrived from victory at Rhode Island. *Adventure* received anchors, stocks, cables and sails from the aptly named 382-ton storeship *Elephant*. Cannonballs, grapeshot and other 'ordinance stores' were loaded. The

---

★ Colnett had sailed as a midshipman in *Resolution* for Cook's second voyage, so he must have known *Adventure* well, at least by sight.

ship's cutter was sent up East River for wood. Four frigates and more transports sailed in. *Adventure* was scrubbed, hogged, breamed and payed.*

The 24-year-old Liverpudlian able seaman Peter Foster who had joined the crew of *Adventure* at Boston in December 1775 was clearly finding it all too much: he received twelve lashes for being drunk on 17 March, a further dozen two months later for 'drunkenness and neglect of duty' and a few weeks later another twelve lashes for 'absenting himself without leave' (a catch-all phrase which covered a range of faults, from spending too long in a dockside pub or brothel to making an unsuccessful attempt to desert).

Another serial offender was the 27-year-old Thomas Cousins from Nottingham who had been punished for 'Neglect of Duty' in January of 1776, 'Mutinous behaviour to the officer on watch' (June 1777) and 'disobeying orders' (August 1777), with the statutory twelve lashes each time.

Water was taken aboard, and on 21 July *Adventure* sailed with the fleet under command of General Howe which was commissioned to take Philadelphia, the capital city of the new republic. It was believed this would sap the Americans' morale and possibly end the war. The Americans had anticipated such an attack and, according to the British press, in late 1775 the inhabitants of Philadelphia had been 'put to a final Test of their Principles, having been compelled either to enter themselves in the military Roll, and attend military Exercises or to quit the Province'.[12] If true, it would have been a difficult decision for the city's numerous Quakers.

Instead of taking the shortest route, up the Delaware, the British fleet sailed all the way down the coast, into Chesapeake Bay and up to its northern shore near Elk River. This was possibly a more strategic passage as Howe wished to bring Washington to a battle, but it was certainly a longer one which took his troops further from the northern army of General Burgoyne, which was still anticipating a rendezvous with Howe at Albany.

The journey was unpleasant; high winds and lightening impeded and damaged many ships. Benjamin Franklin had invented a 'lightning rod' some twenty-five years previously, but it would be well into the next century before effective lightning conductors were routinely used on ships. The foul weather caused delays which meant the provisions were in short supply. Many horses had to be thrown overboard through being damaged by the fury of the sea or starved with the shortage of hay.

Eventually, on 25 August 1777, *Adventure* and the rest of the fleet 'anchored at ye head of Chesapeak Bay'. The soldiers were landed as speedily as possible, and they were no doubt glad to be on dry land. Hallum helped the disembarkation by contributing *Adventure*'s large cutter.

---

* Hogging meant scrubbing the underwater parts of a ship with a flat bristly brush. Breaming was heating the side of a ship with a little fire to soften the pitch, which enabled any embedded accretions to be more easily removed. Paying was caulking with pitch or tar.

General Howe's army met Washington's army, which was larger and drawn up on advantageous ground, in good order at Brandywine. The ensuing battle was furious, but ended in a decisive victory for the British. There were other subsequent clashes, but Washington withdrew, leaving Howe's army to march unopposed and with the band playing into Philadelphia from which the members of the American Congress had made a speedy departure.

While this was going on, *Adventure* was at anchor with the other ships. On 2 and 3 September, seventeen 'Negroe Refugees' came aboard *Adventure* and 'Claim'd Protection'.

It was not unusual for African-Americans to seek to escape slavery by enlisting in English ships, and the 20-year-old John Whitby, a 'negro man' who was buried at Whitby on 12 June 1776, was probably just such a one. It was generally believed that the Mansfield case of 1772 had freed all slaves in England, whereas it had only made it illegal for a master to 'take a slave by force to be sold abroad because he deserted from his service, or for any other reason whatever', which is exactly what had happened to Olaudah Equiano after serving in the navy during the Seven Years War.

After Howe had taken Philadelphia, it became imperative that the Delaware River was made safe to ensure provisions could be brought directly into the city. The fleet embarked troops and sailed down Chesapeake Bay and out into the Atlantic. This journey back was also marred by terrible weather with 'Hard Gales' which scattered the ships. On 30 September, Hallum recorded that at noon the sailors had been set to the pumps as *Adventure* had taken in a foot of water in the previous four hours; the following day the log entry was 'a high sea ye Ship labouring very much & Ship'd a great Deal of Water'. Delaware Bay was finally reached, and the task of controlling the river began. It was not easy; there was much 'smart cannonading' and HMS *Augusta* and *Merlin*, sloop of war, were both lost when they beached, and were set alight and exploded, their crews having managed to escape.

The 'Negroe Refugees' were put off the *Adventure* at 'Schuylkill', presumably where the Schuylkill River joins the Delaware, which was possibly safe for the time being; but perhaps this was not what they had hoped for.

Once *Adventure* had reached Philadelphia, Lieutenant John Hallum was granted leave to go home for benefit of his health, and was replaced as commander by Hugh Tonken. Life was difficult over-wintering in Philadelphia; the crew spent time clearing snow from the decks and keeping busy with useful time-consuming tasks such as making plats (plaits), gaskets and grummetts.* The American resistance fighters were still active, setting fire to some of the British foraging boats (Tonken:

---

* A gasket was a plaited cord used to tie up (furl) the sails to the yards. A grummett (grommet) was a loop of triple rope that attached a sail to the mast, enabling it to be raised and lowered (Information from Gill).

'Sent our people with buckets'.); it wasn't until 15 March that Tonken reported 'Flag of Truce from ye Rebells'. Three members of the crew were punished in less than three weeks in freezing January: one being John Proctor, a seasoned sailor of 58 years, for 'absence without leave'; he was never to see his home town of Newcastle again. There were other casualties in this mortally cruel spring: John Oddy (30) from Chelmsford was taken to Philadelphia hospital where he died in April 1778; less than three weeks later James Collins (24) from Topsham in Devon, died on board ship, and a fortnight later Robert Steell (42, a Cornishman) died in the Philadelphia hospital.

By that time, things had changed. News had come that Burgoyne who, buoyed up by his capture of Fort Ticonderoga and his initial success in pursuing its fleeing garrison, had plunged recklessly south through difficult terrain, stretching his supply lines beyond breaking point, possibly still fantastically imagining that General Howe, or General Clinton from New York, would be waiting for him at Albany. Instead, the American General Gates was waiting for him with a larger army. After some fierce fighting, Burgoyne's proud army of the north, reduced to half its initial size and weak with hunger and exhaustion, surrendered at Saratoga on 17 October 1777.

20

Lord Sandwich and *Leviathan*

If old England is not by this lesson taught humility then she is an obstinate old slut, bent on her ruin.

(General Horatio Gates, in a letter to his wife, 1777)[1]

Saratoga changed the war. France, which had been waiting since 1763 to avenge its humiliation suffered in the Seven Years War, had been supplying the American Revolutionary army with weapons and ammunition, but had stopped short of boots on the ground in case the British won. The new American Republic had now shown to the world that it had a sufficiently large, well-trained, well-disciplined, and well-led army which could defeat the British. France and America signed treaties of Commerce and Alliance on 6 February 1778. War was declared between France and Britain on 17 June. The French, with one of the most rigidly autocratic political systems in Europe, had no ideological reason for supporting a republican revolution. Their motives were anti-British more than pro-American, though they realised that there would be benefits in stealing the American trade from Britain. For the Americans, the alliance with France was crucial, and would enable them to win their independence. They appropriately celebrated, as was made clear in the General Orders from the Heads Quarters, Camp, Valley Forge, 5 May,[2] giving instructions for the following day's celebrations:

It having pleased the Almighty Ruler of the Universe propitiously to defend the Cause of the United American States, and finally by raising us up a powerful Friend among the Princes of the Earth, to establish our Liberty and Independence upon a lasting Foundation, it becomes us to set apart a Day for gratefully acknowledging the Divine Goodness, and celebrating the important Event which we owe to his Divine Interposition.

The celebrations involved:

> a Discharge of thirteen cannon [for the thirteen states], when the thirteenth has
> fired, a running Fire of Infantry will begin … [and] upon a Signal the whole
> Army will huzza 'Long live the King of France'.

This was followed by huzza 'Long live the friendly European powers' and huzza
'For the American States'.

In May 1778, Howe sailed from Philadelphia, and Clinton replaced him as
commander-in-chief. One of the first things Clinton did was to evacuate
Philadelphia, which had not been as welcoming as expected, and New Jersey was
positively antagonistic. The numerous ships, including *Adventure*, prepared for the
return journey to New York. The Loyalists mostly went by ship, but the British
army of some 15,000 men returned to New York overland, a less risky strategy.
On 18 June, the British left Philadelphia which was reoccupied peacefully by the
Americans the following day.

The land route meant that the British forces were out of reach of the French
navy; but they were still vulnerable to the newly trained, enlarged and remotivated
Continental army. There was another close-fought engagement (the Battle of
Monmouth, 28 June) where the initiative swung back and forth. It looked as if
Washington was going to win, but nightfall put a pause to the fighting. When
dawn broke the Americans realised that Clinton had 'done a Washington' and
slipped away in the dark, arriving safely at New York.

Adventure's journey was uneventful, and from 8 July she was anchored off
New York. Everything seemed much the same as it had been when she was last
there, except that then it looked as if Britain might suppress the revolution and
now it didn't.

Adventure, with several invalids aboard, left New York in a convoy of eighty-
nine sail with HMS *Leviathan*, bound for Britain. The atmosphere was edgy and
morale low. Tonken even had to punish one of the invalids for drunkenness and
mutiny. Fog and squally weather meant that it was difficult for the ships to keep
together. Strong gales carried away *Adventure's* 'topmast steering sail and the main
topsail braces', keeping the carpenter and sailmaker busy. It must have been a great
relief when the Scillies were sighted on 22 November; five days later *Adventure*
moored at Spithead. Unfortunately, having endured the dreadful passage, two of
the invalids died before they could be disembarked. On 14 December, she took
on board '3 Tons of Beer', broaching a cask the next day, and a second one six days
later. *Adventure* reached Deptford on 13 January 1779, and her people were set
busy unloading. After a long time away, her voyage was over.

Howe was right to worry about Newport, and the British had taken it. But
Rhode Islanders were an independent people, and there is a difference between

capturing a city and subduing its inhabitants into quiescent acceptance. In a post-Saratoga defensiveness, other British outposts in Rhode Island were withdrawn to Newport, and in the summer of 1778 it became clear that – in a combined operation – the Continental army planned to attack overland, while the French would move in from the sea. In order to avoid being caught in this pincer movement the British decided to sink a number of vessels in the outer harbour to keep the French at bay so they could neither land troops nor concentrate effective firepower. One of the vessels sunk had been used as a prison ship which suggested she was not in the best condition. She was *Lord Sandwich 2*, previously *Endeavour*, previously *Earl of Pembroke*.

The French ships arrived but were troubled by fierce winds and by the (belated) appearance of a British squadron. The British stayed put in Newport,

Farewell, *Endeavour*.

until they decided to evacuate the city on 25 October 1779 in order to focus on the southern colonies.

John Wilkinson was owner/agent for a number of transports, including *Lord Sandwich 2*. He put in a claim for compensation, and the Navy Board provided the ship's original valuation when she became a transport of £2,682 made up of £1,752 15*s* for Hull, Masts & Yards, and £929 5*s* for Furniture & Stores.[3] Wilkinson received the amended sum of £2,421 0*s* 3*d*.

Meanwhile, the French were concentrating on conquests of more immediate importance to themselves. On 8 September 1778, they captured Dominica which had been gifted to Britain by the Treaty of Paris. Britain retaliated by taking St Lucia a couple of months later.

In March 1779, Benjamin Franklin wrote to all American ships requesting them not to interfere with Cook's expedition as it was 'an Undertaking laudable in itself as it facilitated Communication between distant Nations, the Exchange of useful Products and Manufactures, and the Extension of Arts, whereby the common Enjoyments of human Life are multiply'd and augmented, and Science of other kinds increased to the benefit of Mankind'. Franklin had clearly stated that science and trade are universal, and essential for the pursuit of happiness.

At the same, time the French issued a similar instruction to their navy, which was not an Enlightenment manifesto like Franklin's, but much more cautious and suspicious: 'It is the King's pleasure, that Capt. Cook shall be treated as a Commander of a neutral and allied Power' and that any captain 'who may meet that famous navigator, shall make him acquainted with the King's orders on this behalf' adding that it should be made clear to Cook that 'he must refrain from all hostilities'. For these kindnesses Benjamin Franklin and Louis XVI were later (1784) to receive gold medals from Britain. Even though, in fact, Cook was already dead by the time their orders were written, they show the quandary that the Enlightenment thinkers believing in science as an international enterprise were faced with during the nationalism of warfare.

Botanists and botanical specimens had varying experiences on their travels. During the Seven Years War, Peter Collinson lost 'a great many' seeds he was sending to Linnaeus when the French captured two North American ships which were carrying them. Francis Masson (1741–1805), sponsored by Banks on *Resolution* to botanise in South Africa in 1772, had sent home over 500 species by the time he returned to Britain in 1775. Three years later he was sent off by Banks as a plant hunter to Madeira, the Canaries and the Caribbean; he was in Granada when the French captured the island in July 1779, and he was imprisoned. Although he was eventually released by the French, the majority of his specimen plants had died. Thomas Blaikie (1758–1832), a Scottish botanist and gardener as was Masson, had served his apprentice at Upton House with Fothergill, who sent him to find new alpine plants in Switzerland in 1775. Blaikie settled in Paris as a garden designer the following year, where he was very popular even after the French declared war on Britain. He recorded in his diary that he 'Received a large quantitie [of seeds] from Sir Joseph Banks of those brought home by the Discovery ships which went out with Captain Cook'. Blaikie added that he regretted that he had no 'Hottehouse for several sorts of seeds from the friendly Islands and Ottahiette'.[4] He later designed the gardens at Malmaison for Josephine, the wife of Napoleon Bonaparte.

Spain had even less interest in nurturing the young American republic than France; but she was very keen to overthrow the terms of the Treaty of Paris. On 21 June 1779, Spain declared war on Britain (but did not form an alliance with America) and started besieging Gibraltar.*

The entry of Spain into what started out as the American War of Independence, and was rapidly being hijacked as a Revenge War of the Seven Years War Losers, was potentially fatal for Britain. The fleets of Spain and France, if combined, outnumbered and outclassed the British navy. Lord Sandwich, First Lord of the Admiralty, suffered a seemingly endless attack on his competence; he was accused of mismanagements and corruption. It was alleged that while in office he had destroyed more ships than had been built and that vast sums of money paid by the government had disappeared. Sandwich retorted that he had inherited a fleet that was numerous and effective only on paper, and that the money had gone on repairs and replacement of ships built of green, unseasoned wood and on repayment of debts. Largely, that was right; but it is true that there had been false accounting, but not for personal gain. Parliament had voted extra money to the Admiralty when the Falkland Crisis looked like total war with Spain, which (dishonestly) they had not given back; though it had been spent (honestly) to pay off debts – so Lord Sandwich was not keen on transparency, as there would have been a demand for the much needed money to be repaid. He also thought that, in times of war, details of naval expenditure should be state secrets, but the opposition claimed that he was using this argument as a cover-up (which, to a certain extent, he was).

The financing of the navy was something of a nightmare as, especially in war time, it was impossible to foresee what expenses were going to arise in all

---

* The military significance of Gibraltar had not prevented John White, chaplain to the garrison, from cherishing its scientific significance. He studied the flora and fauna of the island, sending information and specimens to his brother Gilbert at Selborne. From these data Gilbert was able to learn much about bird migration; in a letter to Thomas Pennant (26 November 1770) he wrote, 'the rock of Gibraltar is a great rendezvous, and a place of observation, from whence they [the migrating birds] take their departure each way towards Europe or Africa' (White, p.69).

the various departments the Admiralty was responsible for. There was always a shortfall. For example, Deptford Yard listed their bills unpaid by Michaelmas 1776 to a large number of providers including Mary Eastman for 'Poop Lanthorns' (£42 10s), Mary Beaufoy* for vinegar (£49 10s) and several suppliers of canvas including two from Whitby: Jonathan Saunders (£51) and Christopher Preswick (£231 6s). The total owed for canvas supplied was £2,984 4s (c. £5.3 million).

A year later some creditors (including Mary Eastman) were still unpaid, as the same sum appears. The Beaufoy's bill was the same in 1777 though the creditor was Mark Beaufoy (presumably Mary's son). Messrs Mount and Page supplied brown paper** in 1776 to the amount of £6 10s and in 1777 this had risen to £16 5s, but whether this was a new debt or an ongoing tab is not stated.

The Navy Board's unpaid debt for canvas alone had escalated to £3,977 8s 5d (c. £6.7 million), an increase of about about 33 per cent. Christopher Preswick's bill had been paid, but he was not given another contract. Indeed, of the eighteen suppliers of canvas in 1776, only seven were on the 1777 list of twenty-one names, perhaps those that did not reappear either did not fulfil the contract on time, or could not afford to wait too long for their bills to be paid, and did not tender for the business in 1777.

Jonathan Saunders appears in both lists, the value of the canvas he supplied rising to £231 6s. Another Whitby canvas supplier in 1777 was the firm of John and William Chapman (sons of Abel Chapman and Elizabeth née Walker), based at Spital Bridge near the Dock Company's shipbuilding yards. It had provided canvas to the value of £359 17s 6d by Michaelmas 1777, and within a week made a further contract for 160 bolts (about 6,000 yards, or roughly 3.5 miles) of canvas of varying grades for which he eventually received £450 11s (c. £760,000).[5]

The flourishing, and growing, business of sail canvas manufacture in Whitby was built firmly on the work of women, perhaps mainly spinsters as the name implies, spinning the flax whenever they had 'free' time, to keep the voracious looms weaving the valuable sailcloth. Increasingly weaving, the province of men, was done in manufactories, but at least 50 per cent of Whitby weavers seem to have been working from home at this time.[6]

---

* What is interesting is the number of women in charge of large enough businesses that they could make contracts (some of which were of a three-figure value) with the Navy Board. The following appear, in addition to Mary Eastman and Mary Beaufoy: Mary Ayres (handspikes and wedges), Elizabeth Cook (watchglasses), Ann Creed (lead), Dorothy Turner & Son (canvas), Mary Higginson (canvas) and possibly Ellis [Alice?] Bent. They would mainly have been widows, but some might have been spinsters.

** When ships were copper-bottomed, the hull was coated with tar and brown paper before the copper plates were nailed on. This was to reduce electrolytic damage between the copper and iron fitments on the ship's bottom.

The site of the Chapman sailcloth factory, Spital Bridge, Whitby.

For all the 'Rule, Britannia!' and popular patriotism, the British were not happy to pay increasing taxes, whether they had representation or not. The North government was in something of an economic and political crisis; they wanted to continue the war, but it was proving to be very expensive. Lord Sandwich was the target in 1779, the opposition believing that if Sandwich was ousted, the government would fall. The year 1778 had seen several motions in Parliament criticising the conduct of the war which were defeated but only by the narrowest margins, and there were calls for making peace. Sandwich stayed, and was a very effective First Lord of the Admiralty,* and the North government survived, but this was mainly due to the influence of the king who had engineered the fall of the Rockingham administration and had no wish to have it back again.

It is hardly surprising that the opposition fought back; a king meddling in politics and manipulating Parliament was not in accord with the Bill of Rights. Not only was Britain's status of ruler of the waves under serious threat but so

---

* Sandwich had instituted a policy of copper-bottoming all ships-of-the-line. This was expensive, but ensured that not only were the vessels preserved from the depredations of the wood-boring mollusc *Teredo navalis*, but also their hulls acquired fewer accretions (such as barnacles) with enabled them to go faster and outsail enemy ships.

was her title as the land of the free – the latter having been unchallenged (except perhaps by the Netherlands) since 1688. The French and the Spanish might make Britain's navy look decidedly second rate, but America was making Britain look like a tyrannical power. In 1780, John Dunning, a sympathiser with the American colonists, put forward a resolution in Parliament that 'the influence of the crown has increased, is increasing, and ought to be diminished' which was carried – albeit by a small majority.

In Britain the desire for reform was growing. The Yorkshire Association was formed in 1779 to press for shorter parliaments and a more equal and honest representation. They did not wish to extend the franchise but to increase the number of county members who, because their constituencies were large in number and extent, were less likely to be bribed, influenced and cajoled. The Yorkshire Association was copied by other counties.

The storeship *Adventure* over-wintered at Deptford. From the beginning of February 1779, she began to be prepared for the year's voyage: cleaning, scraping, taking on stores which included coal, deals, plank, drumhead pieces for capstans, anchors, sails, beds, slops, topmasts, spars and several 'Bundels of Hammocks' – all firmly packed into the holds with dunnage. James Colnett, the master, was promoted to lieutenant, and left *Adventure* on 23 February for HMS *Bienfaisant*,[*] taking his servant William Hester with him. He was replaced by William Williams, whose servant was Thomas Wilson.

Adventure, fully stocked, sailed down the river on 10 April, was at Dungeness on 15 April, Beachy Head the next day and 17 April she anchored at Spithead. The company was paid for six months, and then *Adventure* sailed out into the Atlantic with a large fleet which included ships and transports heading for three separate destinations: one group sailing for Newfoundland parted company on 10 June, those for Québec 22 June, and *Adventure* continued with those for Nova Scotia. She passed Sambro Island, and entered Halifax harbour on 17 August, but too late for 28-year-old American able seaman Thomas Garrett who had died twelve days earlier. Within a few days of arrival, the troublesome bosun James Gibbs had been discharged to HMS *Licorne*, a recent capture from the French.

Having unloaded all her varied stores, *Adventure* made sail on 26 October and, in spite of fresh gales and 'a Great Sea', was safely moored at Spithead by 22 November. On New Year's Day she was moored off Sheerness and all her cargo – including guns and anchors – was unloaded without her coming up the

---

[*] *Bienfaisant* had been captured from the French at the Siege of Louisbourg (1758). When Colnett joined her in 1779 she was commanded by John McBride who had been at Port Egmont in 1766–67 in HMS *Jason*.

river. This was presumably to avoid any more sailors deserting; five, including Samuel Croker, had 'run' at Halifax. Tonken transferred all the remaining crew to HMS *Brune*, including Peter Foster (mentioned above for receiving punishment) as well as Melburn Mennel, the only Whitby sailor aboard, who had entered *Adventure* on 13 April 1776 and had never had occasion to be mentioned in the captain's log.

On 18 January 1780, Hugh Tonken 'put the ship out of Commission'. What happened to *Adventure* after this is not clear, especially as *Adventure* was a very common ship's name. George Young, Cook's biographer, commented that *Adventure* 'belonged several years to a Mr Brown of Hull, and more recently to Messrs Appleton and Trattles of Whitby' and that she 'underwent a thorough repair in the dock of Messrs Langbourn in 1810, but was wrecked in the gulf of St Lawrence in 1811'. There certainly was a ship *Adventure*, 344 tons, which was recorded in *Lloyd's Register* (LR) for 1799–1800 as being 16 years old, built (in 1767–68)★ at Whitby, which could be the same vessel as the *Marquis of Rockingham*, 336 tons, built at Whitby in 1769. LR gave further details; namely, that she was a ship, owned by T. Brown, the master was H. Lisk, and that she had a single deck. She had been given a number of repairs: new upper works (in 1780?), good repairs in 1795 and 1797 and was part sheathed and doubled in 1800 – the latter probably because she was a transport ship armed with six guns. Much the same information appeared in LR for 1801 and 1802 except the master's name was given as H. Lesk, and the ship was listed as having a single deck with beams (SDB). In 1803, she gave up being a transport, had a repair, and sailed between Hull and Onega – as she continued to do in 1804. The 1805 LR reported that H. Lesk was replaced by Appleton as master, and that the ship had had some repairs in 1803. Appleton remained master until 1806, with the ship sailing between Hull and Memel, but in 1807 T. Jameson took over as master for a year, after which Appleton appeared as both master and owner – they were perhaps father and son. *Adventure* had another good repair in 1808 and she sailed to Québec. In 1809, her master was J. Shaw, who sailed her from Hull to Québec and, in 1810, to St Johns. In 1811, for her last voyage, Snowden was master and she had six 6-pounder guns (but there is no mention of repairs made in 1810). The *Naval Chronicle*[7] added that she was travelling from Leith for Québec when she was lost on 24 May 1811, without loss of life. It also states that she was 'the identical ship which sailed around the world with Captain Cook'; this is the sort of affirmation which invites scepticism.

★ *Lloyd's Register* was published in the middle of the year to which was attributed, so the 1800 volume covered mid 1799 to mid 1800.

There seem to be no clear links between the *Adventure* which Hugh Tonken put out of commission in January 1780, and the *Adventure* which appears in the record twenty years later, owned by T. Brown, and which was lost in 1811; they are separated by two decades, which seem to have no evidential bridge connecting them.

Indeed, apart from the regular mentions in *LR*, there is no mention of a ship *Adventure* with a master Lisk, Lesk or near variant in *Lloyd's List*, the London newspapers or in the local newspapers of Hull and Newcastle – which is unusual. Their first newspaper link with *LR* is the 1805 voyage when *Adventure*, Appleton, sailed to Narva[8] Although the tonnage of the two ships is similar, they are not identical. It seems unusual that Brown's *Adventure* was only partially sheathed and doubled in 1800 when Cook's *Adventure* had been totally sheathed for her voyage. Brown claims his ship was built in 1767–68 whereas *Adventure/Marquis of Rockingham* was built at least a year later; if they were the same ship then it would be a very unusual example of an owner submitting his ship as a transport and exaggerating her age, whereas the custom often was to subtract a few years. John Robson, in his *Captain Cook Encyclopaedia*, states that Cook's *Adventure* was broken up in 1783, which could be possible, though the evidence is not readily available.[9]

By 1780, *Freelove* was over 50 years old and the longest surviving ship in which James Cook had sailed as a servant; she had a fairly varied career. After her spell as a transport ship in the Seven Years War she reverted mainly to the collier trade, but in 1761–63 she was trading with the Baltic and Norway. This would mainly be importing timber, and (from Riga) also masts, flax and hemp. These commodities, crucial for shipping, could have been sold to merchants who dealt with government shipyards. Robert Walker, servant on *Freelove* from April 1762 to October 1763, was probably the son of the owner John; Robert was born in 1747 and would have been known to James Cook as a baby and toddler from his days in the Walker house at Haggersgate.

In 1764, John Swainston left *Freelove*, and the new master was Robert Broderick, aged 34, the son of Thomas and Elizabeth. His first year as master seem to have been restricted to the Shields–London collier run, but the following year *Freelove* brought 'Fir, Timber, Masts, [and] Wainscotts' from Riga to Hull. In 1766, it was back to coal and she continued as a collier to the end of 1768 when Robert Brodrick left to be master of *Peace and Plenty* of Whitby. James Tayler, mate in 1767, took over command of *Freelove* in March 1768, a couple of months before the murder of John Beattie. In 1769, *Freelove* had a radical change, sailing to New England then to Québec before moving on to Barbados and then back to Québec before returning to England. It looks as if Walker was making the most of the new markets available in Canada after the Treaty of Paris, and sending *Freelove* as far away from the London coal market as possible.

In 1770, Valentine Kitchingman became master. The Whitby ships' muster rolls tended to become less informative as time went by, and *Freelove* was no exception: after December 1766 when it was noted that she finished the year at Whitby no places are mentioned until 20 March 1771 when she was recorded as being at London. Fortunately, the Receivers of Sixpences accounts, *Lloyd's List*, and the Burney collection of eighteenth-century newspapers are helpful to fill in the gaps. In 1770, *Freelove* was at Onega, and in 1771 at Petersburg. In 1772, she was back trading in New England, followed by a traditional coal trip, before sailing to Petersburg. She was at Gravesend on 1 November, and the crew were paid off on 18 November, presumably at Whitby. In 1773 and 1774, she was again a collier, but intriguingly was at Liverpool in June 1773. In 1771, Robert Kitchingman, possibly Valentine's brother, had appeared in *Freelove's* muster roll as a seaman, and the following year he was upgraded to being the ship's cook – a position he held until the end of 1774.

In 1775, *Freelove* entered a new sphere of shipping; she became a whaler. The government had given a bounty of £1 per ton to whalers from 1733, which had lured some into a business which had previously been something of a monopoly of the Dutch. When the bounty was doubled in 1750, British shipowners began to take notice in some numbers.

There was not much expertise among the Whitby sailors, but some had sailed on whalers before. James Todd, seaman on *Friendship* from October 1747, had returned from an eventful whaling voyage to Greenland in the *Eliza & Mary*. Adamson, who was the master, described (in a letter of 3 June 1746) how the whalers had 'met with a violent storm of wind whilst in the ice', that his ship was 'almost tore to pieces', and three English ships were lost. He remarked that the Dutch seemed keener to rescue the dead whales than the live sailors from the stricken English ships.[10] Daniel Campbell, who enrolled as a seaman on *Friendship* (Richard Ellerton, master and James Cook, mate) at Shields in 30 July 1752 gave his previous employment as being in *Resolution* (of Newcastle), Anthony Skinner, from Greenland.

Whitby began whaling in 1753 when two ships, *Sea Nymph* and the Walker-owned *Henry & Mary* were altered and strengthened to be whalers. *Sea Nymph*, built 1742 or before, was owned by William Reynolds who was for a while the ship's master. George Ward sailed on *Sea Nymph's* second whaling voyage in 1754, before joining *Freelove* as mate in September of that year. *Henry & Mary*, James Todd, captured three whales on her maiden whaling voyage. This early adventure had met with some success, and other vessels took to whaling, introducing Whitby seamen to the necessary skills. When John Jackson's Whitby-built ship *Three Brothers* (not Cook's ship) was sold in 1756 one of its main selling points was that it was 'very fit for the Whale Fishery'. In 1757, *John & Ann*, William Gaskin, owned by John Yeoman (Henry Walker's son-in-law), sailed to Greenland to catch whales. However, with the advent of the Seven Years War and the consequent French privateers, the east coast was becoming unsafe. An even more dissuasive factor was the damaging Arctic storms which had destroyed the Whitby ship *Leviathan* in 1758, so the Whitby whaling fleet petered out.

It was revived in 1767 when *British King*, owned by William Swales, sailed to the Greenland seas. The following year, *James & Mary* and *Jenny* followed suit, and thence the Whitby whaling fleet grew and grew. Notable ships were *Volunteer*, William Coulson, (owner Richard Moorsom) in 1772; *Freelove*, John Brown (owned by John Walker & Co); *Henrietta* (built by the Langbourns, Nicholas Piper master & owner); *Friendship*, George Ismay, in 1776: and *Speedwell*, John Steward (owned by Thomas Holt) in 1777.

Whaling was an important industry which is why the government was keen to encourage British ships into the business, and why it was so profitable. Whale oil, sometimes called 'train oil' (from a Dutch word), was of vital importance for lighting and – increasingly – for lubrication. The machinery of the Industrial Revolution turned smoothly on whale oil. There were other chemical uses as well, for example, in soap manufacture. Baleen, often confusingly called 'whalebone' or 'whalefin', is the feathered-edged strips in the mouths of filter-feeding whales. They were useful where strength and flexibility were required, as in umbrellas and in stiffening corsets. Proper whalebone (the bone of whales) was used as a cheaper alternative to ivory (and also used for scrimshaw by sailors on whaling ships).

Volunteer's whaling voyage of 1772 was recorded by William Kidd, the ship's surgeon, in an 'Authentick Narration' which was later published. It begins with a traditional voyage-style poem:

Massive iceberg off the misty coast of Greenland.

The North Atlantic right whale, *Eubalaena japonica*.

Farewell you jolly sailors bold,
For now you needs must go,
To try your luck on Greenland Seas,
In quest of Whales that blow.
With Plenty, I do hope you'll meet,
Such as give you Pleasure;
That you may home rejoicing come,
Fill'd with Greenland's Treasure.

Kidd's account gives insight into whale fishery (a whale was traditionally called a whalefish, from the Dutch *een valfis*). The main fishing ground at this time was the Greenland Sea between Spitzbergen and Greenland, but some ships ventured into the Davis Straits between Greenland and Canada. The actual killing was done from the ship's boats (*Volunteer* had eight boats), each of which had a crew of a harpooner, a line manager, a boat steerer, two men and a boy.

The favoured whale to hunt was called the 'right whale' for the reason that it was the easiest and best to catch. A man would be posted on the topmast as a lookout and as soon as he saw a whale 'blowing', he would cry out 'A fall! A fall!' (again from the Dutch). The men would lower their boats into the sea and set forth. As whalers tended to congregate for mutual safety, there could be a rush of boats from a variety of ships, Dutch as well as British, descending upon the innocent pod of whales. Like an explorer planting a Union flag on a Pacific

island and claiming it for Britain, so the harpooner by being the first to plunge his
harpoon into a whale claimed possession of it for his ship. It was only as the barbed
harpoon was thrust deep into its flesh that the whale realised it was under attack,
but its response was sudden and dramatic – with a smack of its massive fluke,
which could slap a boat into splinters – it would dive at great speed. The harpoon
was attached to a long sturdy coiled rope which was fixed at its other end to the
boat, and this is where the line manager's skill came into operation, he had to pay
out the rope at speed without it snagging or the boat would be dragged under the
icy waves. Sometimes the whale sank to the bottom of the sea, sometimes it would
swim underwater for miles, pulling the boat behind it with a white-knuckled crew
hanging on perilously and travelling faster than any other mode of transport then
experienced by humankind. Eventually the wounded creature would surface, and
the boat would come alongside for the kill, then dragging the corpse back to the
ship where a once magnificent whale was processed into commodities.

Seals were also a saleable. There was a market for sealskin, and seals also provided
blubber; however, it was reckoned that it took a thousand seals to produce as
much oil as a large whale.

If a ship had not caught any whales, or if the opportunity presented itself, then
she would go after seals. If a colony of seals could be surprised on the ice, a gang
of sailors could kill scores of them before they could get into the safety of the sea.
The wholesale slaughter of seals in this way was not a pleasant business. In 1774,
Volunteer brought 4,200 seals back to Whitby.[11]

Whaling was a test of endurance: of the cold, the storms, and the often
seemingly endless days searching for whales; so how often the sailors were 'jolly'
in the Arctic Circle is debateable. The whaling ships were strengthened and

Common Seal, *Phoca
vitulina.*

A nineteenth-century print of seals being killed.

double-hulled, but nonetheless could be crushed in a fist of ice. Some ships returned with no whales, which was called 'clean', and some never returned.

Some, like *Volunteer* in 1772, which had caught five whales, returned 'home rejoicing'. She was a ship of 302 tons and there was a crew of forty men; she had been over five months at sea and would have sailed with all the food and other necessities required for at least that period of time, so the ship was fairly cramped. The dismemberment of the whales, chopping up the blubber and putting it into casks for later processing, storing the saleable parts and throwing the rest overboard must have made a considerable mess and a vile stench. It was said you could smell a whaler long before you could see it; no wonder that a ship which had caught no whales was called 'clean'.

No matter how filthy, there was lucre to be distributed. On the *Volunteer*, 1772, Matthew Smith, the mate, would have received about £40 (*c*. £73,000) for the voyage, the 'successful harpooners' between £32 and £33, but Richard Moorsom, the owner, would have made a clear profit of some £1,250 (*c*. £2.3 million).[12] The spectioneer (chief harpooner, again a whaling term adopted from the Dutch) was the 35-year-old John Brown. He stayed as a spectioneer in *Volunteer* in 1773, and on 18 February 1775 sailed from Whitby to the Davis Straits as master of *Freelove* on her first whaling trip, one of fifteen Whitby whalers that year. He was obviously missed by *Volunteer*, as she was a clean ship in 1775.

The boom of British whaling had slumped with the outbreak of the American war, but *Freelove* continued. In 1776 and 1777, HMS *Lion*, Lieutenant Walker

Whalebone arch at Whitby.

Young, convoyed the British whalers to the Davis Straits; by 1777, there were only nine of them, six from Whitby. Young's orders were, that, once he had escorted the whalers to their destination, he was to attempt the North-West Passage and if possible meet James Cook who had been instructed to do the same from the Pacific end.[13] Unsurprisingly, Young failed on both occasions.

The year 1777 was a good one for *Freelove*, partly because so many former whaling ships had been submitted as transports in 1776. On 11 June, she returned from the Davis Straits with the produce of eight whales, viz. 340 butts of blubber which produced 113 tuns (over 28,000 gallons) of oil, and 6.75 tons of baleen. At that time, the price for whale oil was £24 per tun and whalebone (baleen) was £300 per ton.[14] This meant that the voyage had made £2,712 for the oil, £2,025 for the baleen, plus the bounty of £476; in total £5,213 (*c*. £8.8 million). Expenses and wages had to be deducted from this, but even so it was a massive profit for the owners. Who exactly the owners were is interesting. The early musters simply give John Walker as the owner as he would be the main owner, the ship's husband; but most ships were owned by a small group of family members and business colleagues, and this was true for *Freelove*; we know that Joseph Colpits and the rope-making firm of John & Thomas Dawson of Newcastle owned shares in her early years, and it would have been very strange if several of the Walker family, in addition to John Senior, were not also shareholders. From 1775, the owners are called 'John Walker & Co.', which may (but need not) imply a change in the ownership. In 1778, the muster roll does not mention any ownership, and from 1779 it is given as 'Wakefield Simpson & Co.' It seems likely that Walker had bought out the other owners and redistributed the shares among the next generation: his sons Henry, John and Robert, his two unmarried daughters Helena and Elizabeth, and Wakefield Simpson, the husband of John's eldest daughter Dorothy. Wakefield Simpson, as an established banker and the oldest and richest of the next generation, was a suitable person to take over the job of *Freelove*'s husband. These were listed as the part-owners when *Freelove* was registered in January 1787.

Once the French had joined the war, privateers both French and American were more of a problem. The British whaling fleet shrunk from ninety-five ships in 1775 to fifty-two in 1780. In March 1778 *Freelove*, owned largely by Quakers, was 'fitted out with guns and close quarters' and again sailed to the Davis Straits, returning to Whitby in late July with 'three fish'. In 1779, the nine Whitby whalers bound for the Davis Straits decided to sail as a fleet,* with Thomas Franks of *Marlborough* in command. The *London Chronicle* reported that they were 'the best fitted out for the whale fishery of any in England' and intended 'to take, sink, or burn any enemy that should oppose them'. When *Freelove* returned home she was stopped by the British armed ship *Content* who 'pressed twelve of their men but sent fourteen on board in their room'. Seamen on whalers were prized for their skill and were clearly men who would be useful for the navy. However, although it was legal to impress men from a whaler, they had to be returned to their ship when the next season's whaling began – though how strictly this was observed is not clear. The fourteen men *Content* gave them were almost certainly not suitable as sailors and were given to *Freelove* not as a kind gesture (*Freelove* was fairly near home with a crew of forty men; they would have had no problem reaching Whitby with twenty-eight).

No sooner had this dubious transaction taken place than a French privateer appeared, which *Content* engaged; *Freelove* made for home. A fierce battle ensued between *Content* and the Frenchman, until the latter veered away. Later, in the press, the captain of *Content* complained that had *Freelove* remained and joined in the fighting, they could have taken the privateer as a prize. *Freelove* contained a crew which had suffered intense cold and fierce storms; they had not seen

---

* Whitby also sent five whalers to the Greenland seas. This was the second largest whaling fleet that year after London, which sent twenty-three ships to Greenland, two to the Davis Straits and nineteen to 'Falkland's Island in the South Seas' (*Public Advertiser*, 18 June 1779).

their home and family for several months. Had they joined in the battle the navy would not have paid for any damage incurred, and any prize money would have gone to *Content*. The master's prime responsibility was to the owners, and Brown's decision to head for home was humane and wise, and not the act of cowardice that the commander of *Content* had imputed. After this incident *Content* pressed men from all the other returning Whitby whalers.

The war was going badly for Britain. The French captured St Vincent and Granada in the summer of 1779, and 'the Insurance on all Ships, both outward and homeward bound, rose three Guineas per Cent more than it was before, occasioned by so large a French Fleet being out'.[15] John Paul Jones was plundering the English coast, and the appearance (albeit fleeting) of French and Spanish ships in the Channel fuelled panic and despondency. In 1780, the Armed Neutrality was formed to resist with force the British navy's 'stop and search' policy with regard to neutral ships, which involved seizing any cargo belonging to her enemies.

Originally consisting of Sweden, Denmark and Russia, this alliance later included not only Austria, but also Britain's erstwhile friends Prussia, Portugal and Holland.

The Dutch were taking advantage of Britain's entanglement in the war, and not just in the whale fishery. They were supplying weapons and provisions to Britain's enemies, and had their eyes on Britain's lucrative Baltic trade. There were even rumours that the Dutch intended to invade England. In December 1780, Britain declared war on Holland: the Fourth Anglo-Dutch War. This was intended not only to teach a lesson to the members of the Armed Neutrality, but also to protect Britain's trade with Norway and the Baltic ports, so crucial to the building and maintenance of ships, and to have an opportunity to reduce Dutch mercantile territories. The British attempted to capture the Cape of Good Hope from the Dutch but their 'secret fleet' was intercepted by the French at the Battle of Porto Praya (Praia) in the Cape Verde Islands on 16 April 1781, which delayed the British Fleet, allowing the French to reinforce the Cape. In August 1781, British and Dutch men-of-war, both of whom were protecting merchant ships, clashed in a conflict later known as the Battle of Dogger Bank. It was a bloody conflict, with many killed but – like the Four Days' Battle of 1666 – both sides claimed a victory. The British fleet under the command of Hyde Parker was the first to leave the fray, but had inflicted greater damage and death upon the Dutch – who sent no more merchant ships to the Baltic until the end of the war.

The Battle of Dogger Bank was effective, but Hyde Parker was commander of ships that were in very poor condition. Britain's claim that she ruled the waves was over; she did not have enough battle-fit ships to control all the maritime areas of the world where she was involved. Of necessity, the British were largely reduced to fighting a reactive war; it had become a matter of strategy, insight, priority and sea luck to ensure the right ships were in the right place at the right time. And British priorities were the perceived priorities of trade: the Channel, the North Sea, the West Indies, the Mediterranean, Canada and India. Britain captured Dutch bases at Negapatam and Trincomalee in India.

One of the main reasons that Spain had joined the war was to recapture Gibraltar and Minorca. A siege of Gibraltar was instituted almost before the ink was dry on Spain's declaration of war in June 1779, and, although their morale was high, the inhabitants of Gibraltar were increasingly suffering from hunger and scurvy during the winter. Some food was smuggled in by enterprising Moroccan merchants but, because of the risk, their prices were understandably high. Some relief came from Minorca, which itself was under attack.

A British fleet of twenty-four warships and a large number of transports and storeships, commanded by George Rodney, set out for Gibraltar. Off the coast near Cape St Vincent (the furthest western point of the south coast of Portugal) they met a Spanish fleet of about half their size. Realising their danger, the Spaniards sought to escape, but, thanks to Lord Sandwich, all the British ships-of-the-line were copper-sheathed and Rodney's squadron easily caught up with their enemy. In the ensuing battle, fought on 16 January 1780, the British inflicted terrible damage on the Spanish, capturing at least four of their ships and taking many prisoners.

Rodney sailed on with the convoy of transports to Gibraltar where they were able to supply the beleaguered garrison with more troops and a considerable amount of provisions and military equipment. Rodney's fleet then sailed to Minorca to resupply the island, before moving on to the West Indies, where he captured the Dutch islands of St Eustatius in February. In June, the French took Tobago, and in October they recaptured St Eustatius.

Ownership of Gibraltar was becoming a symbol of macho national pride for Britain and Spain. The Spanish had committed several of her ships-of-the-line to retaking it, with the result that the Franco-Spanish invasion of England planned for 1779 had to be postponed. The British committed several serviceable vessels towards keeping Gibraltar, which arguably might have been better used elsewhere.

In August 1781, the British general Charles Cornwallis decided to settle his forces in America at Yorktown, as a strategic base with easy access down the River York to Chesapeake Bay. He built suitable fortifications round the town, as well as setting up a stronghold across the river to secure his position. He had a sizeable army based there, with a number of transport ships, so the town could be easily supplied and reinforced. All this depended upon the British being securely in command of Chesapeake Bay, which was not the case.

A large Franco-American army marched on Yorktown. The French Admiral de Grasse left the West Indies, sailed into Chesapeake Bay unopposed, and landed more troops. Shortly after this a British fleet arrived in the bay and engaged the French who had more ships which were in better repair. It was a rather confused battle, but the British withdrew to New York for repairs and reinforcements. Meanwhile, a second French fleet, under de Barras, sailed into the bay from Newport, with artillery for the army. Cornwallis was outnumbered and outgunned at Yorktown, unable to escape or receive help as the French were in firm control of Chesapeake Bay. The British sank some of their transports to prevent the enemy attacking them from the river, the same tactic as had been used before at Newport, when *Lord Sandwich 2* was sunk. The battle was furious, every day Cornwallis hoping that reinforcements would come to the rescue; eventually, realising his hope was in vain, he surrendered.

In 1780, Cook's ships, *Resolution* and *Discovery* had arrived back in England, but without Cook, commander of *Resolution*, and without Charles Clerke, commander of *Discovery*. Omai had been taken home, some of the west coast of America had been charted, the non-existence of a northerly passage between the Atlantic and the Pacific had been fairly decisively proved and the Hawaiian archipelago was discovered and charted. Cook had vindicated the effectiveness of Harrison's chronometer for measuring longitude with remarkable accuracy, even though he had not taken Harrison's watch (H4) but Larcum Kendall's copy of it (K1) which Cook referred to as his 'trusty friend the Watch'.[16]

Measuring longitude accurately was one of the great discussion topics and the greatest contribution to safety at sea of the century; but it wasn't always easy to discern a ship's latitude, as this involved measuring the altitude of the sun at noon, which was fine if the sun was clearly visible at that time, but 'frequently the mariner [was] prevented by clouds obscuring the sun, for many days together, at noon'. The *London Chronicle* reported in April 1787 that 'a method for determining the latitude of a place, at any hour of the day, when the sun can be seen at one altitude only' was to be presented by the Astronomer Royal Maskelyne at the next meeting of the Commissioners of Longitude. The inventor of this potentially valuable method was not named, but was described as 'a Gentleman at Staithes, near Whitby, in Yorkshire'.

The tragic visits of Cook to Hawaii, comprising deification, assassination and a grisly sort of theophagy, have been well and often told. It has been suggested that, had *Resolution* been better prepared at Deptford for the voyage, she would never have had to return to Hawaii for repairs, and the tragedy there would have been avoided. On Cook's death (14 February 1779), Clerke had taken over the command of *Resolution*, and John Gore of *Discovery*; when Clerke died in August, Gore took over *Resolution* and James King became commander of *Discovery*.

Once the crew had all been paid off (24 October 1780), *Resolution* was changed from being HM Sloop *Resolution* into HM *Resolution* Armed Transport Ship, with Lieutenant Robert F. Hassard, commander; William McQueen, master; Thomas Whitly, mate; James Hayes, boatswain (possibly the same man who

The record of James Cook's death in *Resolution*'s muster, 1779–80. DD stands for 'discharged dead'. (TNA ADM 36/8049)

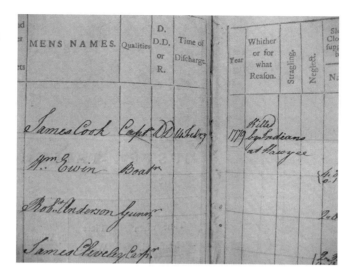

sailed in *Resolution* as a seaman on Cook's second voyage); Peter Langa, gunner; Thomas Turnbull, surgeon; Alex Bell, surgeon's mate; Robert Morris, cook (the only member of the previous crew to stay on); and James Wallis, presumably the carpenter, who had served as such in *Resolution* on Cook's second voyage. Also on the muster was John, transferred from *Apollo*. As he had only a given name, the inference is that he was a slave working his way to freedom.

Resolution's first task, in her latest avatar, was to transfer a number of new Greenwich pensioners down river to the Deptford Hulk where, presumably, they would be held until either space could be made for them at Greenwich Hospital as in-pensioners, or they could show themselves eligible for out-pensions. Greenwich Hospital was the naval equivalent of Chelsea Hospital. It was largely supported by the compulsory contribution of 6*d* a month from every sailor, and the paperwork for this – the Receivers of Sixpences accounts – are very useful sources of information; they only cover contributions from merchant mariners, who were not eligible to be Greenwich pensioners – a source of understandable grievance.

After that, the trail of *Resolution* becomes more complex, the ship's muster book[17] runs only from December 1780 to February 1781, though the last muster recorded was on 15 January at Longreach (south of the river, near the present Dartford crossings) with twenty-one men mustered and one sick.

Of interest is that 'Nicholas Shallice, of his Majesty's Arm'd Transport *Resolution*', made a will signed 12 March 1781,[18] signed by James Wallis (?carpenter), Robt Fitzt Hassard (commander), Wm McQueen (master), and James Hayes (boatswain). Nicholas himself is not mentioned in the January muster, which implies he was enlisted after the end of January, which in turn suggests that *Resolution* was taking on crew for another voyage. The will is of standard phraseology: 'I commend my Soul into the hands of Almighty God hoping for Remission of all my Sins ... and my Body to the Earth or Sea as it shall please God' and his estate includes 'all such Wages Sum and Sums of Money as now or hereafter shall be due to me for my Service or otherwise on Board the said Ship or any other Ship or Vessel'. Such a will was usually made as a matter of course when first a sailor joined the navy, or, if no will had been made previously, before a voyage which could be potentially life-threatening. Nicholas left all his property to his wife, who was also his executrix. The will was not proved until December 1785.

The problem of tracking this ship is that vessels called *Resolution* were as common as men called John Johnson. They included HMS *Resolution*, 72-gun man of war, commander Chaloner Ogle, which was at the Battle of Cape St Vincent and the Battle of the Saintes; and a 358-ton merchant ship *Resolution*, built at Whitby in 1766 and owned by members of the Walker family. She contracted as a transport ship in 1775, Robert Walker master, and again in 1777, with Francis White. This ship appeared in *Lloyd's Register* for 1778, owned by Robert Walker, as a transport armed with six 4-pounder guns, sailing between Québec, London and Cork, and for 1779 with largely identical data, travelling from Cork to Philadelphia. She survived to appear in the compulsory ship register of 1787 and was a whaler, master John Steward. There are two more Whitby-built vessels called *Resolution* at this time, one of which was a sloop, which can cause confusion, but it was only 54 tons. There was also an armed ship *Resolution* which seems the most likely to be Cook's ship.

On 28 January 1781, a number of ships were anchored at Deal. Among them were *Pondicherry*, *Manila* and *Resolution*, all described as 'armed ordnance storeships', and the East Indiamen *Locko*, *Asia* and *Hinchinbrook*. On 12 February, there was a gale of wind at Deal and *Resolution* (now described as an 'armed Ship') lost her 'Bowsprit' and 'received other Damage'. Two days later 'the *Southampton*, East Indiaman' arrived and joined '*Resolution* and *Experiment*' (now referred to as 'armed Cutters') 'and other Ships as before'. On 17 February 1781, *Resolution* ('armed Ship') sailed from Deal to London; she was still referred to as an armed ship when she was back at Deal on 12 March.

The various ships which had been assembling at Deal were to join Commodore Johnstone's previously mentioned 'secret' attempt to seize the Cape from the Dutch. His grand fleet included, five ships-of-the-line, four frigates, a bomb, a fireship, two cutters, a sloop, thirteen East Indiamen including *Locko*, *Asia*, *Hinchinbrook* and *Chapman* (the 558-ton ship built by Thomas Fishburn in 1777 for Abel Chapman), as well as seven armed ships including *Pondicherry*, *Manila* and *Resolution* – each of which carried eighteen guns. Supporting these were four transports, three storeships, and five victuallers including *Admiral Keppel*, Hammond, each with between six to ten guns.

One of the transports was *Content*, Harrison Chilton master, owned by James Atty of Whitby, whose recently indentured servant, Silas James, was aboard this ship and wrote an account of his experiences.[19] The fleet set sail from Spithead on 13 March 1781, one day after Nicholas Shallice made his will.

On 1 April, they arrived at Mayo (Maio) in the Cape Verde Islands; part of the fleet anchored there while the larger part went on to St Jago (Santiago) anchoring in the bay at Praia. *Content* was at Maio where they replenished the water supplies as well as purchasing 'goats, fowls and pigs, besides many monkeys, with some oranges, plantains, milk, honey, yams and Indian corn' in return for 'six 4lb pieces of salt beef and about two-thirds of an old checked shirt' – a bargain so impressive that it borders on exploitation. On 15 April, she sailed to Porto Praia, joining the main fleet there that evening and mooring on the outside of the bay.

The commodore thought she was rather exposed there, so ordered her to 'weigh anchor and run farther into the bay, that in case any thing should happen, the *Content* might be more immediately under the protection of the men of war'. This was done first thing on the following morning, and it was well done, as something did happen almost immediately after her anchor was dropped – a 'fleet of strange ships' appeared. They were the French, under Admiral Pierre de Suffren. The British fleet was taken totally by surprise; all their men-of-war were unrigged, their gun decks cluttered with water butts, and most of the seamen ashore. The French were also taken by surprise at finding the British there, but the existence and the destination of the secret fleet was already known to them, and Suffren's mission was to protect the Cape. A 'tremendous action' ensued. As Commodore George Johnstone was to write[20] after the battle was over: 'The

The bay at Porto Praia, Santiago, Cape Verde.

action bordered upon a surprise, and the nature of the service in which we were engaged, rendered us liable to much confusion: yet upon the whole, until the enemy was beaten off, I saw nothing but steady, cool, determined valour.' The British indeed drove the French away, but not without losses, and the secret position of the secret fleet was secret no more.

Johnstone stayed at Porto Praia to repair the damage to his ships, but Suffren sailed straight for the Cape, doing running repairs. Consequently, the French reached the Cape first and fortified it, before moving on to India. When Johnstone arrived he found the Cape ready and virtually impregnable. However, he did track down a number of Dutch merchant ships hiding in Saldanha Bay some miles up the west coast, and he managed to capture most of them. He then sailed back to Britain with some of his ships and the captured merchantmen, sending the rest to India, which included *Resolution*. On June 2, 'His Majesty's Armed Transports the *San Carlos*, *Resolution* and *Raikes*, with the *Porpoise* Storeship' (all ships previously in Commodore Johnstone's fleet) had arrived safely at Madras.

On 9 June 1782, about a month before the sea battle by which the British foiled Suffren's attempt to take Negapatam, a ship called *Resolution* fell into French hands, which Suffren confided to his journal was 'the very same which had circled the globe with Captain Cook',[21] and he was probably right. Vice Admiral Sir Edward Hughes, commander-in-chief of His Majesty's ships in the East Indies, sent a letter which was widely reproduced in the British press, from HMS *Superb* on 15 July 1782 giving updated information and an account of the Battle of Negapatam. He wrote: 'His Majesty's Armed Transports the *Resolution* and *Raikes*, on their passage to join me at Trincomalee with Stores and Ammunition, had very unfortunately been fallen in with by the French Squadron, and captured.' *Resolution* sailed, as a French ship, for Manila on 22 July 1782 but did not make her destination. On 5 June the following year, Suffren expressed an opinion that she had either foundered or been recaptured by the British. There was a ship called *Resolution* which foundered on a voyage from Bengal to England in October 1783; she returned to Bombay 'in a shattered condition' and was 'condemned as unfit for Service'. She was described as an East Indiaman, so possibly a different ship. She must have been repaired, as the *Public Advertiser* (13 July 1785) reported that 'The *Resolution* East Indiaman which has been given over for lost, and has been out on a trading voyage, for three years [*Resolution* had disappeared three years previously], is returned into the Thames, with the Gunner as Captain, and one of the foremast-men as acting Mate, who were the only Europeans of the crew who survived the voyage.'

A news item of May 1780, based on information from Fort St George dated 19 July 1779, reported that the *Seahorse* man-of-war with the 'ships *Morse* and *Success* were preparing to sail from Madras to China with the *Resolution* armed ship to convey them through the Straits of Messina'. Clearly if this *Resolution* was sailing from India in July 1779 she cannot be Cook's *Resolution* which was sailing through the Bering Strait at that time. So it appears there were two armed ships called *Resolution*, and possibly that this one was the same as that mentioned in the previous paragraph.

One traditional tale is that Cook's *Resolution* became a French whaler called *Marie Antoinette*, a name that was changed to *La Liberté* after the Revolution; and she finally ran aground in Newport Harbour in 1793. The evidence for this, though, is somewhat tenuous.

It seems likely that the fate of Cook's *Resolution* will never be incontrovertibly determined.

Discovery, the nippy little ship which had received such praise from Cook, became a transport ship with John Pennal as master, Matthew Bass (later Thomas Leech), his servant, and Joseph Bennett as mate, a crew of eighteen in total. From 1781, she shuttled between Woolwich, Deptford, Plymouth and Portsmouth carrying timber, stores and supernumeraries, including Greenwich pensioners. After her famous voyage in 'remote parts' *Discovery* was confined within these limits until finally she was broken up in 1797.

The surrender of Cornwallis at Yorktown was de facto the end of the American War of Independence. In February 1782, a motion in the House of Commons that it was impractical to continue the war with America was passed. Lord North resigned after a dozen years as prime minister, and the Whig Marquis of Rockingham came to power again, with Shelburne at the Home Office, and Charles James Fox at the Foreign Office. Lord Sandwich was replaced as First Lord of the Admiralty by Viscount Keppel who resigned, to be replaced by Viscount Howe. Rockingham died in July and a new administration was formed by Shelburne, with William Pitt (the younger) as Chancellor of the Exchequer.

America had agreed with France not to make a separate peace with Britain, so technically the war continued, but Britain was mainly occupied with evacuating troops and Loyalists – a complex logistical exercise which involved numerous transports.

The focus for Britain was then to snatch as much as they could from the French, Spanish and Dutch before peace treaties were signed, and of course her enemies were trying to do the same. Generally speaking, the starting point for such treaties was the status quo, followed by some shrewd swapping of territories, followed by a lot of argument and compromise. Britain had taken Negapatam and Trincomalee from the Dutch, and St Lucia from the French. The French had taken St Vincent, Granada, St Kitts, Nevis, Dominica, Montserrat, Tobago, St Martin and St Eustatius (which the British had taken from the Dutch). Franco-Spanish forces took Minorca in 1782.

It didn't look good for the British: not many bargaining points with the French and the Spanish. Gibraltar was a clash point; the Spanish saw it as clearly part of their territory which had been unjustly snatched from them by the Treaty of Utrecht in 1713. For the British, it was a legitimate prize of war which was crucial for the Mediterranean trade and also for ensuring some measure of control there, without which the French and Spanish fleets could safely hide and multiply without being blockaded. Tangier had been given up in 1684 and Minorca had been taken (again), so Gibraltar was the last remaining British base in the area. The Spanish siege had begun in 1779 and they had failed to capture the peninsula or starve out its garrison. In September 1782, they decided to deliver the *coup de grâce*. A vast Franco-Spanish force of soldiers and ships of war was assembled; their new secret weapon consisted of ten specially commissioned floating batteries each with more than 100 guns. They were designed with triple-layered sloping sides, which ensured that cannonballs could not penetrate, and simply rolled harmlessly into the sea. The plan was to destroy the defences with a massive barrage from all sides, and then to send in the infantry.

The British also benefited from technology and engineering. They had mined out tunnels in the rock from which they could observe and fire at the enemy. More significantly, a gun carriage which enabled cannon to be fired downwards without the recoil sending it dangerously upwards had been invented by Lieutenant Koehler for the purpose of defending Gibraltar using the height advantage. It was called 'Koehler's depressing carriage', and its innovation was to have a sliding gun carriage which also ensured speedier reloading. It was of crucial importance in the defence of Gibraltar.

Gibraltar.

The battle was hard-fought. A pivotal breakthrough was when the British discovered that if cannonballs were heated until red hot and then fired at a floating battery, the balls could embed themselves in the outer protective layer which could set the ship alight, and because the batteries were enclosed, it was difficult to put out fires. Once a floating battery, carrying enough gunpowder for all those cannon, was burning uncontrollably, they exploded violently with horrendous loss of life. This was the fate of three of them; the other seven were scuttled. The so-called 'Grand Assault' failed. A large British fleet arrived a few weeks later and, although the siege lasted until a peace settlement was agreed, there was no disputing the fact that Britain held Gibraltar.

Adam Smith was not impressed:

> The protection of the Mediterranean trade was the original purpose or pretence of the garrisons of Gibraltar and Minorca … The garrisons at Gibraltar and Minorca have never been neglected, though Minorca has been twice taken, and is now probably lost for ever … [Neither] of those expensive garrisons was ever, even in the smallest degree, necessary for the purpose for which they were originally dismembered from the Spanish monarchy. That dismemberment, perhaps, never served any other real purpose than to alienate from England her natural ally the king of Spain, and to unite the two principal branches of the house of Bourbon in a much stricter and more permanent alliance than ties of blood could ever have united them.[22]

But, as the various combatants groped their way towards a peace treaty, it still looked as if Britain didn't have much to offer. And then there was the Battle of the Saintes. A Franco-Spanish fleet of thirty-five ships of war and numerous transports, commanded by de Grasse, who had so successfully prevented Britain from commanding Chesapeake Bay, planned to invade Jamaica. They were intercepted by a fleet under Admiral Rodney, resulting in a fierce battle on 12 April 1782. It was a decisive victory for the British, destroying France's control of the Caribbean Sea. It was clear that it was going to be difficult for France to retain control of all the lucrative West Indian islands it had gained if Britain controlled the waves that surrounded them.

However, the preliminary peace agreement between Britain, France and Spain, signed in January 1783, was not widely popular and was attacked by an ill-matched coalition of the Tory Lord North and the Whig Fox. Shelburne resigned and the Duke of Portland became Prime Minister, with North and Fox, respectively, at the Home and Foreign Offices, and Keppel back at the Admiralty. On 3 September 1783, the Treaty of Versailles was signed, ratifying preliminary treaties by France, Spain, the United States and Britain, with the terms more favourable to the latter than might have been supposed. Britain recognised America as an independent state, agreed its border with Canada, and guaranteed its rights to the lucrative fishing ground off Newfoundland. In the West Indies, France kept only St Lucia and Tobago, all the other islands formerly owned by Britain were returned to her, as was Gambia. Britain ceded to France Senegal and Gorée, the former French bases in India which had been captured, and a share in the Newfoundland fishing rights. Spain retained Minorca and Florida. In 1784, the Fourth Anglo-Dutch War was concluded; Britain kept Negapatam but returned to Holland all the other territories captured during the war. All these treaties became known, confusingly, as the Peace of Paris. By this time, the Fox–North coalition had also collapsed, and William Pitt the Younger became Prime Minister. He called a general election in that year and won a landslide victory. Pitt remained Prime Minister until 1801.

Freelove continued as a whaler. Although the competition was increased with more ships returning to whaling after being transports, the war had reduced international competition. The number of American and Dutch whalers declined, and the British Greenland whalers increased from fifty-one in 1783 to 250 in 1787.

21

Liberty

The merchants of the world are waxed rich through the abundance of ... [their] merchandise of gold, and silver ... fine linen, and ... all manner of most precious wood ... and iron ... and wine ... and beasts, and sheep, and horses ... and slaves, and souls of men.

(*The Book of Revelation*)

The Treaty of Versailles had witnessed the major powers vying for the sugar-rich islands of the West Indies which generated their wealth by slave power, and for the most profitable pitches on the slave-purchasing coast of West Africa.

The Quakers had made an official declaration that slavery was wrong in 1727, almost a century before Britain made slavery illegal in its empire. In 1761, the Quakers forbad members to own slaves, on pain of expulsion. With its strong emphasis on morality and kindness to all, and its absence of dogma, The Society of Friends was able to hold up a clear light in an age when religion was often befogged.

The English Presbyterians, who had won the Civil War, had dwindled to a small band, many of whom, like the scientist and minister Joseph Priestley, became Unitarians, abandoning belief in the Trinity as unbelievable – a sensible assertion, perhaps, but absolutely not acceptable at that time to the Christian majority.

The deists, so strong at the beginning of the eighteenth century with their rational religion of God, the uncaused causer, who made an ordered universe evidenced and progressively revealed in the discoveries of science, had thought themselves to a standstill. The French mathematician and astronomer Pierre-Simon La Place was able to explain the stability of the universe without having to resort to an interfering god;* and even though he probably did not say, '*Je n'avais*

---

* Newton realised that his laws of motion and gravitation were flawed, in that motion 'is always upon the decay'. In other words, his mechanistic universe needed its creator to wind it up again from time to time. As Hampson put it, 'If God said, "Let Newton be!" Sir Isaac returned the compliment' (p.77). La Place's stable solar system needed no divine interference.

pas besoin de cette hypothèse-là' ('I had no need of that hypothesis'; i.e. he had not needed God to explain the stability of the solar system), he probably wished he had.

Adam Smith wrote that, 'Science is the great antidote to the poison of enthusiasm [fanaticism] and superstition' and advocated that a requirement for entry to all 'liberal professions' should be an understanding of 'the higher and more difficult sciences' on the assumption that a desire for understanding science would filter down from the top until everyone would be keen to understand science and think rationally.

Hume had kicked away the support struts of the design argument for the existence of God, which claimed that the ordered nature of the universe was proof of a good and rational God. He took the popular expression of this argument, namely the analogy that a large artefact, such as a ship, was evidence of a designer★ and therefore the existence of the universe is evidence for the existence of God, its designer. Hume argued that, in fact, a ship designer was often 'a stupid mechanic, who imitated others, and copied an art, which, through a long succession of ages, after multiplied trials, mistakes, corrections, deliberations, and controversies, had been gradually improving'.[1] Extending the simile, he claimed that there could be other 'botched and bungled' universes, or indeed that our universe may well be one such, as we are not aware of other universes with which to compare it. He stated that the analogy was flawed in that a ship was not designed and built by a single person, and therefore the argument cannot prove the existence of just a single god; it is more likely to suggest a whole pantheon. Additionally, he argued that what looks like order and design is simply a matter of what works; for example, it is not an amazing miracle that fish can live in water without drowning because, if they were not able to do so, there would not be any fish. The Church of England did not rise to the bait, preferring to reiterate its dogmata rather than review and rethink its theology – which, sadly, has tended to be its default position ever since.

The Church of England, that all-encompassing, slow-moving, self-deceiving solid foundation of a liberal society, demanded little from its clergymen and less from its laity. Provided a clergyman was sufficiently competent, educated, personable and well connected to obtain the goodwill of someone who had the patronage of a parish, and acknowledged the truth of the 39 Articles, he had a security of tenure, which meant it was very difficult to remove him. The 39 Articles which sought to define the beliefs of the Anglican Church were cobbled together in the white heat of religious controversy between 1536 and

---

★ The simile of a watchmaker was the creation of Archdeacon William Paley, some twenty-five years later.

1571, and were included in the official 1662 *Book of Common Prayer*. Increasingly, prospective incumbents must have had their fingers crossed when they assented to these articles; for example, Article 7 asserts that 'The Old Testament is not contrary to the New' which must have been a surprise to anyone who had clearly read both. More truly in line with traditional Anglicanism was Article 34: 'It is not necessary that Traditions and Ceremonies be in all places one, or utterly like; for at all times they have been divers, and may be changed according to the diversities of countries, times and manners, so that [provided that] nothing be ordained against God's Word.' An attempt to liberalise this position was made in 1771 with the submission of a petition (known as the Feathers' Tavern Petition after the place where it was signed) to Parliament with 200 signatures, initiated by Francis Blackburne, Archdeacon of Cleveland, 'to allow the clergy to interpret the Bible in the light of reason and conscience instead of being bound by creeds and formulae'.[2] It was rejected (mainly as a result of a powerful speech by Edmund Burke) as granting too much liberty to tender consciences and potentially allowing Anglican clergy to preach Unitarian views.

One of the benefits of the Church of England was to ensure there was an educated man in each parish, and (though subverted by absenteeism and arrogant placemen) this often did provide a leavening of society by men of wisdom and concern for others – until the parish system was swamped by the squalid urban pustules of the Industrial Revolution. Intellectually, the eighteenth-century Church provided an income for several scholars, such as Gilbert White, many of them scientists whose motivation was to explore the wonders of a God-created world. Many, as Ronald Blythe wrote of Parson Woodforde, were country gentlemen occupying a living and doing their duty in a 'spiritually comatose' Church.[3] The laity were expected to attend Church services regularly, know the Lord's Prayer and the Apostle's Creed, be confirmed in due course, pay their tithes, be outwardly obedient and behave well.

But in the late eighteenth century the mood in Europe was changing; in Art it became known as Romanticism, in Religion its counterpart was Evangelicalism. It was an outpouring of feelings, of aspiration and inspiration, of love, passion and sympathy (but sometimes rather short on empathy). The ideal religious life became one of drama, beginning with a Pauline moment of conversion, a personal life-changing experience that fires up the soul to labour ceaselessly in the service of God, caring for the poor, the hungry, the exploited and the marginalised. The Church of England may have neglected its theology, its form of worship and its organisation, but the evangelical revival was resuscitating English religious life.

The combination of Quakers and (mainly evangelical) Anglicans eager to put a stop to slavery became louder and more organised. Granville Sharp (1735–1813), son of an archdeacon, had been instrumental in bringing the James Somerset case to court, which resulted in Mansfield's influential judgement. He worked closely with his American counterpart, the Quaker Anthony Benezet, and both produced seminal anti-slavery publications.

The slave trade was thought by many to be an unpleasant but essential element of British trade, and although being master of a slave ship was not an enjoyable job, it was considered a difficult and demanding one and therefore a possible step towards promotion – something that would look good on a résumé. John Paul Jones served as a mate in a couple of slaving ships. John Newton was master of two slavers, and after two religious experiences, he gave up his rather chequered life at sea to be ordained an Anglican clergyman in 1764. He became a popular preacher, a writer of hymns, and an important campaigner for the ending of slavery.

Another sailor who was very influential in the abolition of slavery was Luke Collingwood, who had sailed with James Cook as a fellow servant. Luke, born in Leith, had entered *Friendship* in 1747, probably in July, as a 14-year-old, four years younger than Cook. Luke remained in *Friendship* in 1748, but joined Cook in *Three Brothers* in June of that year. Collingwood saw out his apprenticeship in that ship. In 1754, he was a seaman in a ship called *Norfolk*, before returning briefly to serve in Walker's *Freelove* in the same year. He moved to Liverpool (along with Bristol, one of the main ports for slavers) and served as ship's surgeon on the slaver *William*. In 1781, he was master of the newly acquired 110-ton slave ship *Zong*, sailing from Africa on 17 September with a seventeen-man crew and 442 slaves, many times the optimum number for a ship of that size.[4] Fever broke out among the slaves and the crew; by late November, sixty of the slaves had died, and the crew was reduced to ten men. Collingwood decided that the best policy was to discard the sick slaves; 133 of them were callously thrown into the Atlantic, while ten others leapt to their deaths rather than endure the further indignity of being tossed overboard like rubbish.

Collingwood's motives were to reduce the spreading of the fever (and thus preserve the value of the remaining slaves), to protect the lives of the massively outnumbered crew, and to save money for the owners. It was also an insurance scam. If Collingwood could claim that the slaves were thrown overboard to protect the ship, then the insurers paid for the loss; if they died on board, the owners paid. Collingwood asserted, untruthfully, that the ship was short of water so some slaves were sacrificed for the preservation of the ship, its crew and the rest of the 'cargo'. No doubt he thought that what he did was a shrewd piece of business, and the owners would be pleased; after all, it was just trade, as evidenced in the *Public Advertiser*'s chillingly matter-of-fact report:[5]

The following ships are arrived at Jamaica, viz. the *Adventure*, Muir with 360 slaves; *Champion*, Abrams, with 685 ditto; *Othello*, Johnson, with 190 ditto; *Zong*, Collingwood, with 208 ditto, and *Ulysses*, Fisher, with 390 ditto

When the owners sought to claim the statutory £30 (*c.* £46,000) a head for the drowned dittos, the underwriters contested it, and the matter was taken to court in March 1783. Olaudah Equiano brought the case to the notice of Granville Sharp, and what started as a fraudulent insurance claim became a national scandal.

The London Quakers had submitted a petition to Parliament that year, and petitions were to form a vital part of the anti-slavery movement. However, the Quakers realised that forming an alliance with the Anglican abolitionists would give them greater influence and political power, and in 1787 the non-denominational Society for the Abolition of the Slave Trade was formed. William Wilberforce of Hull, Evangelical Anglican and MP for Yorkshire, was particularly useful in relentlessly bringing abolitionist bills before Parliament, the first being in 1791. After the bill was rejected – by a substantial majority – Anna Barbauld, teacher and poet, wrote *An Epistle to William Wilberforce Esq. On the Rejection of the Bill for Abolishing the Slave Trade*, which included the lines:

> The Preacher, Poet, Senator [i.e. Wilberforce] in vain
> Has rattled in her [Britain's] sight the Negro's chain;
> With his deep groans assail'd her startled ear,
> And rent the veil that hid his constant tear;
> Forc'd her averted eyes his stripes to scan,
> Beneath the bloody scourge laid bare the man,
> …
> She knows and she persists—Still Afric bleeds,
> Uncheck'd, the human traffic still proceeds;
> She stamps her infamy to future time,
> And on her harden'd forehead seals the crime.

William Bligh's 1787 expedition in the *Bounty* was to bring breadfruit from Tahiti to the plantations in the West Indies as cheap food for the slaves. The voyage was the plan of Joseph Banks who was not simply into finding new plants, but also into ascertaining their properties and, if possible, transplanting them into different places where they could be useful and profitable. For example, when he was at Tahiti on the *Endeavour* voyage, Banks had sowed seeds there of lemon, orange, lime and watermelon which had come from South America.[6]

Bligh, who was known as a brilliant navigator and who had served as sailing master and later lieutenant on *Resolution*, was an obvious choice. Unfortunately, circumstances were against him. The *Bounty*, previously a Hull collier, was only 214 tons, and classed as an 'armed vessel' with the status of a cutter. This meant that there were no marines aboard, and Bligh was the only officer until he upgraded the mate, Fletcher Christian, to a temporary lieutenant. The crew was forty-five men, of whom twenty-five were seamen, the rest included the warrant officers and the two gardeners. The first of these two was David Nelson who had been gardener-botanist on Cook's third voyage, and Bligh would have known him and admired his professionalism; since then, Nelson had been working for Banks at Kew. His was the responsibility of caring for the breadfruit plants, and finding and recording new plants. The other gardener was William Brown. Because she was such a small ship, *Bounty* was 'simultaneously overcrowded and undermanned',[7] which tended to exacerbate stress and conflict. Some of the warrant officers, particularly John Fryer the sailing master, were not helpful, but Bligh had no alternative but to work with them.

Bounty finally sailed from Spithead on 24 November 1787, two months later than originally planned. Bligh had learnt much from James Cook, and in many ways they were similar; both were good navigators* and mapmakers, both were true professionals knowing and doing what was needed, and expecting the same high standards from the crew. And when the people responsible failed to reach these standards they were cross. Cook got angry, and in his third voyage his anger on occasion seemed to be out of control, but Cook had the common touch and a certain gruff charisma, and he was very ship-wise. Bligh did not really understand human nature; if he had to reprimand someone he used unseemly language and did not care who was listening – a sure way to make enemies. Bligh thought that if he was cheerful and friendly the next day, the unpleasantness was in the past and forgotten. Fletcher Christian was particularly touchy and unforgiving, and not good at taking orders that were blunt and tactless.** The weather did not help; Bligh spent a month trying stubbornly to battle his small ship round Cape Horn before taking the route round South Africa. *Bounty* reached Tahiti on 26 October 1788, to a rapturous welcome; but the delay meant that he would have to remain on the island for longer than had been planned, which was not good for keeping discipline.

Bounty eventually sailed with on 4 April 1789 with 774 pots of breadfruit plants.

The story of the mutiny is well known, as is Bligh's amazing achievement in navigating the boat over 3,800 miles to Timor with just a sextant, losing only one man – who was killed by natives on Tofua where they had landed to find food.[†]

---

* Cook had taken on board *Resolution* the Chronometer K1, which he called a 'never failing guide' (Sobel, p.150); it later travelled with the First Fleet to Botany Bay. Bligh took on board *Bounty* K2, which had previously been on the polar voyage of Constantine Phipps (Lord Mulgrave). After the mutiny, it was taken to Pitcairn Island.

** It may have run in the family: Fletcher's brother Charles had been a mutineer. He was on a merchant ship, and mutiny was a capital offence only in Royal Navy ships.

† David Nelson was in the boat with Bligh; he arrived at Timor safely, but died there after catching a fever while botanising. William Brown was one of the mutineers; he was killed on Pitcairn Island.

A breadfruit tree, *Artocarpus altilis*.

Bligh was stubborn and persistent, and when he returned to Britain he was troubled that he had failed to fetch and deliver the breadfruit which he had been ordered to do. In 1791, in HMS *Providence*, he was able to achieve this successfully, with the support of Joseph Banks, who never lost faith in him. On July 1792, he sailed from Tahiti with over 2,000 potted-up breadfruit and over 500 other plants. For his successful transplanting of the breadfruit plants William Bligh was awarded the Royal Society Medal. The breadfruit prospered, but the slaves refused to eat them. However, since then the breadfruit, which is a high-yielding plant whose fruit is rich in vitamins B and C (as well as the bark having medicinal properties), has gradually become a part of the diet in the Caribbean.

In all this time, *Freelove* continued her whaling career. John Brown remained master. William Anderson, who had been a servant on *Freelove* in 1768, and then a seaman, was a harpooner in 1787. Alexander Sinclair's apprenticeship ended in 1787, and he was to become a line manager in 1789.

In 1788, the early news from the first whalers from the Greenland Seas brought bad news, 'Many ships were beset in the ice, and it is feared there will be much loss amongst them.' The *Chance* of Whitby was lost 'in a heavy north gale', and *Freelove* returned from the Davis Straits with only one 'fish'. The following year, Whitby sent eighteen ships, the third largest British whaling fleet (after London and Hull); but four of them, including *Freelove*, returned 'clean'.

In 1790, *Freelove* reverted to being a collier, making at least six coal runs between Shields and London. In 1791, John Brown, after twenty years of captaining *Freelove*, was replaced by Henry Charter for another year as a collier, again with at least six trips culminating in over-wintering at Whitby. In 1792, with a new master, Thomas Smith, *Freelove* made another foray to the Davis Straits – in spite of the reduction of the bounty to 25*s* per ton. Some of the crew members were old hands in Whitby whaling ships: the chief mate Joseph Paxton had been a boatsteerer both in *Volunteer* (1772) and in *Speedwell* (1775); spectioneer Robert Mann had been a harpooner in *Marlborough* (1791), and boatsteerer Francis Beverly had fulfilled the same post in *Whitby* (1787). Others had sailed in *Freelove* in her whaling days: Magnus Sinclair, line manager (1787); Paul Hodgson, harpooner (1787–89), and Miles Townsend, carpenter (1790).

The expedition seems to have been unsuccessful, as shortly after she arrived back at Whitby in August *Freelove* set out for Petersburg with Robert Jackson as captain, arriving at Elsinore on 6 September. Benjamin Bridekirk, who had been harpooner in *Freelove* (1787–88), had been mate of *Marlborough* in 1791 and it is possible he continued in that role in 1792, as he only joined *Freelove* for the Baltic voyage. He would have known Magnus Sinclair well, and Paul Hodgson very well, having been working on *Freelove* as fellow harpooners for twelve months.

Etching by W. Miller, from Turner's *The Shipwreck*.

The Halifax gibbet.

Freelove was in London on 29 November, and probably was on the run back to Whitby (perhaps with only the permanent crew) when she was 'lost on or about 3 Dec'. She was a fine old ship of 64 years, one of many victims of the treacherous North Sea. There is no information about the crew.

One hundred and fifty years after Charles I raised his standard in war against his Parliament (an action that was to lead to his execution outside the Banqueting House in Whitehall) the French king Louis XVI was deposed, and a republic was declared. Louis was brought to trial on December 26 1792, and executed on 21 January, using a device which had been invented, and long since abandoned, in Halifax, Yorkshire.

On 1 February 1793, France declared war on Britain, which found itself for the second time in two decades in conflict with an enemy which believed it was fighting for liberty; and once again Britain had to rethink what it means to live in a free society.

Appendix

The Measure of Things

Money

Bxritish money at this time was in pounds (£), shillings (s) and pennies or pence (d). There were also farthings (a quarter of a penny) and halfpennies. Apart from the demise of the farthings in late 1950s, this continued to be the case until early 1971. There were 12 pennies in the shilling and 20 shillings in the pound. Three hundred and fifty pounds nine shillings and sixpence would usually be written £350 9s 6d or £350-9-6.

When our monetary system changed to the present decimal one, the pound remained the same, with 100 new pence in the pound. One new penny (p) was equal to 2.4 old pennies (d). However, this equivalence was only relevant at the time; to say in the twenty-first century that 10 shillings is equivalent to 50 pence is a meaningless comment. What we want to know is what the old money at a given time in the past is worth now. However this is no easy task.* Generally, there are two main, but different, ways of calculating this: using the retail price index, and by using average earnings. They differ considerably.

The retail price index (RPI) tells us what the price of a commodity was compared to today's price so, for example, a small family car in 1950 might have cost around £500 whereas to buy one now might cost about £13,000. So using these figures one might say that £1 in 1950 is worth £26 today. But not many families had cars in 1950 compared with car ownership today, not because they didn't want a car, but because they couldn't afford one. So if we want to know what share of an average person's income would have been be taken up with this purchase (i.e. how *affordable* it was) compared with today the equivalent would be about £41,000. As Adam Smith put it, 'The real price of everything … is the toil and trouble of acquiring it.'

---

* I have used 'Measuring Worth' on www.measuringworth.com. At the time of going to print the latest year ('today's value') is 2011.

The further back in time one goes, the more difficult it is to make meaningful comparisons, as those who lived in the eighteenth century lived in a world with different retail demands and a different distribution of earnings. At the time covered by this book, the average earnings index gives a value in excess of ten times the retail price index value. Where sums in old money are mentioned in the text, the approximate modern value usually appears immediately after in brackets. The retail price index is possibly more useful for small items, so for anything under a pound the equivalent in modern value uses this index. For sizeable amounts I have used the average earnings index, which gives a more realistic estimate. Sometimes, I have used both values, in which case the retail price value is the first, and the average earnings value the second.

Length

The units of length were mainly inches (in), feet (ft) and yards. Two feet and 6 inches can be written as 2ft 6in or as 2'6". There were 12 inches to a foot, and 3 feet in a yard. A mile was 1,760 yards. A fathom, used in measuring depth, was 6 feet.

Their approximate modern metric equivalents are:

1 inch = 2.5cm
1 foot = 30.5cm
1 yard = 0.91m
1 fathom = 1.83m

Speed

Speed of ships at sea was and is measured in knots; a knot is a nautical mile per hour. A nautical mile is a minute of longitude at the equator, which is approximately 2,027 yards. One knot is approximately 1.15mph (1.85kph).

Weight

The imperial pound (lb) is the smallest unit of weight which appears in this book, it was divided into 16 ounces. Cargoes were often measured in hundredweight (cwt) which was 112lb; a 'quarter' was a quarter of a hundredweight (i.e. 28lb), and 20cwt made a ton.

Their approximate modern metric equivalents are:

1 pound (lb) = 0.45kg
1 hundredweight (cwt) = 50.8kg
1 ton = 1.02 metric tonnes

Volume

Imperial measurements of volume:

4 gills = 1 pint
2 pints = 1 quart
4 quarts = 1 gallon (gall)
1 anker = 10 gallons
1 barrel = 31½ gallons
1 hogshead = 2 barrels
1 pipe (also 1 butt) = 2 hogsheads

Dry measure:

1 bushel = 8 pints

Approximate metric equivalents:

1 gill = 142ml
1 pint = 568ml
1 gall = 4.55 litres
1 bushel = 36.4 litres

Coal was measured in chaldrons, sometimes called chalders. Confusingly, a Newcastle chaldron was different from a London chaldron. Colliers taking coal from Newcastle to London would therefore buy the coal in Newcastle chaldrons and sell it in London chaldrons; an additional complication was that London chaldrons were based on a volume, whereas Newcastle chaldrons were based on weight (though in practice they could be measured either way).

Newcastle chaldron = 52½cwt
Newcastle keel = 8 chaldrons
London chaldron = 36 bushels = approx. 25$^1/_3$cwt

Ship Tonnage

A ship's tonnage was meant to indicate the number of tons of cargo she was able to carry (tons burthen). Finding a way of assessing a ship's tonnage was a very vexed issue, as much depended upon the type of cargo, and what was, in practice, measurable. For colliers, vessels were often, and usefully, rated by the amount of coal they could carry.

There were a number of different methods of finding tonnage in the early eighteenth century, which caused much confusion. So far as the Navy Board was concerned, being able to measure the tonnage of a vessel was crucial, as transports were chartered at so much per ton. From 1695, they would have used the following formula, which was current at the time, to assess tonnage where L is the length of the keel and B is the breadth of the vessel:

$$\frac{L \times B \times \frac{1}{2}B}{94}$$

This was deemed not very accurate and was not compulsory. An Act of Parliament (1772) laid down an official standard way of measuring ships' tonnage. The dimensions were to be measured thus: 'The Length shall be taken on a straight Line along the Rabbet of the Keel of the Ship, from the back of the Main sternpost to a perpendicular Line from the Forepart of the Main Stem under the Bowsprit' and 'the Breadth shall be taken from the outside of the Plank in the Broadest Place in the Ship, be it either above or below the Main Wales, exclusive of all manner of doubling Planks that may be wrought upon the Sides of the Ship'. These measurements were then used in the following equation to find 'the true Contents of the Tonnage'.[*]

$$\frac{(L\ ^3/_5B) \times B \times \frac{1}{2}B}{94}$$

All vessels measured by the Navy Board would have had their tonnage established in this way from January 1776 (though there was a slight change to the way the breadth was measured in 1781). This tended to produce a lower figure than did the former equation, which meant that the Navy Board paid a smaller sum for hiring transports. Both these equations can result in fractional 94th parts; I have taken the liberty of recording these as decimals, i.e. a ship measured as $317^{89}/_{94}$ tons I have transcribed as 317.89 tons.

[*] See Syrett (1970) pp.110–13.

Although Steel in 1805 described the 1772 regulation as being a 'very defective rule' because it meant that all vessels with the same 'length of keel and extreme breadth' will 'appear to be precisely of the same burthen or capacity even if their bodies be extremely full or extremely sharp', the system persisted. The next significant change in standardising tonnage measurement was the Moorsom Rule, in the mid-nineteenth century.

The Calendar

Although New Year's Day was customarily celebrated on 1 January, the official beginning of the year in England, Ireland and Wales was 25 March, which was Lady Day, one of the four Quarter Days, the others being Midsummer Day (24 June), Michaelmas (29 Sept) and Christmas. Quarter days were when accounts had to be presented, debts and rents paid, and were usually the times when the contracts of employment, especially for manual workers, began and terminated. Beginning the year on 25 March caused confusion as, for example, the day after 31 December 1728 was followed by 1 January 1728 and the day after 24 March 1728 was 25 March 1729. Wisely, the Scots began their year on 1 January, as they had since 1600, but the rest of Britain did not join them until 1752.

The Quakers disapproved of the pagan names for the days of the week and (most of) the months of the year, so they replaced them with numbers – Sunday being the first day of the week. They called March the first month of the year until 1752 when January became their first month.

The old Julian calendar was used throughout Europe in the Middle Ages even though it was clear that it was becoming increasingly out of synchronisation with the solar year. In 1582, Pope Gregory XIII introduced a better calendar (the Gregorian calendar), now fairly universally used, which benefited from the work of Kepler and other astronomers. It was readily adopted by Catholic countries (and Holland), but Protestant and Orthodox countries were loath to follow a Catholic calendar. Britain did not adopt it until 1752 by which time she was eleven days out of step with the solar calendar, and a day behind the Catholic countries of Europe. Eleven days were taken out of September, though the days of the week continued so the day following Wednesday 2 September 1752 was Thursday 14 September. Much fun is made of the protests with the slogan 'Give us back our eleven days'; but those who rented a cottage at a fixed rate per calendar month paid for eleven days they never had, and agricultural labourers employed until Michaelmas, if paid by the day, not only lost eleven days' earnings but also prematurely faced the long hungry months from Michaelmas until Lady Day when there was less chance of finding winter work. For many, losing eleven days was not a joke. It probably did not affect transport ships which seem to have been paid by the lunar month.

Notes

Abbreviations

Burney   The Burney Collection of Early Newspapers, British Library. Digitised by Gale Group.

ECCO   Eighteenth Century Collection Online, Gale Group.

TNA   The National Archives, Kew.

NMM   The National Maritime Museum, Greenwich.

Chapter 1. *Present Succession*

1.   Hazard, p.121.
2.   From *Records of the Colony of Rhode Island*, i, pp.374–8. Quoted in Rufus Jones, pp.54–5.
3.   Dryden, *Annus Mirabilis*, v.12.
4.   Bryant, Arthur, *The Fire and the Rose*. Collins. 1965. p.129.
5.   Quoted in David Salmon, *The French Invasion*, p.133.
6.   Evelyn, *Diary*, 31 May 1672.
7.   Patent Rolls, 26 Charles II. Quoted in Jeffrey, pp.85–6.
8.   *Contemporary Parliamentary Records*. Quoted in Jeffrey, p.84.

Chapter 2: *Liberty* and *Property*

1.   Braithwaite, p.437.
2.   Quoted in Cragg, p.237.
3.   *Spectator*, No. 465, Saturday 23 August 1712.

Chapter 3: *Brotherly Love*

1. Fiennes, p.101.
2. TNA E190/159/8.
3. Gaskin, p.234.
4. Davis, p.49.
5. Davis, p.54.
6. *Windsor August 13 1704 The Lord Tunbridge Arrived.* ECCO.
7. *Ibid.*
8. *The Conduct of the Allies*, 1711, Internet Archive, p.48.
9. Ventress (a), p.50.
10. St John, Letters, IV, 369, to the queen, 27 Sept 1711. Quoted in Duguid.
11. *Ibid.*, pp.122–3.
12. Ridley, Matt, *The Origins of Virtue.* Viking. 1996.
13. Clarke, pp.39–40.

Chapter 4: *The Prospect of Whitby*

1. *A Description of England and Wales.* London. 1770. p.270.
2. Pepys, *Diary*, 6 August 1662.
3. *Statutes at Large*, Vol III. ECCO.
4. Thornton (2009), pp.11–13.
5. Raistrick, p.32.

Chapter 5: *Good Agreement* and *Truelove*

1. Besse, Ch.4, p.142.
2. Quoted in Ventress, p.45.
3. Fielding, *Tom Jones*, p.265.

Chapter 6: *Peace and Plenty*

1. 1713, 25, pp.7–10. Quoted in Duguid.
2. *Review of the Affairs of France*. 1704 (i) 86. Quoted in Duguid, p.14.
3. Boswell, *Life of Johnson*. 7 April 1779.
4. TNA CUST 90/1.
5. Quoted in Ventress (a), p.64.
6. Young, p.495.

7. Clarke, p.40.
8. *Ibid.*, p.39.
9. *Leviticus*, 25.10.
10. *London Evening Post*, 15 October 1734. Burney.
11. Will of Margaret Holt, widow of Joseph, 1749. Borthwick.

Chapter 7: *Fair Trader*

1. Davidoff & Hall, p.198.
2. Defoe (1728), p.68.
3. Hausman, p.473.
4. Cremer, p.127.
5. Oldroyd, p.15.
6. Pope, *Imitations of Horace*. Book II, Epistle II, ll.270–3.

Chapter 8: *Mars*

1. Quoted in Plumb, pp.19–20.
2. TNA ADM 106/3305.
3. Quoted in Plumb, p.40.

Chapter 9: *Enterprise*

1. Grigson, p.294.
2. Archbishop Herring's *Visitations* 1743. Quoted in 'The Established Church' a chapter from O'Sullivan, Dan, *Great Ayton – A History of the Village*. http://greatayton.wdfiles.com/local--files/churches/Religion-The-Established-Church.pdf.
3. Letter from James Cook to John Walker, 19 August 1775. Quoted in Beaglehole, p.445.
4. TNA C 12/857/14. Transcribed by Dave King.
5. See Thornton (2000) and Great Ayton website.
6. Baines, 2010, pp.27–8.
7. Young, p.851. He says he received this information from Mrs Dodds of Boulby, Mr Sanderson's daughter.
8. Prebble, p.221.

Chapter 10: *Freelove*

1. TNA ADM 68/194.
2. TNA ADM 106/3312.
3. TNA C103/205. Transcribed by Dave King.
4. TNA E 190: 248/9, 248/10, 252/1 & 253/7.
5. Hausman, p.465.
6. Miller, p.14.
7. The artefacts are in the Maritime Museum, Gdańsk. See Ossowski (2008) and Baines (2010).
8. Gaskin, pp.266–7.
9. Russell, P., *England Displayed*. 1769. Vol. II, p.158.
10. *A Short Account of the Life and Death of Nathanael Othen*. London. 1758. ECCO.

Chapter 11: *Three Brothers*

1. 'Authentic memoirs of the late celebrated Captain Cook' in *London Chronicle*. 11 May 1780. Burney.
2. Julia Rae, 'Wapping' in Robson, J.
3. TNA E190/248/2.
4. TNA E190/249/5.
5. *An Account of the Life, Travels, and Christian Experiences in the Work of the Ministry of Samuel Bownas*. London. 1756. pp.182–3.

Chapter 12: *Flora*

1. *Letter to John Rodes*. 1690. Quoted in Raistrick, p.254.
2. Letter from Thomas Lower. Quoted in Raistrick, p.244.
3. Preface to the Reader in *Catelogus Plantarum circa Cantabrigiam nascentium*. Ewen, A.H. and Prime, T. (eds), *Ray's Flora of Cambridgeshire*. Hitchen, Wheldon and Wesley. 1975. p.22. Quoted in Armstrong, p.46.
4. Ray, J., *Observations Topographical, Moral and Physiological*. 1673. p.122. Quoted in Armstrong, p.127.
5. TNA ADM 106/278. Deptford Letter Books. Letters dated 29 August & 2 September 1762.
6. Quoted in Raistrick, p.256.
7. Much of this information is from the Natural History Museum Website.

8. Fissell, Mary and Cooter, Roger 'Exploring Natural Knowledge: Science and the Popular' in Porter, Roy (ed.), *The Cambridge History of Science. Volume 4. Eighteenth-Century Science.*

9. *Ibid.*, p.152.

10. Jennings, p.3.

Chapter 13: *Mary*

1   Taylor, H., p.2.

2. *Joshua*, Ch. 10, vv.12–14.

3. *Job*, Ch. 9, v. 8.

4. 'On Miracles', section 10 of *An Enquiry Concerning Human Understanding*. 1748.

5. Barker (2011), Appendix 2.

6. *A Voyage to the Pacific Ocean, Undertaken by the Command of His Majesty for making Discoveries in the Northern Hemisphere Performed under the direction of Captains Cooke Clerke and Gore In the Years 1776,7,8,9, and 80. In Four Volumes.* Printed by R. Morison junior for R. Robinson and Son. 1785. Vol. I, p.37. See also Gaskin p.386: 'In 1750 he [Cook] was in the *Maria*, belonging to Mr John Wilkinson of Whitby, employed in the Baltic trade under the command of Captain Gaskin, a relation of Mr Walker.'

7. TNA ADM 106/244, 28 December 1758.

Chapter 14: *Friendship*

1. From a speech made in 1800 about Napoleonic France. MacArthur, pp.193–5.

2. Cook to Walker, 19 August 1775; Phillips coll. Salem, Mass.; transcribed in Beaglehole, J.C. (ed.), *Journals of Captain James Cook* (with *Addenda and Corrigenda*). Quoted in Beaglehole, *The Life of Captain James Cook*. p.445.

3. Cowper, William (1731–1800). *The Diverting History of John Gilpin*. ll.98.

4. Equiano, p.74.

5. TNA ADM 106/3312, 15 September 1758.

6. Beaglehole, p.10.

7. Syrett (2008), p.3.

8. TNA ADM 106/3312.

9. Taylor, H., p.11.

10. Smith, p.700.

Chapter 15: *Earl of Pembroke*

1. Wilkinson, p.10.
2. TNA ADM 106/3305. 7–8 July 1741.
3. Rae, p.237.
4. TNA ADM 106/244.
5. Campbell, John, *A Political Survey of Britain*. Vol. III. 2nd Edition. Dublin. 1775. p.32.
6. R.B. Sheridan. Quoted by O'Toole, p.84.
7. Watkins, p.8.
8. Byron, *Don Juan*, Canto I, LXIII.
9. *Newcastle Courant*. 4 July 1767.
10. *The Westminster Journal and London Political Miscellany*. 16 July 1768. Burney.
11 TNA ADM 106/1168.

Chapter 16: *Marquis of Rockingham* and *Marquis of Granby*

1. Mantel, Hilary, *Bring up the Bodies*. Fourth Estate. 2012. p.79.
2. O'Brian, pp.168–9.
3. Rachel Wilson. Quoted in Thornton (1998), p.1496.
4. Thornton (1998), p.1497.
5. *Morning Chronicle and London Advertiser*. 14 June 1773. Burney.
6. *Voyages of the Tamar*. http://www.brucehunt.co.uk.
7. Goldsmith, p.202.
8. http://www.brucehunt.co.uk.
9. Windsor, Royal Archives 1323. Quoted in O'Brien, p.159.
10. Sobel, p.145.
11. Bakewell, p.70.
12. *Elegy XXI*. These lines refer to the Welsh Hills.
13. O'Brian, p.165.
14. O'Brian, p.154.
15. Kew Royal Botanic Gardens website.

Chapter 17: *Endeavour*

1. NMM ADM 354/185/190.
2. TNA ADM 106/1205/364.
3. These details from the master's log TNA ADM 52/1720.
4. TNA ADM 33/641.
5. *A Short Description of Falkland's Islands, their Produce, Climate and Natural History*. TNA ADM 7/704.

Chapter 18: *Diligence*

1. State Library New South Wales: http://www.sl.nsw.gov.au/discover_collections/history_nation/voyages/wallis/index.html.
2. Dr Samuel Johnson on Phipps' voyage, from Chapman, R.W. (ed.), James Boswell, *Life of Johnson*. Quoted in Savours, p.403.
3. Phipps, p.11.
4. Equiano, p.172.
5. Alexander, pp.34–7.
6. TNA E 379/5. Hull Port Book. 1774. Overseas. Inwards.
7. TNA ADM 106/3318.
8. O'Brian, pp.219ff.

Chapter 19: *Freedom* and *Adventure*

1. MacArthur, pp.77–80.
2. From Sichel, Walter, *Sheridan*, Vol. 1. London. 1909. pp.624ff. Quoted in O'Toole, p.98.
3. TNA ADM 49/125.
4. TNA ADM 106/3318.
5. *Ibid.*
6. Presumably a contemporary newspaper, but Weatherill does not attribute it.
7. Pfister, Albert & Seume, Johann Gottfried, *The Voyage of the First Hessian Army from Portsmouth to New York 1776*. Project Gutenberg.
8. TNA ADM 1/487.
9. Abbass, Part II, p.317.
10. *Ibid.*, p.318.
11. Brogan, p.180.
12. *The Public Advertiser*, 3 January 1776. Burney.

Chapter 20: *Lord Sandwich* and *Leviathan*

1. Quoted in Hibbert, p.196.
2. From the *New Jersey Gazette*, 13 May, quoted in *St James' Chronicle*, 2–4 July 1778. Burney.
3. TNA ADM 106/3404.
4. Blythe (1989), p.113.
5. TNA ADM 106/3318, 5 October 1776 & 6 October 1777.
6. Baines, pp.56ff.
7. Vol. 26, p.152 & Vol. 32, p.308. Quoted by Grocott, p.314.

8. Mentioned in *Lloyds List*, *The Hull Packet* and the *York Herald*.
9. R.O. Morris gave a lecture *Surveying Ships from Cook to the Computer Age* at the National Maritime Museum, Greenwich which appeared later in the *Mariner's Mirror*, Vol. 72, November 1986, pp.385–410 in which he stated that 'The *Adventure* ... became a fireship, and was eventually sold out of service in 1783'.
10. Lubbock, p.85.
11. Young, opposite p.568.
12. Data from Barrow, p.24.
13. Lubbock, pp.115–6.
14. Prices from Stephanie Jones, p.305.
15. *Public Advertiser*, 18 June 1779. Burney.
16. Sobel, p.150.
17. TNA ADM 36/8049.
18. TNA PROB 11/1136/109.
19. James, Silas, *A Narrative of a Voyage to Arabia, India, &c.* ECCO.
20. To the Earl of Hillsborough, Secretary of State for the Southern Department, dated 16 April 1781. Quoted by Silas James, p.19.
21. '*Le même qui avait fait le tour du monde avec le capitaine Cook*', *Mariner's Mirror*, Vol. 17, No.1, p.84 (1931). Quoted by John F. Allen.
22. Smith, Adam, Book 5, Chapter 1, Part 3, Article 1, pp.739–40.

Chapter 21: *Liberty*

1. Hume, p.77.
2. Cragg, p.169.
3. Blythe, p.75.
4. John Robson, *The Zong Affair*. Cook's Log, Vol. 35, No. 1 and Hullwebs History of Hull, www.hullwebs.co.uk.
5. *The Public Advertiser*, 13 March 1782. Burney.
6. Holmes, p.33.
7. Kennedy, p.17.

Bibliography

Books and Articles

Abbass, D.K. *Rhode Island in the Revolution: Big Happenings in the Smallest Colony.* 4 Vols. Rhode Island Marine Archaeology Project (RIMAP). 2006 (2007).

Alexander, Michael. *Omai, 'Noble Savage'.* Collins. 1977.

Allen, Richard C. '"Remember me to my good friend Captain Walker": James Cook and the North Yorkshire Quakers' in Williams, Glyndwr (ed.). *Captain Cook Explorations and Reassessments.* Boydell. 2004.

Armstrong, Patrick. *The English Parson-Naturalist.* Gracewing. 2000.

Atkinson, J.C. *Memorials of Old Whitby.* Macmillan. 1894.

Badeslade, Thomas & William Henry Toms. *Chorographia Britanniae, or A Set of Maps of all the Counties in England and Wales.* 1742.

Bakewell, Sarah. *The English Dane.* Chatto & Windus. 2005 (Vintage. 2006).

Barker, Rosalin. *The Rise of an Early Modern Shipping Industry; Whitby's Golden Fleet, 1600–1750.* Boydell Press. 2011.

Barrow, Tony. *The Whaling Trade of North-Eastern England 1750–1850.* University of Sunderland Press. 2001.

Barton, Simon. *A History of Spain.* Palgrave Macmillan. 2004.

Beaglehole, J.C. *The Life of Captain James Cook.* A.&C. Black. 1974.

Besse, Joseph. *A Collection of the Sufferings of the People called Quakers.* 1753. (Facsimile. Intro by William Session, 'Sufferings of Early Quakers; Yorkshire 1652 to 1690'. York. 1998.)

Besse, Joseph. *A Collection of the Sufferings of the People called Quakers.* 1753. (Facsimiles. Intro by Michael Gandy. York. 'Sufferings of Early Quakers … Durham & Northumberland 1658 to 1690 [et al]'. York. 2000.)

Blythe, Ronald. *Each Returning Day, the Pleasure of Diaries.* Viking. 1989.

Boreham, Ian. 'William Sanderson of Staithes' in *Cook's Log.* Vol. 18. No.4 1995.

Boswell, James. *Life of Johnson.* (ed. Charles Osgood. Project Gutenberg. 2006.)

Braithwaite, William C. *The Second Period of Quakerism.* CUP. 1919. (Internet Archive.)

Brand, John. *Observations on Popular Antiquities.* Newcastle. 1777.

Bray, William (ed.). *Memoirs Illustrative of the Life and Writings of John Evelyn.* Vol. 2. 2nd edn. London. 1915. (Internet Archive.)

Brogan, Hugh. *The Longman History of the United States.* Longman. 1985 (1999).

Capper, Paul. *A Cook Chronology.* Captain Cook Study Unit. 1997.

Chapman, Colin R. *Marriage Laws, Rites, Records & Customs.* Lochin. 1996.

Clarke, Lilian. *Family Chronicles.* Wellingborough. 1911.

Convey, Sheila. *North East England Local History.* www.otherworldnortheast.org.uk

Cragg, G. R. *The Church in the Age of Reason (1648–1789).* Penguin. 1960.

Cremer, John. *Ramblin' Jack.* (Transcribed by R.R. Bellamy. Jonathan Cape. 1936.)

Davidoff, L. & Hall, C. *Family Fortunes: Men and Women of the English Middle Classes 1780–1850.* Routledge. 1987.

Davis, Ralph. *The Rise of the English Shipping Industry In the Seventeenth and Eighteenth Centuries.* David & Charles. 1962 (1972).

Defoe, Daniel. *A Journey Through the Whole Island of Great Britain.* 1724–26. (Penguin. 1971 (1986).)

Defoe, Daniel. *A Plan of the English Commerce.* London. 1728.

Duguid, Paul. 'The Making of Methuen: The Commercial Treaty in the English Imagination'. people.ischool.berkeley.edu/~duduid/articles/M_OF_M.pdf.

Edwards, Philip (ed.). *The Journals of Captain Cook*, prepared from the original manuscripts by J.C. Beaglehole for the Hakluyt Society, 1955–67. Penguin Books. 1999.

Equiano, Olaudah. *The Interesting Narrative, and Other Writings.* London. 1789. (Ed. V. Carretta. Penguin. 1995 (2003).)

Evelyn, Helen. *The History of the Evelyn Family.* London. 1915. (Internet Archive.)

Fiennes, Celia. Manuscript (ed. Christopher Morris, *The Illustrated Journeys of Celia Fiennes c.1682–c.1712.* Macdonald. (1982) 1984.)

Fox, George. *Journal.* 1694. (Online by Street Corner Society www.strecorsoc.org. See also Nickalls, John L.)

Frank, Peter. *Yorkshire Fisherfolk.* Phillimore. 2002.

Freeth, John. *The Political Songster, or A Touch on the Times.* Birmingham. 1790. (ECCO.)

Garnett, R. (ed.). 'Correspondence of the Archbishop Herring and Lord Hardwicke during the Rebellion of 1745' in Poole, Reginald. (ed.). *The English Historical Review* Vol. XIX 1904. Part 1 No. LXXV pp.528–554. Part 2 No. LXXVI. pp.719–747. Ascanius. 1904.

Gaskin, Robert Tate. *The Old Seaport of Whitby.* Whitby. 1909. (Caedmon. 1986).

Gibson, William. *Religion and Society in England and Wales, 1689–1800.* Leicester University Press. 1998.

Gill, Claude (ed.). *The Old Wooden Walls: An Abridged Version of Falconer's Celebrated Marine Dictionary (1769).* London. 1930.

Goldsmith, Oliver. *A History of the Earth and Animated Nature.* London. 1774. (Ed., with copious notes. 1850.)

Gregory, Jeremy & Stevenson, John. *Britain in the Eighteenth Century 1688–1820*. Longman. 2000.

Grigson, Geoffrey (ed.). *Before the Romantics, an Anthology of the Enlightenment*. Salamander. 1984.

Grocott, Terence. *Shipwrecks of the Revolutionary & Napoleonic Eras*. Chatham. 1997.

Hampson, Norman. *The Enlightenment. An evaluation of its assumptions, attitudes and values*. Penguin. 1968 (1990).

Hausman, William J. 'Size and Profitability of English Colliers in the Eighteenth Century' in *The Business History Review*. Vol. 51, No 4 (Winter 1977) pp. 460–473.

Hazard, Paul. *The European Mind 1680–1715*. Penguin. 1964.

Herring, Thomas. *A Sermon Preach'd at the Cathedral Church of York, September the 22d, 1745 On the Occasion of the present Rebellion in Scotland. London. 1745*. (ECCO.)

Hibbert, C. *Redcoats and Rebels: the War for America 1770–1781*. Grafton. 1990. (Penguin. 2001.)

Hoare, Philip. *Leviathan, or The Whale*. Fourth Estate. 2008 (paperback 2009).

Holmes, Richard. *The Age of Wonder*. Harper. 2008.

Hough, Richard. *Captain James Cook, a biography*. Hodder & Stoughton. 1994 (1995).

Hume, David. *Dialogues Concerning Natural Religion*. 1779. (Ed. Martin Bell. Penguin. 1990.)

Hunt, Bruce. *Voyages of the Tamar*. http://www.brucehunt.co.uk.

Jackson, Ralph. *Diaries*. (transcribed by the Ralph Jackson Research Group, greatayton.wikidot.com/ralph-jackson-diaries.)

Jardine, Lisa. *Going Dutch: How England Plundered Holland's Glory*. Harper Perennial. 2009.

Jeffrey, Percy Shaw. *Whitby Lore and Legend*. Whitby. 1952.

Jennings, Anne. *Georgian Gardens*. English Heritage. 2005.

Jones, Rufus M., *Quakers in the American Colonies*. London. 1911. (Questia. www.questia.com.)

Jones, Stephanie K., *A Maritime History of the Port of Whitby, 1700–1914*. Unpublished PhD thesis. London University. 1982.

Kennedy, Gavin. *Captain Bligh, the Man and his Mutinies*. Duckworth. 1989.

Kidd, William. *An authentick narration of all the occurrences in a voyage to Greenland in the year 1772 in the* Volunteer *of Whitby, Mr W. Coulson, Master*. Durham.

Lamb, Christian. *From The Ends of the Earth*. BFP. 2004.

Lubbock, Basil. *The Arctic Whalers*. Glasgow. 1937.

MacArthur, Brian (ed.). *The Penguin Book of Historic Speeches*. Penguin. 1996.

Mackie, J.D. *A History of Scotland*. Penguin. 1964 (1978).

McLaren, Moray. *Bonnie Prince Charlie*. Granada. 1972.

McLynn, Frank. *The Jacobite Army in England 1745, The Final Campaign*. John Donald. 1983 (1998).

McLynn, Frank. *1759, The Year Britain Became Master of the World*. Cape. 2004. (Pimlico. 2005.)

Mead, Hilary P. *Trinity House.* London.

Miller, Amy. *Dressed to Kill.* National Maritime Museum. 2007.

Milton, John. *Paradise Lost.* 1674. (Mentor. 1961.)

Morris, Derek. 'Whitby and Wapping in the 18th Century' in *Whitby Literary and Philosophical Society Annual Report.* 2006.

Naphy, William G. *The Protestant Revolution.* BBC. 2007.

Neal, Daniel. *The History of the Puritans.* London.1822.

Nickalls, John L. (ed). *The Journal of George Fox.* London. 1975.

O'Brian, Patrick. *Joseph Banks.* Collins Harvill. 1987 (1994).

Oldroyd, D. *Estates, Enterprise and Investment at the Dawn of the Industrial Revolution.* Ashgate. 2007.

Ollard, S.L. and Walker, P.C. (eds). *Archbishop Herring's Visitation Returns, 1743,* vv71–2, 75,77,79. Yorks Archaeological Society Records Series.

Ossowski, Waldemar (ed.). *The General Carleton Shipwreck, 1785. Wrak Statku General Carleton.* Dual Language English/Polish. Polish Maritime Museum, Gdańsk. 2008.

O'Sullivan, Dan. *Great Ayton – A History of the Village.* 1996. (See Great Ayton website.)

O'Toole, Fintan. *A Traitor's Kiss, The Life of Richard Brinsley Sheridan.* Granta. 1997 (1998).

Padfield, Peter. *Maritime Supremacy and the Opening of the Western Mind.* Murray. 1999. (Pimlico. 2000.)

Paine, Thomas. *Rights of Man.* 1791. (CRW Publishing, 2004.)

Penrose, Bernard. *An Account of the Last Expedition to Port Egmont, in Falkland's Islands, in the Year 1772, Together with the Transactions of the Company of the Penguin Shallop During Their Stay There.* London. 1775.

Phillips, Patricia. *The Scientific Lady. A Social History of Women's Scientific Interests 1520–1919.* Weidenfeld & Nicholson. 1990.

Phipps, Constantine. *A Voyage towards the North Pole.* 1773. Internet Archive.

Pickvance, Joseph. *A Reader's Companion to George Fox's Journal.* QHS. 1989.

Plumb, J.H. *Chatham.* Collins. 1953 (1965).

Pocock, Tom. *Battle for Empire. The Very First World War 1756–63.* Michael O'Mara. 1998.

Porter, Roy. *Enlightenment; Britain and the Creation of the Modern World.* Allen Lane. 2000.

Porter, Roy (ed.). *The Cambridge History of Science. Vol. 4. Eighteenth-Century Science.* CUP. 2003.

Prebble, John. *Culloden.* Penguin. 1967 (1985).

Rae, Julia. 'Wapping' in Robson, John. *The Captain Cook Encyclopaedia.* London. 2004. pp. 236–9.

Raistrick, Arthur. *Quakers in Science & Industry.* David & Charles. 1968.

Richardson, George. *The Annals of the Cleveland Richardsons.* Newcastle. 1850.

Robson, John. *The Captain Cook Encyclopaedia.* London. 2004.

Robson, John. 'The Zong Affair' in *Cook's Log,* Vol. 35, No. 1. 2012.

Roger, N.A.M. *The Command of the Ocean*. Penguin. 2004 (2005).

Rogers, Glen M. 'Benjamin Franklin and the Universality of Science' in *The Pennsylvania Magazine of History and Biography*. Vol. 85, No. 1 (Jan 1961). pp. 50–69.

Savours, Ann (Mrs Shirley). 'A very interesting point in geography: the 1773 Phipps Expedition towards the North Pole' in *Arctic*, Vol. 37, No. 4 (Dec 1984) pp. 402–28.

Smith, Adam. *Wealth of Nations*. 1776. (ed. Tom Griffiths. Wordsworth. 2012.)

Smith, William (ed.). *Old Yorkshire*. London. 1884.

Sobel, Dava. *Longitude*. London. 1995.

Spavens, William. *The Narrative of William Spavens, a Chatham Pensioner*. Louth. 1796. (Ed. & Intro. N.A.M. Rodger. Chatham. 1998.)

Syrett, David. *Shipping and the American War 1775–83*. Athlone Press. 1970.

Syrett, David. *Shipping and Military Power in the Seven Years War*. Exeter University Press. 2008.

Taylor, Henry. *Memoirs of the Principle Events in the Life of Henry Taylor*. North Shields. 1811.

Thornton, Cliff. 'The Diary of Ralph Jackson (1736–1790) Part IV: Commodore Wilson of Great Ayton' in *Cook's Log*, Vol. 21, No. 2 (1998).

Thornton, Cliff (ed.). *Bound for the Tyne: Extracts from the Diary of Ralph Jackson*. Newcastle. 2000.

Thornton, Cliff. *Captain Cook in Cleveland*. The History Press. 2009.

Traherne, R.F. and Fullard, Harold (eds). *Muir's Historical Atlas*. George Philip. 1965.

Uglow, Jenny. *A Little History of British Gardening*. Chatto & Windus. 2004. (Pimlico. 2005.)

Ventress, Monica. *A Great Convincement*. Whitby. 2008.

Ventress, Monica. 'A Whitby Quaker Mariner, 1631–1693' in *Whitby Literary & Philosophical Society, Annual Report*. 2008.

Walvin, James. *Black Ivory, A History of British Slavery*. Harper Collins. 1992. (Fontana. 1993.)

Walvin, James. *The Quakers; Money & Morals*. John Murray. 1997.

Watkins, W. 'Life, Writings and Genius of the late Francis Gibson', preface to Gibson, F. *The Poetical Remains*. Whitby. 1807.

Watts, Isaac. *The Improvement of the Mind*. London. 1795.

Weis, C. McC & Pottle F. (eds). *Boswell in Extremes 1776–8*. London. 1971 digital.nls.uk/scotlandspages/timeline.17762.html.

White, Gilbert. *The Natural History of Selborne*. 1788. Ed. Richard Mabey. Dent. 1993.

Wilkinson, Clive. *The British Navy and the State in the Eighteenth Century*. Boydell. National Maritime Museum. 2004.

Williams, Glyndwr (ed.). *Captain Cook, Explorations and Reassessments*. Boydell. 2004.

Wilson, A.N. *God's Funeral*. Murray. 1999.

Wright, E. Perceval. *Animal Life, being The Natural History of Animals*. Cassell. 1884.

Young, George. *A History of Whitby*. Whitby. 1817. (Caedmon Reprint. 1976.)

Websites

Ascanius; The Jacobite Rebellions. www.yourphotocard.com/Ascanius/documents

British Newspaper Archive. www.britishnewspaperarchive.co.uk

Bryn Mawr College. 'Quakers & Slavery : George Fox'. trilogy.brynmawr.edu/speccoll/quakersandslavery/commentary/people/fox.php

Captain Cook Society. CaptainCookSociety.com

Falkland Islands – History & Timeline. falklandstimeline.wordpress.com

Family Search. familysearch.org

Geni. www.geni.com

Great Ayton. greatayton.wikidot.com

Historic Britain. www.historic.britain.com/vendor/fulhampalace.aspx

History of Parliament. www.histparl.ac.uk/research/members

Hullwebs History of Hull. www.hullwebs.co.uk

Internet Archive. archive.org/details/texts

Kew Royal Botanic Gardens. www.kew.org

Literature Network. www.online-literature.com/booksearch.php

Maritime History Virtual Archives. Lars Bruzeliu. www.bruzelius.info/Nautica/Nautica.html

National Archives. www.nationalarchives.gov.uk

National History Museum. Nature Online. www.nhm.ac.uk/nature-online/science-of-natural-history/biographies

National Maritime Museum. www.nmm.ac.uk

Official Non-Conformist and Non-Parochial BMDs Service. www.bmdregisters.co.uk

Old Bailey Online. www.oldbaileyonline.org

Open Library. openlibrary.org

Oxford Dictionary of National Biography. OUP. 2004. www.oxforddnb.com

Peerage. www.thepeerage.com

PoemHunter.com. www.poemhunter.com

Project Gutenberg. www.gutenberg.org

Royal Society. royalsociety.org

University of California, Museum of Paleontology. Carl Linnaeus. www.ucmp.berkeley.edu/history/linnaeus.html

Whitby Group. uk.groups.yahoo.com/neo/groups/thewhitbygroup/info

Acknowledgements

I am grateful to numerous institutions which have given me help, especially The National Archives at Kew, the National Maritime Museum at Greenwich, the Whitby Pannet Park Museum, Library and Archive, and the United Kingdom Hydrographic Office. I am also indebted to the libraries of Cambridge University and the University of Essex, and to the public libraries of Colchester and Lancashire.

Anyone who writes history owes a deep debt of gratitude to Sir Tim Berners-Lee, and all those who have made information available on the internet. Noteworthy are Internet Archive, Gutenberg, Open Library and British Newspaper Archive; but my especial gratitude goes to the Gale Group for their digitisation of the Burney Collection of seventeenth- and eighteenth-century newspapers (held in the British Library), and for their Eighteenth Century Collections Online (ECCO) which is an impressive source for historians of this period.

So many people have been helpful to me in the writing of this book that I cannot list them all, but the following need a mention: D.K. Abbass, Rosalin Barker, Ian Boreham, Roger Dalladay, Margaret Holmes, Dave King, Yvonne Leck, Amy Miller, Robert and Jane O'Hara, Waldemar Ossowski, John Robson, Ann Thirsk and Cliff Thornton. Also my four favourite people: my wife Susan and our daughters Claudia, Eleanor and Philippa, without whom I would probably never have finished this book.

Illustrations

I am grateful to the following for permission to publish illustrations:
Wotton House Hotel (p.39).
Portsmouth Royal Dockyard (p.42).
Jill Greenwood (pp.58, 240).
Barrie Wright (p.95).
Centralne Muzeum Morskie, the Polish Maritime Museum in Gdańsk (p.113).
Harvey Taylor (p.117).
The National Archives (pp.122, 147, 151, 152, 202, 209, 211, 245).
Chatham Historic Dockyard Trust (p.148).
The Marquis, Colchester (p.149).
Parks Canada (p.151).
Colleen Baines (p.185).
United Kingdom Hydrographic Office archive (pp.215, 217, 219).

Other illustrations are taken from the following books:
The Book of Common Prayer, OUP. 1711 (pp.10, 13, 33).
Badeslade & Toms, *Chorographia Britanniae* (pp.56, 116).
The Gallery of Nature and Art. Vol. 2. London 1823 (pp.26, 156).
Atkinson, *Memorials of Old Whitby* (p.57).
Smith, *Old Yorkshire* (pp.131, 261).
Wright, *Animal Life* (pp.193, 216, 239).
Goldsmith, *A History of the Earth and Animated Nature* (pp.181, 197, 237, 238).

Other photographs have been taken by me of public places and of prints, documents and artefacts in my possession. The maps and charts are made by me using existing data, the sources where appropriate are attributed in the text.

While great care has been taken, if I have unintentionally omitted sources or infringed copyright I apologise, and will ensure such errors are amended in future editions.

Index